Irish Drama:

Local and Global Perspectives

Irish Drama:

Local and Global Perspectives

Edited by
Nicholas Grene and Patrick Lonergan

Carysfort Press

A Carysfort Press Book
Irish Drama: Local and Global Perspectives
Edited by Nicholas Grene and Patrick Lonergan

First published in Ireland in 2012 as a paperback original by
Carysfort Press, 58 Woodfield, Scholarstown Road
Dublin 16, Ireland

ISBN 978-1-904505-63-1
©2012 Copyright remains with the authors

Typeset by Carysfort Press
Cover design by eprint limited
Printed and bound by eprint limited
Unit 35
Coolmine Industrial Estate
Dublin 15
Ireland

This book is published with the financial assistance of
The Arts Council (An Chomhairle Ealaíon) Dublin, Ireland

Contents

Acknowledgements

This book arises from a conference that was held as part of a project funded by the Irish Research Council for the Humanities and Social Sciences. The project was entitled 'The Internationalization of Irish Drama, 1975-2005' and the conference took place at National University of Ireland, Galway in April 2009. We gratefully acknowledge the support of the Council. We also wish to thank Lisa Coen and Shelley Troupe, who co-organized the event.

Thanks to Rough Magic theatre company and Colm Hogan for permission to reproduce images from *A Solemn Mass for a Full Moon in Summer*. Thanks to Blue Raincoat, Quay Street, Sligo for kind permission to reproduce an image from *The Third Policeman*, taken by Joe Hunt. We also wish to thank Bisi Adigun and Roddy Doyle for permission to quote from their script of their 2007 adaptation of *The Playboy of the Western World*.

We are grateful to the members of the Irish Theatrical Diaspora organising committee and advisory board. We also wish to thank the peer reviewer who commented in detail about all of the papers in the book.

Finally we wish to record our thanks to the editors of Carysfort Press for their continued support for the Irish Theatrical Diaspora series of books.

NG
PL

List of Illustrations

Introduction

Since the late 1970s there has been a marked internationalization of Irish drama, with individual plays, playwrights, and theatrical companies establishing newly global reputations. Opportunities to travel internationally have led to a continuing re-invention of Ireland as it is represented on the world stage and, as a result, a growing number of theatre companies and writers are seeking to exploit and re-evaluate international constructions of Irishness. Simultaneously, the increased globalization of Irish society has led to a new awareness within the Irish theatre of international dramatists and practices – which have in turn have helped to shape and reshape Irish awareness of its place in the world. These new forms of cultural mobility, to and from Ireland, have also affected Irish dramatists' and practitioners' considerations of social and cultural identities within Ireland. Such developments have been widely celebrated and, following the collapse of the Irish 'Celtic Tiger' economy in late 2008 have (perhaps surprisingly) intensified, with the Irish government investing significant resources in promoting Irish culture abroad in the hope of restoring the country's reputation.

In 2009, members of the Irish Theatrical Diaspora network gathered in Galway to discuss these developments. Our aim was to chart and analyse the growing presence of Irish drama on the world stage – but also to consider how the international success of Irish theatre was being reflected at a local level. It is often assumed that the success of an Irish play on Broadway or in London's West End must be of benefit for theatre within Ireland itself, we had noted – and to a great extent we found that assumption borne out by the evidence. Yet we also discovered some evidence of an impoverishment of theatre in parts of Ireland: a homogenization of the kinds of plays being produced, a reduction in the number of new works by leading authors being premiered in Ireland, and a gradual decline or disappearance of companies with strong links to their localities. It seemed to us that our understanding of the health of Irish theatre could vary greatly, depending on whether one viewed it from a global or local perspective.

The conference was an attempt to consider these issues in detail. We invited contributors to explore specific case studies, most of them from the period 1975-2005. Those papers have subsequently been rewritten and reviewed, and are gathered in this book.

Immediately evident at the conference was the fluidity of terms that were used to speak about the movement of Irish theatre around the world. Some contributors spoke of Irish theatre as functioning in ways that might be termed *international*: that is, they considered theatre that involves a movement from one specific national space to another. For others, Irish theatre has become *globalized*: it is based on a conception of the world as a single place with one broadly shared culture – so that an Irish play can mean much the same thing in Ballina as it does in Bochum, Broadway, or Birmingham. We heard from some scholars who explored the increased multiculturalism of Irish drama, and from others who saw Irish theatre as having benefited from entering into intercultural dialogue with non-Irish practitioners and performance practices. Some speakers also sought to historicize Irish drama, and thus to consider it in its colonial and postcolonial contexts. In each case those terms were used precisely, but what was fascinating was the extent to which they converged, overlapped, and sometimes contradicted each other.

We do not promise to resolve those contradictions in this volume, but our hope is that by placing case studies in dialogue with each other we may reveal surprising affinities and new areas for investigation. For instance, we were aware when organizing the conference that there was already enormous academic interest in the 2007 Abbey Theatre adaptation of *The Playboy of the Western World*, which had been co-authored by the Irish writer Roddy Doyle and the Nigerian director Bisi Adigun. Christopher Murray's paper in this book provides a detailed reading of the adaptation, but also situates it in terms of the work of the Dublin-based theatre collective The Passion Machine. He thus allows us to view the Doyle/Adigun production through several prisms: the local (that is, Passion Machine's relationship with its Dublin audience), the national (the staging of the play at the Abbey Theatre), and the intercultural (the interrelationships between the Irish and Nigerian elements of the script). He also shows us how the treatment of race in 2007 can be mapped back on to the Passion Machine's approach to social class in the 1980s and 1990s.

It has sometimes suggested that the Doyle/Adigun *Playboy* is one of the earliest intercultural productions on the Irish stage, but many papers in this book show that Irish theatre has drawn from non-Irish traditions throughout the contemporary period. Rhona Trench explores Blue Raincoat's adaptation of Flann O'Brien's *The Third Policeman*, showing how that Sligo-based group staged one of the most innovative Irish novels of the twentieth century. Trench reveals how that adaptation features many traits that can be construed as characteristically Irish: the verbosity and eloquence of the characters, a mischievous attitude to authority, the use of a cyclical rather than linear conception of time, and so on. Yet she also provides a discussion of how Blue Raincoat's work has been influenced by French ideas about movement and performance from such practitioners as Jacques Copeau, Marcel Marceau, and Étienne Decroux. The group thus uses their Sligo base to connect with a major European performance tradition – and the result is a significant re-evaluation of a key Irish text.

Blue Raincoat was one of a wave of Irish companies formed in the late 1980s and early 1990s, partly inspired by the success of Druid Theatre, the Galway-based company founded in 1975. In her essay, José Lanters shows how Druid used their west of Ireland location to allow the Irish theatre to re-connect with the works of John Millington Synge. *DruidSynge*, the company's day-long staging of all of Synge's plays, premiered in Galway in 2005 and subsequently toured internationally, and here Lanters provides an investigation of its time in the United States. What emerges is a theme that runs through this book: that theatre tends to provoke a variety of responses, even as its mediators – marketing people, academics, journalists – seek to impose a single meaning upon what is being performed. As Lanters shows, *DruidSynge* provoked markedly different reactions as it toured. The critical response as recorded in newspapers can only give us a partial insight into the reactions of audience members; we are therefore faced with the difficulty of retrieving accurately and comprehensively the conditions in which a play was produced and received.

That variety of reactions is also notable in Martine Pelletier's consideration of Field Day Theatre Company. Field Day has both produced and been the subject of a great deal of academic criticism, much of it focused on the interpretation of text. Yet as Pelletier shows, the meaning of a Field Day play could vary considerably – not just from one country to another but from one community within Ireland to another. As Field Day developed it started to engage in the production of anthologies and literary criticism. Pelletier identifies an intriguing contrast between the living conditions in which performance is created and the more static conditions in which the acts of canon formation and literary analysis take place.

That variety of response is most obvious in Werner Huber's essay about German productions of Irish plays. As Huber shows, Irish plays have been very popular in Germany since the mid-1990s (if not before), with works by Enda Walsh, Martin McDonagh and other young dramatists finding favour in that country. Notably, however, their plays are not always seen as Irish: they are instead misidentified as English or their nationality is disregarded. This is not to suggest, however, that German audiences are unaware of Irish plays. Huber provides a fascinating account of a fake Irish play entitled *Die Blinden von Kilcrobally* (*The Blind People of Kilcrobally*). At the time of that play's premiere, the public was told that the author was called 'George O'Darkney', but it was later revealed that it was written by the German scriptwriter and dramatist Jörg Graser. It is notable that Graser was able to do something that McDonagh and Walsh found more difficult: to write a play that could be seen as self-evidently Irish.

McDonagh and Walsh are of course not the first Irish dramatists to be misidentified as English: the long tradition of traffic between Ireland and Britain makes such mistakes inevitable. Two papers in this book seek to explore that tradition from different perspectives. Richard Cave provides an account of Abbey tours to London since the 1980s, identifying a relationship that can broadly be seen as national – not just in the sense of the Abbey functioning as Ireland's national theatre, but also in that producing plays in London locates Irish plays at the heart of British drama. There has been a tendency to see Irish drama as a sort of smaller offshoot of the British tradition, and Cave's essay shows how for some practitioners and writers success in London still matters more than success in Dublin – and not just because of the financial rewards available in the larger city. Yet James Moran also reveals that Irish drama can often be seen as inspirational within Britain, by showing how the development of the Birmingham Repertory Theatre was influenced by the emergence of the Abbey in Dublin. Where Cave gives a focussed account of one historical period, Moran ranges across the twentieth century, showing how the changing status of the Irish in Britain was reflected on the stages of the Birmingham Rep.

Moran thus identifies a dynamic that dominates this book, and which is the subject of the first essay, by Chris Morash: the relationship between theatrical space and other kinds of space (social, virtual, political, historical). Morash explores a 2009 Dublin production of *Solemn Mass for a Full Moon in Summer* by the Quebecois dramatist Michel Tremblay. He invites us to consider how our understanding of theatre can be conditioned by space: not just the horizontal and vertical spaces of the stage, but also by such spaces as websites and social media, which are used to promote those productions but may also extend their performance outside the theatre. By focussing on a play that provides a secularized version of the Catholic mass, Morash points to the affinities between two different national cultures (the Irish and the Quebecois) but also gestures out towards immaterial spaces, such as those occupied by ritual within a community's imagination.

If our understanding of a performance is determined by 'where we're coming from', then the perspective of the originator of the work is especially significant. As plays travel internationally, their meanings often shift and are altered, both through translation and as a result of local resonances. How, then, does the role of authorial intention fit into this dynamic? The three playwrights who contribute to this book seem not just unthreatened but actively energised by the ways in which their works change meaning from place to place. Enda Walsh, for instance, has been produced far more often in Germany than in Ireland, but the essay by Elizabeth Kuti – an English dramatist who lived and wrote in Ireland – reminds us that Walsh's experience abroad has been matched by dramatists who have travelled to Ireland from elsewhere. And as Ursula Rani Sarma reminds us, the experience of being produced outside of Ireland – of being translated or adapted – presents writers with a recurrent challenge: that of 'redefining which box I fit into', as she puts it.

'We need theatre,' writes Chris Morash, 'to make space for us'. These essays aim to make space too: room for us to reconsider our own processes of categorization and definition. Our objective is not just to shed light on the present, but also to draw attention to the fact that many of the challenges faced by our writers are not new: the fashionable distinction between local and global may have important equivalences in the past. That observation may lead to a consideration of the possible futures of Irish theatre. If Irish theatre is to be created mainly for a global audience, how will that process affect Irish audiences, especially those living outside the major centres for theatre on the island? If theatre is increasingly used to promote the Irish state abroad, how can it protect its independence, its power to critique the government that funds it? And, as identities shift and change, will the concept of a specifically 'Irish' play continue to have meaning and value for audiences or authors? We cannot answer these questions comprehensively yet – but our hope is that this book might initiate a conversation which seems likely to become more urgent during the years ahead.

1 | Making Space: Towards a Spatial Theory of Irish Theatre

Chris Morash

Theatre Diaspora and Theatre Space

When the Irish Theatrical Diaspora Project first began to take shape a number of years ago, its most obvious value seemed to be that it created a framework for drawing a global map of Irish theatre.[1] This could encompass everything from the Smock Alley tours to Oxford in the late seventeenth century, through the London-Dublin theatre axis of the eighteenth century, to the touring circuits, defined by rail lines and steam ships, of the nineteenth century; and then on to the early Abbey tours, initially to England, and later to the US; and, finally, through to the Irish theatre world of today, which nominally has a Dublin centre, but in which major Irish plays very frequently premiere in London, and in which the major event of early 2009 was arguably the Dublin premiere of a Sam Shepard play, *Ages of the Moon*.[2] When this range of theatrical activity comes into focus, the value of the Irish Theatrical Diaspora Project seems self-evident.

However, there is a sense in which there is a more fundamentally structuralist value in conjoining the terms 'theatre' and 'diaspora'. To put it simply, space is more than just part of the language of theatre; it is one of its conditions of being, as much ontological as semantic. Indeed, we could argue that along with time, language, the body, sound, and memory, it constitutes one of the five irreducible elements of theatre, the earth/air/fire/water of what takes place on the stage. Theatre does not just occupy space, or take place in space; nor does it simply use space – although it does all of these things. In a sense that I will attempt to define more fully as I go along, theatre *produces* space, and in that sense theatre *is* spatial.

Perhaps the best means to remind ourselves of the ways in which theatre is a spatial medium is to begin with an actual production: Rough Magic's staging of Michel Tremblay's *Solemn Mass for a Full Moon in Summer*, which ran from 5 to 28 March 2009 in the Project Arts Centre in Dublin.[3] Of course, the first thing to say is that this is not an 'Irish' play in the sense of a play written by an Irish writer about Ireland; in another sense, Bryan Delaney's acclaimed translation makes it as much an Irish play as Brian Friel's versions of Chekhov, for instance, or Frank McGuinness's translations of Ibsen – neither of which any but the most dogmatic purist would like to rule out of court as part of Irish theatre. Indeed, part of the attraction of using this play as a means to explore the space of Irish theatre is that it forces us to step outside our standard assumptions as to what constitutes an 'Irish play'. In this case, let it suffice that *Solemn Mass for a Full Moon* is a translation by an Irish writer in Irish production by an Irish company with an Irish cast.

Any consideration of theatre space will always at some point turn to the actual physical space of the stage, so this is probably a good place to begin. Paul O'Mahony's set for *Solemn Mass for a Full Moon in Summer* follows the script in reorienting the theatrical space by creating a set of six apartment balconies, two by two, three stories high, moving the play from the more usual horizontal to a vertical axis, and this in turn makes the production very spatially self-conscious from the outset. What is more, the play's engagement with space goes beyond this obvious vertical orientation. *Solemn Mass* is not structured as a linear narrative, but as a series of micro-dramas, vignettes from the lives of six couples, with the play as a whole given structure by the transit of the moon. We never see the moon, only its light, from an initial red glow over the stage, to a dazzling, monochrome white light in the sky, crossing the zenith, and finally as fingers of a deeper red, seeping through shadows, leaving the set in darkness. Light in *Solemn Mass for a Full Moon in Summer* (and, indeed, this is often the case on the stage) both creates space, by defining areas on the stage, while simultaneously structuring the passing of time. This in turn can remind us that *time* – one of the other pure, irreducible structural elements of theatrical production – is not only not separate from (much less opposite to) space; it can be inextricably a part of the production of space.

Physical Space

Figure 1: *A Solemn Mass for A Full Moon in Summer*
(Photograph by Colm Hogan)

In other words, the space of the stage, particularly as produced by light (although the same can also be true of movement or sound) is what Andy Merrifield (writing of Henri Lefebvre), refers to as space 'redescribed not as a dead, inert thing or object, but as organic and fluid and alive; it has a pulse, it palpitates, it flows and collides with other spaces. And these interpenetrations – many with different temporalities – get superimposed upon one another to create a *present* space'.[4] As the unseen moon crosses the sky, it thus creates what we may call an ontogenetic space.[5] Within this space, the play picks up moments – ranging from short scenes, to monologues, to a snatch of an incantatory phrase, collectively weaving together the six microdramas of love, sex, and death, played out across the balconies.

On one level, then, the play is almost devoid of movement. There are, however, two exceptions to this: the play is book-ended by two moments of epiphany, in which a pair of characters step into the open space in front of the apartments. In these moments, the play creates two spaces: one that foregrounds its own spatiality through its vertical orientation, and the other which goes from being a non-space – simply a piece of floor between the front row of the audience and the set – to being a theatrical space. The first time this second space is used, the characters are a pair of young lovers in the first throes of passion, whose speech circles around the chanted phrase: 'Let's do it.' The second time around, the characters are a gay couple, played by Arthur Riordan and Darragh Kelly; Riordan's character is in the final stage of AIDS, so when the two step into the open space in front of the stage for a kind of ironic tango, the openness of the space becomes that of which the theatre speaks most powerfully when it is most theatrical: the possibility of transformation. In this particular case, it is not the characters who are transformed. Indeed, no one is transformed in Tremblay's play, and in this regard the confining, atomising space of the balconies is the play's defining image. However, if the characters are not transformed in the play as a whole, the space is utterly transformed in those two brief moments, and the play exists in the tension between these two different kinds of space. As Anne Ubersfeld puts it, 'Theatre constructs space that is not only structured, but in which structures become signifying'.[6]

**Figure 2: *A Solemn Mass for A Full Moon in Summer*
(Photograph by Colm Hogan)**

This, then, is one way of speaking of theatrical space. And, indeed,
quite often when we talk about stage space, the analysis does not go
very far beyond what we might call *scenic* or *scenographic* space, the

real, physical space produced on the stage by the performance. To this we might add an analysis of the real, physical space of the auditorium, and the series of spaces produced by architecture, light, and the movement of people in the building as a whole; and the building is located in the real physical space of the theatre building in the city; and so on, in a series of concentric circles, rippling outwards. Indeed, this aspect of physical theatre space – the architecture of theatres, and their location within the (almost invariably) urban space of the city – is one of the great under-researched areas in Irish theatre studies. Having said this, real, physical space, or 'absolute space', is only one of the ways in which we can think about space and spatiality in relation to the theatre.

Fictional Space

For instance, if you were to ask someone who had seen *Solemn Mass for a Full Moon in Summer* where it is set, the most likely response would be that it takes place in Montreal; we can call this the 'fictional space' of the play. Again, discussion of plays very often concentrates on the fictional space of the play: think, for instance, of how much has been written on Friel's Ballybeg, on Synge's Aran Islands, or on Martin McDonagh's Leenane. Indeed, it could be argued that one of the pleasures of Irish theatre since the late eighteenth century has been the production on stage of fictional *represented* spaces. Considered in an historical perspective, a defining moment comes in the 1770s, when John O'Keeffe began producing plays such as *The Giant's Causeway; or, A Trip to the Dargle* which was staged in Belfast on May 25, 1770 and featured a giant capable of flying from the Antrim coast to the Wicklow mountains, thus providing occasion for 'an elegant View of the Giant's Causeway, the Dargle, and the Waterfall of Powerscourt'.[7] Throughout the nineteenth century, one of the primary functions of what was known as 'the Irish Play' – of which Boucicault was only one of many practitioners in his time, along with Edmond Falconer, John Baldwin Buckstone, and others – was to create narrative frameworks to justify the creation of stage landscapes such as the Lakes of Killarney (in the case of Boucicault's *Colleen Bawn*). Such a survey could then continue through Synge's Wicklow, Friel's Ballybeg, to Marina Carr's Offaly.

In other words, one of the enduring pleasures of Irish theatre has been the *representation* of space. Indeed, it could be argued that the critical weight accorded to Brian Friel's *Translations*, for instance, or Tom Murphy's *Bailegangaire* (as opposed to their theatrical effectiveness, which is another matter entirely), has much to do with the centrality of the concept of the 'sense of place' in the wider field of Irish criticism. If we can now look back on this argument, its core principle might be summed up in the idea that, for various historical reasons, Irish landscape has been invested with a dense weave of signification. This – and I'm simplifying here – has given Irish writers something of a head-start on the rest of the world, in that they were starting with spaces that already had meaning: places, not spaces.

'Theatricality constructs a signifying totality out of what, in the world, is in-significance', writes Anne Ubersfeld. 'This reversible signification, so to speak, is perhaps the principal task of theatre'.[8] If there is a defining feature of the fictional spaces of Irish theatre, it may well be the sense that we begin with places already inhabited with signification, which only need to be transferred to the stage for that signification to function (or, perhaps, for it to be magnified). However, this may have masked for us the recognition that representational space is only one form of theatrical space, and by no means the most important. If we are to understand theatrical space, we need to grant it greater agency; so, rather than considering theatrical space as representational, or even as signifying, I would argue that we need to begin thinking about the ways in which the theatre *produces* space.

The silent presence who has been informing my arguments about the production of space has had a much more profound influence among cultural geographers than among theatre scholars: Henri Lefebvre. 'Not so many years ago,' Lefebvre begins in *The Production of Space* (1974), 'the word "space" had a strictly geometrical meaning: the idea it evoked was simply that of an empty area. ... To speak of "social space", therefore, would have sounded strange'.[9] Lefebvre goes on to argue that space is not something that is simply there (or not there). Instead, Lefebvre insists, space is produced, and he goes on to construct what has become known as his 'spatial triad'. In the years since *The Production of Space* first appeared, this theoretical paradigm has been used for exploring everything from organizational structures to urban planning to network theory. He has been mentioned by some theatre scholars – most notably in the historical work of David Wiles and in the ground-breaking work of Gay McAuley, particularly her *Space in Performance*; however, in both cases, Lefebvre's ideas are explored only in passing.[10] This situation is somewhat strange, for even though Lefebvre developed his ideas primarily through an attempt to understand the spaces of everyday life, particularly urban space, his understanding of that space is profoundly theatrical.

Lefebvre sets out his triad in the opening section of *The Production of Space*. He argues that in beginning to think spatially, we run the danger of confusing very different forms of space (something for which he criticizes Foucault, for instance), and hence he is insistent that we need to disentangle and demystify space by distinguishing among three basic ways in which space is produced: space is produced as something *physical*, space produced as something *mental* (including logical and formal abstractions), and space produced as something *social* (11).

The first element of his triad is what Lefebvre calls 'spatial practice', which is sometimes glossed as 'perceived' space, the commonsensical, 'everyday' (to use a loaded word for Lefebvre) space in which we live, and in which social life exists. This can be distinguished from 'representations of space': 'which are tied to the relations of production and to the "order" which those relations impose, and hence to knowledge, to signs, to codes'. Also sometimes called 'conceived' space, this is the space of planners, of cartographers, and, to some extent, to theorists of space themselves. Lefebrve then disrupts what could be a fairly straight-forward binary of spatial relations – the perceived as opposed to the conceived – by differentiating these two categories from what he calls 'representational space', which he later refers to as 'lived' space, but which is ultimately more complex than this suggests (220). For Lefebvre, it 'embodies complex symbolisms, sometimes coded, sometimes not, linked to the clandestine or underground side of social life, as also to art (which may come eventually to be defined less as a code of space than as a code of representational spaces)' (33).

It is at this point that Lefebvre emerges as a figure with potential as a theorist who can help us understand the ways in which the theatre produces space. In one of the very few direct comments on theatre in *The Production of Space*, Lefebvre writes:

> Theatrical space certainly implies a *representation of space* – scenic space – corresponding to a particular *conception of space* (that of the classical drama, say – or the Elizabethan, or the Italian). The *representational space*, mediated yet directly experienced, which infuses the work and the moment, is established as such through the dramatic action itself. (188)

In these few sentences, we get a sense of potential complexity that Lefebvre's model brings to our understanding of theatrical event. In other words, Lefebvre's structuralism does not allow us the sterile pleasure that one so often finds with structuralism, that of simply naming inert objects. Instead, this is a dynamic theoretical model, in which three modes of producing space – the *perceived*, the *conceived* and the *lived* – interact, moment by moment.

Conceptual Space

If we return to the Rough Magic production of *Solemn Mass for a Full Moon in Summer*, we find that it produces a fictional space that is not simply Montreal (although it is that). While the play is not structured around a single narrative, linear or otherwise, it is nonetheless a highly structured piece of work, borrowing rhythms, language, and forms from the liturgy of the Catholic Mass, as the title of the play suggests. This in turn opens up something closer to the idea of a diasporic space than to the more conventional forms of representational fictional space. In order for a play based around the structure of the Catholic Mass to be comprehensible at all, it must assume a certain competence on the part of the audience, a certain familiarity with Catholic liturgy. The late John Devitt once spoke of what he saw as a 'vestigial religious reverence'[11] that Irish theatre has drawn upon in the closing decades of the twentieth century, which he saw as the energizing force in plays such as Kilroy's *Talbot's Box* (1977), Friel's *Faith Healer* (1979), and Murphy's *The Gigli Concert* (1983). It may well be that the Rough Magic production of *Solemn Mass* is drawing on the attenuated forms of these religious energies in a culture that still harbours memories of liturgy, but that has enough distance from the content of the liturgy to be able to channel it toward other ends. Indeed, in *Solemn Mass for a Full Moon in Summer*, there is a moment that even moves towards some definition of this post-Catholic state, when a chorus from all of the balconies beseech the setting moon to 'bring us back your big white lie.' *Solemn Mass for a Full Moon in Summer* 'recognises' wrote Peter Crawley in *The Irish Times,* 'that in these faithless times individual griefs need a new choir'.[12]

By drawing upon what we might call a level of shared liturgical competence, an assumption that the structures and responses of the Mass, if not their content of belief, have been internalized by an audience, the Dublin production of *Solemn Mass* also produced a particular kind of space. In those moments at which the play almost draws to our lips the correct liturgical response – 'And also with you' – *Solemn Mass for a Full Moon in Summer* creates a form of space very different from the physical, or absolute, space of the play, and different from the fictional space of the play (although it arises out of both). When we participate in the post-Catholic communion that is *Solemn Mass*, we recognize that our ability to respond would have been shared by the original Quebecois audience when the play was first performed in Montreal. In other words, when we watch *Solemn Mass for a Full Moon in Summer*, we place ourselves in an alternative map, and a different kind of imaginary geography, in which the Catholic (or post-Catholic) world is connected, able to share, in certain controlled, liturgy-like environments (such as the theatre) a kind of post-Communion. This is something more than the old cliché of finding ourselves in a play from another culture. It is the active participation in a shared culture that is not bound by the absolute space of the nation; it is a form of active participation in a form of diasporic space that is produced by a shared set of beliefs – or, at the very least, the memory of those beliefs.

The idea that we join with a map of imagined audiences in other physical spaces (and, presumably, other times) could equally be used to think about productions by Irish writers, or Irish companies, outside of Ireland. So, for instance, when Druid Theatre Company performs in Sydney, the Australian audience are, at some level, inscribing themselves in the contour lines of a map that stretches back to Ireland. In either direction, the sense of shared communion with imagined audiences elsewhere produces one form – in this case, a very powerful form – of what we might call the 'conceptual space' of the theatre. And if we are to think clearly about the spaces of Irish theatre, we need to demarcate carefully this *conceptual* space of the theatre from the *physical* space of the theatre – the balconies of *Full Moon*, for instance, or the Project Arts Centre – and from the *represented* space of the theatre – whether that be Montreal, Ballybeg, or the Lakes of Killarney.

Virtual Space

When *Solemn Mass for a Full Moon in Summer* was opening, pre-publicity concentrated not on the play's use of liturgy, however, but on the production's use of the internet. Not only did Rough Magic develop a website for the show with full production credits (which is now fairly standard); they also had a 'trailer' uploaded to YouTube, along with three other videos. Going further, a fuller visual archive was uploaded to the photo website Pix.ie, with pictures of the set and of individual cast members, a Twitter feed, a forum within the site itself in which the actors took part, and a Facebook link. 'Rough Magic is at the technological coalface with its promotion of the Irish premiere of *Solemn Mass for a Full Moon in Summer*', reported *The Irish Times*. 'As well as spreading the word through bloggers and twitterers, and a YouTube trailer … the company has set up a dedicated, interactive website solely for the production'.[13]

All of this is part of the production, in the same way that programmes, posters, and reviews are part of a production, and this is a part of the conceptual space that the play produces. However, programmes and posters remain rooted to the location of the production; posters are posted, for the most part, in the city or town in which the production takes place; programmes are purchased in the theatre. A website, on the other hand, has a very different relationship to physical location. The website produces a space that, while it refers to a real (or absolute) space, is everywhere and nowhere. It is in Dublin and Dubai at the same moment; it is, in short, 'virtual space'. Virtual space is, it has been argued, a form of conceptual space. At the same time, it is produced in a way that differs profoundly from the kind of conceptual space that I was describing in relation to the Catholic liturgy in post-Catholic cultures, at least in part because it is the product of a very different technological formation.

Perhaps most crucially, the virtual space of the solemnmass.ie website existed as a website only as long as someone gave it server space (again, that telltale phrase that indicates how deeply our culture is enmeshed in metaphors of spatiality: 'server space' is more metaphorically spatial than it is concretely spatial; the microscopic components that retain binary code as electrical pulses can only really be imagined as something akin to a very tiny set of library shelves). There are elements of the site that were what we might term process-determined, such as the blogs, twitter threads, and forums; over time, these slowly wound down, and for a time the site took on a more or less fixed form. However, when the tweeting finally stopped, the website was not complete (as would be the case with a painting, for instance, when the last brush stroke has been made, and the paint allowed to dry). When the last posting was made to the website, it was not complete; it was dormant, which is quite a different thing – more like a glacier or a volcano than a piece of sculpture. A dormant website is a temporarily dead website, poised for a period between the potential for rebirth, and the recognition that it needs to be buried. When it was finally buried, and the link to the site in the larger Rough Magic website removed, it became, like the performance of the play itself, confined to memory.

In this respect, a website is something like the performance of a play, in that both have duration (and here, once again, time is an element of theatre). However, the performance of the play is even more time-determined than a website, existing for two distinct durations: the duration of the run of a given production, and the duration of a given performance (which will, of course, vary slightly from performance to performance in the same run). This means that both the absolute space of performance and the virtual space of solemnmass.ie are instances of ontogenetic space, space that exists in, or is produced by, processes that have a temporal dimension.

Local/Global

Differentiating among the physical, fictional, conceptual, and virtual spaces of theatre is probably more important now than at any point in the past. In *Theatre and Globalization*, Patrick Lonergan argues forcefully that 'we need a new framework for understanding contemporary developments in theatre in their social and cultural contexts'.[14] If we are to begin to understand the reconfigurations of theatrical space (and, indeed, time) that have been produced by the multiple processes that we understand by the term 'globalization', we need clarity as to the different kinds of space that theatre produces. Without some version of the kind of distinctions outlined here, there is always the danger that we simply identify the physical, absolute space of the performance as *local*, and the conceptual space of reference and reception as *global* (although that makes a good starting point). Instead, as with any binarism, there is a more complex, deconstructive reading possible, and it is with this that I will conclude.

The argument for understanding the theatrical event as fundamentally local in its spatiality is simple, and compelling. Perhaps the best way to think about this is to make manifest the middle term between local and global that has been ghosting this entire discussion: the national. If we compare the ontological status of a play in performance with Benedict Anderson's influential argument about the role of print in the creation of the conceptual space of the nation, we can immediately see the difference made by the rooted, concrete spatiality of the performance. A play in performance takes place in a clearly demarcated space (usually a theatre building) at a clearly defined time. The audience for any given performance is limited to those people who are in the same theatre at the same time. Members of an audience at a play are not, in Anderson's evocative phrase, an 'imagined community':[15] they are a real, *albeit* temporary, community whose relationship to one another is clearly bounded by the temporal and spatial parameters of the performance as event. Hence, the argument would go, theatre in performance is fundamentally local.[16]

So, if theatre in performance creates an event that is by definition local, we need to ask two questions: what enabled us to think about theatre as a national form for so long? And what is now enabling us to think about it as a global form? The answers to both of these questions are effectively the same, bringing us back to the role of other media in creating both a national theatre culture, and a globalized theatre culture. Theatre in performance may not share the features of print that make it so conducive to the production of the national space (much less global space), but this does not prevent the theatrical experience from being translated into print, radio, television, and the internet. The publication of reviews, play scripts, and the accumulation of these sources in theatre histories re-configure the temporally and spatially specific form of performance into the temporally and spatially diffuse form of print, broadcast, and digital media. When we read a review of a play, read a dramatic script, or take part in an online forum, we are sharing with those geographically distant and anonymous others that sense of 'communion' of which Anderson speaks, bringing us all together as an imagined community.

This means that the media into which the theatre is translated become a dangerous, but necessary, supplement to the theatrical event itself (in the sense in which Derrida writes of the 'dangerous supplement': 'the sign is always the supplement of the thing itself'[17]). It is dangerous, because it constantly threatens to supplant the theatrical event, but necessary, because otherwise we cannot talk of either a national or a globalized theatre at all. At the same time, when considering the role of that supplement specifically in creating a national theatre, we need to keep in mind that there is another form of supplementary, or excess, at work here. For instance, in the case of Rough Magic's production of *Solemn Mass for a Full Moon in Summer*, the website solemnmass.ie, by virtue of the medium in which it existed, spilled over the island of Ireland. Although contributions to the forums on the site suggest that most traffic actually came from Ireland, there is an awareness that it could potentially be seen from anywhere in the world (in a way that is not true of the print edition of a national newspaper, for instance, even though copies may well be available in other countries). To put it simply, the website exceeds the conceptual space of the nation, and exists in the virtual space of the global.

Conclusion: Making Space

In the end, however, the great value of theatre is that it relentlessly returns us to real, physical space. This aspect of theatre is irreducible; theatre not only takes place in real space, it produces that space. At the same time, the absolute space of the theatre produces various forms of conceptual space, and the nature of that conceptual space will change with changing media technologies, social and cultural formations. If in an earlier period, Irish conceptual space was dominated by the concept of place, in a period of increasingly mediated globalization, place is being supplanted by virtual space, and by global spaces. However, a play like *Solemn*

Mass for a Full Moon in Summer can remind us that because of the theatre's highly-charged capacity for producing space, it can produce alternative forms of conceptual space – in this case by activating the alternative map of a geographically diffuse post-Catholic community. Once we recognize this, we can see that now, more than ever, we need theatre to perform its acts of spatial conjuration; in other words, we need the theatre to make space for us.

[1] This essay owes a number of debts. In the first instance, I am indebted to my colleagues in the Irish Theatrical Diaspora Project over the years, particularly Nicholas Grene. An early version of some of the material here was delivered to the School of Drama in Queen's University, Belfast, where the discussion afterwards helped me to sharpen my ideas considerably. I have also benefited enormously from the work of colleges in the Department of Geography, and in NIRSA, at NUI Maynooth. Finally, the work presented here is part of a larger project to theorize Irish theatre space on which I have been working with Shaun Richards; much of what has been written here is the product of that collaboration and would not exist in its present form without it.

[2] Sam Shepard's *Ages of the Moon* premiered on the Peacock stage of the Abbey Theatre on 3 March 2009. It was revived on the theatre's main stage on 17 October 2009.

[3] Michel Tremblay, *Solemn Mass for a Full Moon in Summer*, trans. Bryan Delaney, dir. Tom Creed. Rough Magic Theatre Company, Project Arts Centre, Dublin. 5-28 March 2009.

[4] Andy Merrifield, in *Thinking Space*, eds. Mike Crang and Nigel Thrift (London: Routledge, 2000): 171.

[5] I am indebted to my colleague at NUI Maynooth, Prof. Rob Kitchin, for sharing with me his work on ontogenetic space.

[6] Anne Ubersfeld, *Reading Theatre*, trans. Frank Collins, eds. Paul Perron and Patrick Debbèche (Toronto: University of Toronto Press, 1999): 102.

[7] Cited in: W.S. Clark, *The Irish Stage in the County Towns: 1720-1800* (Oxford: Clarendon Press, 1965): 230.

[8] Ubersfeld, *Reading Theatre*, 102.

[9] Henri Lefebvre, *The Production of Space*, trans. Donald Nicholson-Smith (1974; Oxford: Blackwell, 1991): 1.

[10] David Wiles, *A Short History of Western Performance Space* (Cambridge: Cambridge University Press, 2003):9-13; Gay McAuley, *Space in Performance: Making Meaning in the Theatre* (Ann Arbor: University of Michigan Press, 1999): 57-58. Subsequent quotations appear in the text.

[11] John Devitt, in conversation with Nicholas Grene and Chris Morash, *Shifting Scenes: Irish Theatre Going 1955-1985* (Dublin: Carysfort, 2008): 99.

[12] Peter Crawley, Review of Solemn Mass for a Full Moon in Summer, *The Irish Times* 11 March 2009: 16

[13] Deirdre Falvey, 'On the break, or on the make?', *The Irish Times* 28 February 2009: 45. The production website was: http://www.solemnmass.ie/

[14] Patrick Lonergan, *Theatre and Globalization: Irish Drama in the Celtic Tiger Era* (Basingstoke and New York: Palgrave Macmillan, 2009): 30.

[15] Benedict Anderson, *Imagined Communities: Reflections on the Origin and Spread of Nationalism*, revised ed. (London: Verso, 1991): 35, 36.

[16] I have made this argument at greater length elsewhere. See, 'The Road to God Knows Where: Can Theatre be National?', *Irish Theatre on Tour*. Irish Theatre Diaspora Series 1. Eds. Nicholas Grene and Chris Morash (Dublin: Carysfort Press, 2005): 101-115.

[17] Jacques Derrida, *Of Grammatology*, trans. Gayatri Chakravorty Spivak (Baltimore: Johns Hopkins Press, 1974): 145.

2 | Field Day: Local roots and global reach

Martine Pelletier

When Field Day came into existence in 1980 with the premiere of Brian Friel's *Translations* in Derry's Guildhall, the company vigorously proclaimed their northern roots. *Translations* was to prove a national and a global success in the following years, translated into numerous languages, performed and adapted the world over. By 1991, with the publication of the long-awaited *Field Day Anthology of Irish Writing*, which included official launches in Ireland, London, and the United States, Field Day's global reach had been firmly established. Patrick Lonergan's *Theatre and Globalization: Irish Drama in the Celtic Tiger Era* has drawn attention to the impact of globalization on Irish theatre and, in many ways, one could well find, in the company's own progress from Derry's Guildhall to the global critical and theatre stage, echoes of Ireland's trajectory from provincialism to global fame in the 1980s and 1990s. If we look at the Field Day directors themselves, the combination of the local and the international is a striking characteristic of at least five of the seven men, six of whom came from Northern Ireland. Brian Friel, Seamus Heaney, Stephen Rea, and Seamus Deane can rightly be seen as global figures. Friel is an internationally recognized dramatist; Rea's career on the stage and in cinema has turned him into a household name well beyond Ireland; Heaney is undoubtedly Ireland's favourite poet but his Nobel Prize for Literature in 1995 has ensured global recognition. Thomas Kilroy, the only Southerner on the board of directors, regularly has his plays performed outside Ireland. Though Seamus Deane also writes poetry, it is in the globalized world of academia that he has mostly made a name for himself. Tom Paulin and David Hammond both played an important part in the company, though they have remained less well known internationally. Together, they succeeded in making Field Day both an identifiably Irish project and a genuinely global phenomenon.

Field Day first came to life as a theatre company that aimed to present plays and tour them across Ireland, north and south. As Stephen Rea put it: 'It was essentially, I guess, a political statement: we were northern but we belonged to the whole country, whatever we were talking about we wanted to address the whole country. By touring Ireland north and south we were doing something nobody else had done before'.[1] The focus on Derry and the local tours were of vital importance in the role the company saw for itself, as well as in attracting funding from the Arts Councils of both Northern Ireland and the Republic. The political dimension of touring the thirty-two counties did not escape anyone, while Field Day genuinely filled a gap in bringing theatre to small Irish towns that were outside the ordinary touring circuit but which provided exciting venues for the cast. As Stephen Rea recalled:

> If you did *Saint Oscar* in Andersonstown, as we did, you could hear a pin drop. Because people in the North knew that everything you said had implications, had reverberations. When I did this 'speech from the dock' people laughed but they didn't laugh so much in Belfast because they wanted to hear it, they did not want to miss it. For people in the North it was life and death. For that brief time we had a theatre that actually touched people's lives in a very important way

He continued:

> It was important to go to people because instead of making people get into cars and drive to *you*, you went to *them*. We went to a lot of one-horse towns but you were really talking to the people of that place. They weren't coming into a theatre where they felt intimidated, or that they had to have some kind of theatrical understanding that would make things easy for them. They really had an experience. When we did *Making History* [Brian Friel's 1988 play for Field Day] in Dungannon, which is where Hugh O'Neill had his seat of power it was very different from doing it anywhere else. When we talked about the Devlins and the Quinns having a feud they roared laughing in Dungannon because presumably they're still having that feud. It was an intense experience, talking about the conquest of Ireland and the demise of Hugh O'Neill meant something in Dungannon that it couldn't mean anywhere else. (60-1)

The emphasis on addressing local audiences was summed up, perhaps somewhat disingenuously, by Friel in a 1980 interview for

Magill: 'We are talking to ourselves as we must and if we are overheard in America, or England, so much the better'.[2] Instead of pitching their voice for English audiences and outsiders, Field Day first sought to exist in and for Ireland. However, in practice, after the success of *Translations*, the strong local roots and inflections certainly did not preclude efforts to transfer the plays onto other stages, reaching audiences outside Ireland, partly though not exclusively from the Irish diaspora. As Nicholas Grene perceptively showed in his 1999 study, *The Politics of Irish Drama*, Irish drama has long functioned at the juncture between the local and the international; *Translations* was perfectly pitched for audiences both inside and outside Ireland. The play is in one sense a text in which the empire writes back: an Irish playwright uses the English language to commemorate the Irish culture of which the English colonists deprived him and his. Yet Friel addresses metropolitan audiences in their own language, which is handled with assurance and skill. And so, although *Translations* was first staged in Derry, toured through the town halls and improvised stages of both parts of Ireland, it is written with a confidence of being not only 'overheard' but understood and applauded in London and New York.

The company was unquestionably sincere in its determination to address local audiences and issues, and in its desire to put Derry on the map. Yet the tension between those goals and the likely appeal of Field Day productions internationally was unavoidable from the beginning. There can be no doubt that, as Nicholas Grene puts it, 'Field Day was given impetus not just by the warm reception of *Translations* throughout Ireland but by the international attention which went with that reception, and the high-profile productions outside Ireland that followed'.[3] Mainly thanks to Stephen Rea's well-established contacts in the London theatre world and Friel's reputation as a playwright of a truly international stature, Field Day was soon to develop a pattern of exchanges with the English stage – and in particular with the Royal National Theatre and Hampstead Theatre – which allowed them to transfer most of their productions to London in the 1980s. Friel's *Translations*, *Three Sisters* (1981), and *The Communication Cord* (1982); Kilroy's *Double Cross* (1986); Friel's *Making History* (1988); Eagleton's *Saint Oscar* (1989), and Heaney's *The Cure at Troy* (1990) all enjoyed runs on English and sometimes US or other international stages. The effort to bring challenging new Irish plays to London has no doubt been of great benefit subsequently to a number of Irish dramatists, as English theatre directors and audiences took increasing interest in Irish playwrights and their work – though of course one could reasonably argue that the Ireland/England axis is not the best example of a truly global phenomenon.

A clearer sense of their increasingly global perspective may be adduced from their preference for adaptations of classics of world theatre, expanding their horizons to bring on stage Athol Fugard's South Africa and Chekhov's Russia, but also Molière's France as well as the cradle of Western drama, ancient Greece. For their 1983 production, after three Brian Friel plays, the company chose to stage Fugard's *Boesman and Lena*. Field Day's choice of this South African play puzzled and dismayed local audiences who chose to stay away, making the tour a financial failure. The production however won near unanimous critical acclaim. As Marilynn Richtarik argues most convincingly, there were numerous parallels between Fugard's experience and conception of theatre on the one hand, and the ideals of Field Day on the other: the commitment to making theatre accessible to non-conventional audiences, the experience of living in a deeply-divided society, and a focus on the relationship between art and politics.[4]

Other Field Day versions of non-Irish plays were adaptations – and indeed adaptations became something of a hallmark of Field Day's work, partly following their distinguished forebears of the national theatre movement at the beginning of the twentieth century.[5] Thus Friel's adaptation of Chekhov's *Three Sisters* in 1981 greatly contributed to the taste of Irish dramatists and audiences alike for adaptations of Russian plays. Friel's intense admiration for the Russian playwright is well known but the company also saw the adaptation of classics as significant in a variety of ways. Friel's claim for a Chekhov freed from the expected English accent and pitched for Irish ears proved hugely influential, as well as controversial. That claim can be encapsulated in a phrase that seems to echo Ngugi wa Thiongo's famous study, *De-Colonising the Mind*: 'The decolonisation process of the imagination is very important if a new Irish personality is to emerge', said Friel.[6] Thus the power of universal classics was enlisted to strengthen the emergence of a strongly-rooted Irish voice, using the Irish vernacular and confident in its right to appropriate texts often claimed by English voices. Paulin's *Antigone*, produced in 1984 as *The Riot Act*, along with Derek Mahon's version of Molière's *The School for Husbands* as *High Time*, undoubtedly showed what could be achieved by taking a time-honoured classic and emphasising its openness to modern and topical inflections and contexts. Seamus Heaney's *The Cure at Troy* gave political discourse in Northern Ireland and the Republic one of its most popular phrases with the lines 'The longed-for tidal wave / Of justice can rise up / And hope and history rhyme'.[7] Chekhov had the final word, in that the last Field Day production to open at the Guildhall in 1995 was Frank McGuinness's adaptation of *Uncle Vanya*. Initial and later critical responses to such adaptations have proved mixed; where some applauded the effort to make such plays more accessible to audiences and saluted the dramatists' ingenuity in suggesting parallels and proximities across space, time and cultures, others saw these adaptations as manifestations of provincialism, as being patronising towards those same audiences, or downright offensive in replacing the beauty of Shakespeare's language by an 'Irish brogue', as one reviewer put it.[8] What Field Day did undoubtedly succeed in doing through those years was to raise awareness of the stakes involved in adaptations and the need to query, linguistically and politically, the transferability of texts and scripts written by and for users of Standard English to Ireland.

While the plays in their various ways foreground concerns with identity politics as seen from the northern constituency – though with an eye on reception outside of Ireland – the series of pamphlets launched from 1983 onwards indicated the company's desire to step onto the international critical scene at a time when Irish Studies as a discipline was expanding.

Field Day went on to devise a double channel of communication with their audience – or, rather more accurately, they developed ways of addressing potentially different audiences, both at home and abroad: first with the plays and tours engineered by Rea and Friel, then with the pamphlets from 1983 onwards. This double channel initiated a dialogue or rather a dialectic between the two mutually supportive sides of their activities. Seamus Deane, the chief architect of the critical enterprise, sees the two parts of the project as nevertheless having the same aim:

> I see both the pamphlets and the plays as exercises in the critique of various forms of authority that have become illicit or ineffective or anachronistic and yet refuse to concede to new conditions (or to conspire in their own demise). Our belief then was that the northern state never had legitimacy and the Republic's legitimacy was severely qualified. This is still my opinion.[9]

Looking back, Stephen Rea saw this critical, analytical activity as central:

> What was interesting was that, as Kevin Whelan put it, in these colonial situations you are allowed to produce the great poets, the great artists, this explosion of creative energy; but what Field Day did as well was to have a critical position, an analytical position of the situation we were in. So that it wasn't just going to be left to those outside who would see those wonderful creative artists doing things, but that we would actually define what it was we were doing ourselves. (56)

Their critical activities – which allowed Heaney, Paulin, and Deane to participate actively in the project – gradually superseded, and eventually outlived, the theatre project. In this dimension too, one can trace an evolution, as the critical concerns addressed in the first series of pamphlets undoubtedly bear the mark of local, regional, and national perspectives and progressively incorporate – or open up to – international or global perspectives and players. The authors of the first three series were either Field Day members (Deane, Heaney, and Paulin) or intellectuals closely associated with Field Day and its forerunner, the journal *The Crane Bag* (scholars such as Declan Kiberd and Richard Kearney). The two series were published in Derry, courtesy of a printing firm based in Belfast. But when *Ireland's Field Day*, the volume in which the first six pamphlets were brought together, was published in 1985, it was with the London publishing house Hutchinson, which had outlets in Australia, New Zealand, and South Africa. Field Day were aiming for readers further afield. This move was confirmed by the subsequent publication of the same volume the following year in the United States, this time courtesy of University of Notre Dame Press. An afterword – written 'specifically for American readers' as mentioned on the back cover – by Thomas Flanagan, the critic and writer, author of the best-selling historical novel *The Year of the French* (1979), returned to the image of the outsider eavesdropping on a private conversation:

> These are Irish writers debating, without provincialism, the condition and the future of their culture and their country. It is our good fortune that we can overhear what they say, because the debate extends, by implication, well beyond Ireland. They are talking, ultimately, about the place of the imagination in a world like ours.[10]

The third series, 'The Protestant Idea of Liberty' opened the door to critics both outside Field Day's inner circle and outside literary criticism with the inclusion of Terence Brown, Marianne Elliott, and Robert McCartney. Even more bravely, the fourth series ventured well outside the literary and into legal territory with three pamphlets relating to 'Emergency Legislation' and including contributions by Michael Farrell, Patrick McGrory, and Eanna Molloy. The fifth series, 'Nationalism, Colonialism and Literature' (1988), caused much controversy as two of the critics involved could lay no claim to any form of Irishness whatsoever (Palestinian-born and US-based Edward Said and American Frederic Jameson) while Oxford-based Terry Eagleton was better known for his work on English literature and literary theory from a Marxist perspective than for his Irish origins. Edna Longley's criticism that Deane was trying to make

Derry rhyme with Derrida was taken up again, this time deriding Field Day's reliance on outsiders to 'interpret between privacies'. However, this series marked a clear intervention in terms of postcolonial criticism, a critical paradigm that would dominate Irish studies for almost two decades. Here again Field Day were proving they were in tune with global academic debates, and fully able to draw world-famous critics into their intellectual ambit.

From the beginning, Deane had ambitions for the company's critical and publishing arm that were on an altogether different scale. He had greatly encouraged this diversification of activities, convinced as he was of the need to foster, within Field Day and in Ireland generally, better critical, and not exclusively creative or artistic, practices. The introduction to *Ireland's Field Day*, ended with an announcement:

> A central ambition ... will be the production of a large-scale anthology of Irish writing in the last 500 years. This anthology will have the aim of revealing and confirming the existence of a continuous tradition, contributed to by all groups, sects and parties, in which the possibility of a more generous and hospitable notion of Ireland's cultural achievements will emerge as the basis for a more ecumenical and eirenic approach to the deep and apparently implacable problems which confront the island today. (viii)

The anthology was scheduled to come out in 1988 but over time, the chronological span to be covered was expanded, increasing from 300 to 1500 years.[11] The cost of the project rose in proportion to this expansion, forcing the Field Day directors, particularly Deane and Friel, to seek to raise funds in the United States. Their efforts paid off, as is demonstrated by the acknowledgments in the published volume. No fewer than five of the eight major sponsors mentioned were American individuals or organizations, with a special mention for Marianne McDonald. The paragraph on 'Organizational Support in relation to Funding' is almost entirely American in hue, with Boston featuring prominently through various individuals and bodies. In fact, the development of Irish Studies on both sides of the Atlantic held out the promise that a definite market was to be found within the universities. Norton agreed to distribute the anthology in the United States while Faber looked after the British and European markets. More than half of the first print run was destined for the American market.[12]

The *Field Day Anthology* – three handsome, flawlessly presented tomes, adding up to over 4,500 pages – received an official launch in Dublin on 31 October 1991 with Taoiseach Charles Haughey in attendance, confirming that it was seen as a significant political as well as cultural intervention. But there were also in the following weeks various launches in the United Kingdom and in the United States, confirming the global ambition of the *Anthology*.

On the home front however, Field Day were in for a shock. On 11 November 1991, the writer and journalist Nuala O'Faolain launched an unexpected attack in an *Irish Times* article:

> Unfortunately, there are more kinds of imperialism than one. The male editors failed to find women interesting. Of all people, that Seamus Deane, a Northern Catholic, should not be alert to what it's like to be treated as a second-class citizen. The book ends with four up-to-date sections. 'Writing in Irish' covers 88 years: there are two women writers in the section. 'Irish Fiction' covers 25 years: the youngest of the women represented there is 47 years old. 'Drama' covers 32 years: there are no women represented there. 'Contemporary Poetry' contains work from 35 male and three female poets. When that sank in - when I brought myself to believe that they'd really done this - I began to question the whole book. If a compilation as seemingly authoritative as this came out in the USA, with these flaws, American women would not let it stand. They would demand its withdrawal ... While this book was demolishing the patriarchy of Britain on a grand front, its own, native, patriarchy was sitting there. Smug as ever.[13]

The campaign was short but decisive, with numerous academics worried about what they regarded as an unbelievable series of omissions resulting in the systematic obliteration of women's writings, and more generally in the down-playing of the role of women in literary and intellectual history. This concerted action coincided with the growing importance of Women's Studies and of the success of the women's movement since the late 1980s, as exemplified by the setting up of several centres for gender studies in Irish universities or by the creation of Attic Press, in the wake of a similar trend in the UK and US.[14] Deane conceded that the feminist angle had escaped him and suggested the preparation of a supplementary fourth volume entirely devoted to Irish women writers. Eight women editors were identified: Angela Bourke, Siobhan Kilfeather, Maria Luddy, Margaret MacCurtain, Gerardine Meaney, Mairin Nic Dhonnchadha, Mary O'Dowd, and Clair Wills.

This second anthology, like the first, took more time, more space, and more funding than was initially planned. In 2002, two thick volumes of some 1,500 and 1,700 pages respectively, were published by Cork University Press which, in the meantime, had become the publishing partners for *Critical Conditions*, a new series of critical texts edited by Seamus Deane as part of a revamped Field Day. It would be an exaggeration to suggest that the angry reaction to the anthology on the part of the increasingly vocal Irish feminist lobby had a direct impact on the place that legislation relating to gender (divorce, abortion, homosexuality) was to occupy in the following years. Nonetheless, there is an arresting coincidence and the commissioning of two further volumes to correct the gender imbalance of the first three testified eloquently to yet another global shift in critical paradigms, as postcolonial discourse increasingly had to vie for prominence on campuses and in print with women's studies, soon to morph into gender studies.

After Brian Friel officially resigned from Field Day in 1994, the company effectively died a natural though somewhat protracted and acrimonious death. Given the global success achieved by *Dancing at Lughnasa* – the best play Field Day never had – Stephen Rea's despair at seeing this play escape Field Day and the north, to be given instead to Dublin and the Abbey, is fully justified. To some extent, the themes of *Dancing at Lughnasa* bear the mark of encroaching globalization: what the play charts are the shockwaves of the belated industrial revolution hitting Ballybeg in the late 1930s and threatening a whole traditional, communal way of life with imminent and irrevocable extinction – as networks and connections, not yet called global, come into existence with the radio, factories (outsourcing of labour), emigration, and the Spanish civil war. One could well make a case for the success of *Dancing at Lughnasa* being closely connected, consciously or not, with the early tremors of globalization felt by Irish audiences in the 1990s, as Patrick Lonergan argues in *Theatre and Globalization*.[15] While *Lughnasa* went from strength to strength, Stephen Rea and Seamus Deane agreed to try to keep the much-reduced Field Day show on the road, each in his own area of expertise. Thus Stephen Rea went to on direct and act in *Uncle Vanya* which opened at the Guildhall in 1995, then to stage in association with Belfast's Tinderbox a memorable production of Stewart Parker's *Northern Star* in the First Presbyterian Church of Rosemary Street in November 1998, the very church where several of the United Irishmen of the play would have worshipped. Sean O'Casey's *The Plough and the Stars*, which Stephen Rea directed in 2000, was no longer an official Field Day production, though Rea claimed he had worked as he used to work for the company.[16]

But it is in the critical field that the Field Day name lives on. 1996, the same year the Field Day Derry office closed, saw the publication of the first four volumes of a new series of Field Day Essays with Seamus Deane as general editor, published by Cork University Press as 'The Critical Conditions' series, which now runs to fifteen volumes. In 2005 came *The Field Day Review*, launched in the Verbal Arts Centre in Derry, and published annually ever since. As for the Field Day Files, their first issue consisted of the publication of Joe Cleary's

Outrageous Fortune: Capital and Culture in Modern Ireland in 2006 and since then various monographs have been added to the list. It is clear that the new Field Day publishing company is reaching out to a transatlantic constituency, based as it is since 2004 in Newman House, Dublin as part of the Keough-Naughton Institute for Irish Studies at Notre Dame University, Indiana, to which Deane was affiliated from 1993.

The critical spirit of the pamphlets has found other outlets but the intended audience of such books and series is the global world of Irish Studies, particularly well represented in American universities – and not primarily the Irish reader. The current Field Day has little in common with the Friel-Rea project for a Derry-based touring theatre company, but there can be no doubt that, in their trajectory on the page and on the stage through the 1980s and early 1990s, as well as in their present incarnation as an Irish-American, largely academic venture, Field Day have proved that a strong dedication to a local base and 'the matter of Ireland' could be reconciled with a truly global reach.

---

[1] Stephen Rea interviewed by Martine Pelletier, '"Creating Ideas to Live By": An interview with Stephen Rea', *Sources* 9 (Autumn 2000): 52. Subsequent references appear in the text.

[2] Brian Friel interviewed by Paddy Agnew, 'Talking to Ourselves', *Magill*, December 1980: 60. Friel was already at that point an internationally acclaimed playwright and it was unlikely that a new play of his would fail to attract attention outside of Ireland. Moreover, Field Day would rapidly agree to take *Translations* to London and further afield.

[3] Nicholas Grene, The Politics of Irish Drama: Plays in Context from Boucicault to Friel (Cambridge: Cambridge University Press, 1999): 49.

[4] Marilynn Richtarik, Acting Between the Lines. The Field Day Theatre Company and Irish Cultural Politics, 1980-84 (Oxford: Clarendon Press, 1994): 204-5.

[5] See Grene, 266.

[6] Friel, 79.

[7] Seamus Heaney, *The Cure at Troy* (London: Faber, 1990): 77.

[8] See Richtarik, 126.

[9] Deane, letter to the author, 25 May 2000.

[10] Seamus Deane (ed.) *Ireland's Field Day* (South Bend: Notre Dame University Press, 1986): 117.

[11] For a more thorough discussion of the *Field Day Anthology* see Martine Pelletier, 'Acts of Definition: The Field Day Anthologies of Irish Writing' in *The Book in Ireland*. Edited by J. Genêt, S. Mikowski & F. Garcier (Newcastle: Cambridge Scholars Press, 2006): 206-227.

[12] See Conor McCarthy, *Modernisation. Crisis and Culture in Ireland 1969-1992*. (Dublin: Four Courts Press, 2000): 202.

[13] Nuala O'Faolain, 'The Voice that Field Day Didn't Record'. *The Irish Times*, 11 November 1991: 14.

[14] Attic Press was founded in 1984 and was taken over by Cork University Press in 1997. A feminist publishing house, Attic Press both enabled the publication of books on women's issues and contributed to the rise of women's studies and the wider feminist movement in Ireland.

[15] Patrick Lonergan, *Theatre and Globalization: Irish Drama in the Celtic Tiger Era* (Basingstoke and New York: Palgrave Macmillan, 2009): 31-55.

[16] Pelletier, *Sources*, 57-58

3 | 'We'll Be the Judges of That': The Critical Reception of *DruidSynge* in the USA

José Lanters

DruidSynge, Druid Theatre Company's production of the cycle of all six plays written by John Millington Synge during his brief lifetime, premiered at the Galway Arts Festival on 16 July 2005, and in subsequent months was performed in Dublin, Edinburgh, and a range of locations on the Aran island of Inis Meáin.[1] The critical response to the event in all these locations was overwhelmingly positive, as evidenced by Karen Fricker's summary, in the Autumn 2005 issue of *Irish Theatre Magazine*, of Irish and British newspaper reviews of *DruidSynge*:

> It is 'a triumph', according to *The Connaught Tribune*. *The Examiner* gave it five stars. Emer O'Kelly in *The Sunday Independent* imagined it as a 'chariot of dramatic fire' and 'a spinning sun in the theatrical heavens'. Michael Billington declared punningly in *The Guardian* that it is quite impossible to 'have too much of a good Synge'. And Fintan O'Toole, in *The Irish Times*, proclaimed DruidSynge 'one of the most important events in the history of Irish theatre'.[2]

While conceding that '[t]he level of ecstatic critical uniformity generated by *DruidSynge* doesn't come along very often; nor, indeed, does a theatrical project as ambitious and impressive', Fricker went on to ask a series of pointed questions about the nature of Druid's project which, as its name suggests, focused as much on the theatre company as it did on the playwright and his works. Before the show went on the road, aspects of the production, publicity, and marketing were carefully packaged by Druid 'to present a coherent, unified, and attractive theatrical product', and Fricker felt that the entire experience was designed to make 'high praise ... a foregone conclusion' (23-4). The formula worked in Britain and Ireland; Druid's American tour of the Synge cycle in 2006, however, elicited a much more mixed response from audiences and reviewers: not only to the concept of *DruidSynge*, but also to the performances and the plays themselves.

DruidSynge premiered in the United States in June 2006 at the Guthrie Theatre in Minneapolis, Minnesota, where it was the first stage show following the theatre's opening festivities for its new venue on the banks of the Mississippi. The entire cycle of six plays was performed twice, on 27 June and 1 July, while on the three intervening nights the plays were presented in pairs: *Riders to the Sea* and *Deirdre of the Sorrows* on 28 June; *The Tinker's Wedding* and *The Well of the Saints* on 29 June; and *The Shadow of the Glen* and *The Playboy of the Western World* on 30 June. From Minneapolis, the production moved to the Lincoln Center Festival in New York City, where the entire cycle was performed seven times between 10-23 July in the Gerald W. Lynch Theater at John Jay College. The Lincoln Center initially assumed it had the US premiere of *DruidSynge*, and information to that effect, provided by the festival, appeared in *The New York Times*, which subsequently had to print a rectification when it turned out that Joe Dowling had secured the premiere for the Guthrie – an unexpected order of events that led *BroadwayWorld* to print the tortuous headline, 'Pre-Lincoln Center *DruidSynge* Hits St Paul's Guthrie 6/27'.[3] For the Druid Theatre Company, the five-week tour of the USA was the highlight of 2006. For theatre audiences and reviewers in Minneapolis and New York alike, the *DruidSynge* cycle was, in many ways, the conundrum of 2006.

Garry Hynes decided a long time ago to make touring central to Druid's commercial and artistic policy. Irish commentators have tended to respond to Hynes's enterprising spirit with a mixture of mild cynicism and grudging admiration. In 2005, Karen Fricker described the director as 'a woman on a mission' to bring the works of Synge to a larger audience, and pointed out that, because Synge's achievement 'is so difficult to classify, the unifying element – and the star player – in *DruidSynge* becomes Hynes herself'.[4] In 2009, Deirdre Falvey ironically referred to Druid's 'barmy – if really impressive' planned schedule that year of 335 performances in twenty-six venues in five countries as an attempt at 'world domination', and cited the enthusiastic response to this undertaking of Eugene Downes, chief executive of Culture Ireland, one of the funding agents for Druid's international touring programme: 'I can't think of a better way to convince global audiences that Ireland is a world leader in creativity'. Minister for Arts Martin Cullen concurred: 'Druid is now recognised by leading international festivals, venues and critics as a company of world stature'.[5] Garry Hynes herself has described Druid's 'mammoth touring schedule' as a 'testament to the value for money the arts provide'.[6]

The commercial and political interest in Irish theatre on tour cannot be separated from the strategy prevalent during the Celtic Tiger era of selling 'Irishness' as a commodity in the international marketplace. One consequence of the success of this approach is that Irish plays are often 'marketed or received internationally as corresponding to the Irish "brand",' suggests Patrick Lonergan.[7] The limited range of references and conventions associated with that brand has become so well established that audiences expect to encounter them in every play. John Harrington notes with some dismay that the critical response to the Abbey Theatre's production of *The Playboy of the Western World* during its 2004 Centenary Tour of the United States did not stray much beyond references to Yeats, Joyce, Beckett, the Celtic tenors, whiskey, Blarney, and the McCourt brothers.[8] While there certainly is validity in Lonergan's caution that, '[j]ust as Irish critics should condemn stereotypical representations of Irishness on the global stage, we must also be alert to the dangers of essentializing the response of non-Irish audiences',[9] such responses are nevertheless often predictable because in general, as the same author suggests elsewhere, the majority of contemporary theatre-goers, in the USA and Europe alike, 'do not pay for something *new* or unfamiliar, but instead to have their presuppositions ... confirmed'.[10] American (and especially Irish-American) audiences often resist representations of Irishness that do not fall within their experience, expectations, or comfort zone. For that reason, the perceived rural nostalgia of Brian Friel's *Dancing at Lughnasa* worked on Broadway, but the contemporary urban mid-life angst of *Wonderful Tennessee* did not. Marina Carr's characters and her representation of the Midlands often meet with hostility or incomprehension: after seeing a performance of *Portia Coughlan* in Pittsburgh in 2001, one audience member referred to the characters as 'trash' and dismissed them as not 'my kind of Irish'.[11]

Much as in the case of the 2004 Abbey tour referred to above, American reviewers of *DruidSynge* frequently resorted to comparisons between Synge's works and those of better-known figures from the Irish theatrical pantheon, or at least writers whose work had recently been seen on the New York stage, in an attempt to place the relatively unfamiliar playwright in a context that would make sense to their readers (and in some cases, one suspects, to themselves). The names of Samuel Beckett, Martin McDonagh, and Conor McPherson were most often invoked. The reviewer for *The Philadelphia Inquirer* spotted a connection between Synge's *The Well of the Saints* and Brian Friel's *Molly Sweeney*.[12] Only *Deirdre of* the Sorrows posed problems in this regard, and left critics at a loss for better-known Irish equivalents with which to compare Synge's unfinished play: indeed, one frequently heard complaint was that Druid's 'brogue-free' interpretation of Synge's 'Celtic' play was not Irish enough. The phrase critics most often resorted to in relation to Deirdre was 'Shakespearian'.

   To a considerable extent, American theatre critics appeared to limit themselves in their responses to what they thought their audiences would know and expect. An interesting case in point is presented by two different articles written by the same critic in The New York Times: Charles Isherwood wrote a long piece about DruidSynge when the play cycle was first performed in Dublin in 2005,[13] and then reviewed the production again in 2006 when it was staged as part of the New York Lincoln Center Festival.[14] Although both articles are overwhelmingly positive, the difference in tone between them is striking. The piece written in Dublin in August 2005 describes an Irish event staged in Ireland, at a time when no American tour of DruidSynge had yet been arranged. The article written in 2006 was addressed to a New York audience and dealt with the same event taking place in that city. The earlier article is wide-ranging in its historical and cultural references, and almost academic in its tone and in the way it provides a context for the playwright, his oeuvre, and the production under review. It acknowledges the extent to which Garry Hynes's 'enterprising efforts' have been instrumental in reviving interest in Synge's life and career, and it gives a detailed assessment of each play and each performance. When Isherwood writes about the Lincoln Center Festival in 2006, he sounds like a different critic. In this later piece, his attitude towards Synge and the Synge cycle is markedly defensive in anticipation of the response of his fellow New Yorkers. Gone is the urbane, almost academic perspective, to be replaced by a more popular register that does not shy away from cultural clichés. Isherwood clearly feels that New Yorkers will need some persuading to go and see a Synge marathon in the middle of summer. If the alternatives are a trip to the beach or to Shea Stadium, do people really want to enter a dark theatre to spend the day 'submerged in the little-known oeuvre of the Irish playwright J.M. Synge in its entirety? Don't all jump at once, guys: tickets are still available!' In his earlier article about the Dublin performance of DruidSynge, Isherwood had merely stated that experiencing all plays in one sitting is 'vastly more illuminating' than seeing them piecemeal on separate occasions. In the 2006 article, nothing is less self-evident. The prospect of sitting through all six plays, he admits to his readers, 'seems daunting' and rather like 'the theatrical equivalent of a Super Big Gulp'. To convince his readers of the merit of such an endeavour, he resorts to a confession, from one New Yorker to another, about his own first encounter with the play cycle:

> Intimidated myself when I traveled to Dublin last summer, I initially saw the plays in three separate programs, before returning, at the friendly urging of Ms Hynes, to see 'DruidSynge' in a one-day immersion. She was right to persuade me: the cycle was designed to be experienced as a single entity, and is more powerful seen whole. The Lincoln Center Festival has wisely – and bravely – programmed it in full-day installments only.

In the article written in 2005, Isherwood praises the way the production brings the plays together, 'with comedy and pathos emphasized in different measures as one play succeeds another. A vibrant physicality, an earthy, almost exaggerated realism and an idiomatic ear for Synge's rich, folk-lyric language run through them all'. That folk-lyrical quality, discussed in 2005 as a self-evident aspect of Synge's work, is presented in 2006 as a challenge. The production, Isherwood suggests in the later article, 'brings alive a milieu that feels both intriguingly remote and utterly intimate, exotic in the eccentric syntax and unruly lyricism of its earthy dialogue – God bless the Irish! – but familiar in its consoling knowledge of the loneliness and despair that are the sorrowful scars of all humankind'. Synge's dark yet life-affirming vision, he writes later, is expressed 'in some of the most gorgeous rustic language you'll ever hear onstage; language almost Shakespearian in its texture and vitality'. To which he adds as an aside: '(Don't fret if you lose some of the dialogue, as you surely will, given the idiomatic delivery of the actors and the imperfect acoustics of the Gerald W. Lynch Theater at John Jay College; there's plenty more on the way.)'

Isherwood also anticipates that New Yorkers will not be as accommodating of Hynes's theatrically less effective *Deirdre* as he himself had been in 2005, when he saw 'something aptly Syngean in the cycle concluding not with a bravura bang but with quiet letdown'. In 2006, the impatient New Yorker in him states: 'After the intoxicating high of "Playboy", it must be acknowledged that "Deirdre of the Sorrows" comes as a bit of a letdown and, to be entirely honest, a bit of a trial too'. Rather than place the play within the context of Synge's oeuvre and Hynes's vision, as he had done previously, Isherwood provides his readers with a more practical rationale for sticking it out to the bitter end: 'it would be a shame – make that a disgrace – to leave before "Deirdre", pleading fatigue or an early meeting. The plays are not performed with individual curtain calls. So only at the conclusion of the cycle do we have a chance to acknowledge the company's extraordinary work'.

Charles Isherwood knows the New York public. He anticipates, correctly, that audiences will baulk at the length of the performance, its language, and the nature of the final play. Reviewers, however, can have a significant effect on audience response. When Fintan O'Toole saw *The Beauty Queen of Leenane* in New York in 1998 in a preview performance, before it had been reviewed, he noted that those attending 'seemed deeply uncertain about how to respond to McDonagh's blackly comic world'. When he saw the same production again, after reviewers had praised the comedy of the play, 'the audience was laughing its head off in all the right places'.[15] For Charles Isherwood to raise the issues that he does, even in a pre-emptive attempt to encourage audiences to look past them, has the inevitable effect of emphasizing that such issues exist. The reviewer thus perpetuates, even encourages exactly the response he is trying to forestall, and ends up condescending to his audience in the process. Isherwood's own 2005 article in *The New York Times* on the Dublin run of *DruidSynge* indicates that there was no need for such a cautious approach.

All this is not to say that Isherwood was incorrect in his assumptions about how *DruidSynge* would be received in New York – or, indeed, in Minneapolis – because there were few noticeable differences between the responses to the production in these cities. American reviewers overwhelmingly focused on exactly the issues Isherwood had singled out, particularly the length of the performance, and Synge's baroque language. At least a dozen reviewers mentioned the 'authentic' impenetrability of the performers' accents. According to Bloomberg's John Simon, 'the brogue used is so thick it could blunt any knife trying to cut it, and left most of the audience chasing after comprehensible words like sparrows after sparse crumbs'.[16] *The New York Daily News* complained that 'some actors have accents so thick you might regret not knowing Gaelic'.[17] Denis Staunton reported on the problem in *The Irish Times*:

> At the end of *Riders to the Sea*, the first of six plays in DruidSynge, much of the audience at New York's Gerald W. Lynch Theatre made a dash towards the cloakroom. They were not looking for their coats – in the scorching July heat, nobody had one – but queuing for earphones designed for the hard of hearing. By the end of the first interval all the earphones were sold out, as more than 600 New Yorkers strained to decipher Synge's words delivered by Druid's actors in the authentic voices of rural Ireland.[18]

The *Washington Times* critic, who attended the first night of the Minneapolis run, observed that 'more than one theatergoer could be heard grumbling in the lobby about the difficulty of understanding the actors'.[19] Ed Huyck praised the acoustics of the new Guthrie Theatre's McGuire Proscenium stage while confessing in the same breath, seemingly without irony, that he had a problem understanding Synge's language: 'By Tuesday evening, a near-capacity audience filled the theatre for *The Playboy of the Western World* and *Deirdre of the Sorrows* ... And while the thick, unfamiliar accents made much of the dialogue hard to understand, there was no difficulty in hearing the actors or seeing the action'.[20] The muffled acoustics at the John Jay College theatre in New York City did contribute to the problem of audibility. A number of commentators wished for supertitles.

If Michael Billington's declaration in *The Guardian* newspaper, that it is quite impossible to 'have too much of a good Synge', can be seen as representative of the British and Irish response to *DruidSynge*, the comment of the reviewer in *The Philadelphia Inquirer*, by contrast, that 'all of Synge may be too much Synge', can be said to reflect the general sentiment expressed by American critics.[21] 'Synge, Synge, Synge: six plays by one author in eight and a half hours? It might get anybody's Irish up', said the headline of a review in *The Village Voice*, whose author, Michael Feingold, argued that, as a way of enjoying Synge, 'sitting through his entire oeuvre in one day is like a pie-eating contest as a way of enjoying dessert'.[22] For *The New York Post*'s Frank Scheck, sitting through six works that were never meant to be seen one after the other was 'an experience akin to cramming a graduate-level college course into one punishing day'.[23] *The Wall Street Journal* drama critic Terry Teachout confessed, 'Between the strain of understanding some of the actors and the sheer length of the performance, I found "DruidSynge" to be a bit of a slog'.[24]

Inevitably, given the almost unanimous description by US critics of *DruidSynge* as an endurance test, the cast members were praised as much for their stamina as for the quality of their performances. 'If you think it's hard to sit through all six of John Millington Synge's plays, one after the other, ... imagine what it's like to perform them', Barbara Hoffman wrote in *The New York Post*.[25] In the same paper, Frank Scheck praised the actors for their 'admirable versatility and endurance'.[26] For several reviewers, any enjoyment of Synge's work or even of the individual performances was eclipsed by the overwhelming sense that they were witnessing a project. 'It felt like an event for an event's sake', Jeremy McCarter wrote in *The New York Magazine*: 'not an especially shrewd way to savor great writing'.[27] Michael Feingold put it more bluntly in *The Village Voice*: 'Festivals are for pigs ... *DruidSynge* has to have been a festival marketer's idea of a good time in the theater'.[28] For him, the only redeeming feature of the event was Druid's version of *The Playboy*. These negative statements about festivals can be seen as reactions to the phenomenon of event-driven theatre, where 'audiences ... consume the experience of *having been to* the play' rather than engaging fully with the work or the performance.[29] For David Finkle, *DruidSynge* revealed as much about the concept as it did about the playwright:

> Hynes begins each of the six pieces ... with an economical tableau. When the opaque black scrim lifts, the director presents a lone figure holding a pose before beginning an action ... While the lone figure is a striking convention, it is also a giveaway to a problem that occasionally mars *DruidSynge*. Hynes is essentially implying that we're witnessing something iconic: and the unwanted (and unverbalized) response from some spectators may be, 'We'll be the judges of that'.[30]

A number of critics lacked a clear understanding of the socio-historical context of Synge's characters: to call his plays 'bleak, at times darkly comic tales of the downtrodden working class',[31] as the *Washington Times* critic did, was to evoke an inappropriate Marxist register; to call them 'slice-of-life tales of common Irish folk'[32] was to make them sound like an Irish version of the BBC radio soap opera 'The Archers' ('An everyday story of country folk'). In the absence of a cultural context, most reviewers had no concept of the place of 'tinkers' in Irish society, nor was Hynes's decision to represent the characters in *The Tinker's Wedding* as contemporary Travellers well understood. Toby Zinman thought it a clever move, but for the wrong reasons, believing that it created 'a portrait not of "folk" but of the provincial homeless'.[33] Michael Kuchwara's plot summary of the play, in which he describes Marie Mullen playing 'a raucous, drunken hag whose indifferent son is being corralled into marriage by a slatternly younger woman',[34] ignored the 'tinkers' context altogether, as did Joe Dziemianowicz's understanding of the play as being about 'a rural couple and a greedy priest'.[35]

Garry Hynes, 'whom many consider Ireland's pre-eminent theatre director', as *The New York Times* claimed when it profiled her in 2006,[36] was often given special mention by American reviewers for her determination, innovative style, and risk-taking skills. The sometimes slightly sycophantic nature of critical responses to Druid and its Tony-winning director may have been what rubbed Bloomberg's John Simon the wrong way. The unfairly negative tone of his review of the Lincoln Center event seems above all to have been a reaction to the sometimes uncritical reception of everything done by Druid in New York in the wake of the success of the *Leenane Trilogy*. Having dismissed the *DruidSynge* set as 'dismally shabby', the 'rural Irish syntax' as 'monotonous', the leading man as 'both unattractive and undistinguished', and Marie Mullen as 'overexposed in five plays', Simon writes of the nineteen actors that 'maybe three or four belong on a metropolitan stage'. He then goes on to suggest that the show's director 'is not really major league despite her lofty reputation at home and abroad. She gets the job done, but without that inconspicuously convincing extra touch that marks the true master'.[37]

The most important issue for John Simon, however, was that 'poor, tubercular Synge ... did not grow into a significant dramatist'. To question Synge's standing as a playwright is, of course, not a new critical departure, nor is it an American prerogative. Karen Fricker reports that, after the premiere of *DruidSynge* at Galway's Town Hall Theatre, some jokers were heard to wonder 'whether it was really necessary to go to such lengths to prove ... that Synge wrote one great play'.[38] But while opinion varies about the quality of the playwright's entire oeuvre, in Ireland, unlike in the USA, Synge has been an important and constant presence in the national conversation from the beginning of the twentieth century onwards. Certainly, Druid's 1982 *Playboy* rescued the play from overly pious interpretations: up to that point, Fintan O'Toole argues, 'Synge existed in the worst kind of artistic limbo. He was a semi-official figure, paid too much empty homage as a national treasure to be interesting to the young and yet too neglected to be a real, serious presence in the culture'.[39] While Synge was perhaps misunderstood, he was not a forgotten figure, however. Before Garry Hynes put her stamp on his oeuvre, others, ranging from W.B. Yeats and James Joyce to Myles na Gopaleen and Charles Haughey, had appropriated the playwright for their own ends. Druid may have been responsible 'for our fresh understanding of Synge's genius', as Colm Tóibín argues, but it did not have to rescue him from oblivion. [40]

In the United States, Synge does not have the iconic presence he has in Ireland, and *DruidSynge* consequently had a different impact on that side of the Atlantic. Knowledge of Synge's work and reputation varied greatly from critic to critic, and there was little agreement on whether Synge's works were overly familiar or totally unknown to American audiences. The *Washington Times* reviewer argued that Synge is, on the whole, 'not well-known to American audiences'.[41] Michael Feingold's appraisal of *DruidSynge* as an exercise in 'festival tedium', on the other hand, stemmed in part from his sense that, apart from *The Well of the Saints* and *Deirdre*, 'Synge's four other plays are as familiar to me (or to anyone my age who's done time in a drama school or college theater department) as corned beef is to cabbage'.[42] According to Brooke Allen in *The New Criterion*, Hynes restored 'fizz and kick' to a group of plays that all in recent decades 'have become classics, and rather musty ones at that, with the popular *Playboy*, in particular, subjected to countless college and amateur productions'.[43] Terry Teachout argued in *The Wall Street Journal* that in America, Synge has 'vanished into the pantheon of half-remembered masters – none of his plays has been seen on Broadway since 1971'. Since Synge's work 'is no longer familiar enough for Americans to have any preconceptions about it', theatre-goers 'take it for granted when Synge's peasants are played not as poetry-spouting romantics but dirty barefoot louts'. Without the shock value, this reviewer felt that *DruidSynge* came across as a 'mixed bag' – good in parts perhaps, but decidedly uneven.[44]

Although there seems no question that the American tour of *DruidSynge* was successful, what Karen Fricker called 'the level of ecstatic critical uniformity generated by *DruidSynge*' in Ireland and the UK was not duplicated in the USA. If there was critical agreement about the event, it was that the length of the show taxed audience patience; that it was hard to understand; that the performances were admirable; and that, while Druid's interpretation of *The Playboy* made the marathon (almost) worthwhile, Synge's oeuvre came across as uneven. The spectrum of critical responses to *DruidSynge* was broad, ranging from ecstasy (Charles Isherwood, who called the event 'the highlight of ... my theatre-going life'[45]) to exhaustion (*TimeOut*'s reviewer, who felt that 'Garry Hynes's ambitious undertaking doesn't accumulate enough dramatic force to energize its audience'[46]). On a scale from one emotional extreme to the other, most critics were slightly more bored than they were ecstatic.

In interviews with the media on both sides of the Atlantic, Garry Hynes made a point of stressing Synge's modernity and relevance to the contemporary world. In a lengthy profile published in *The New York Times* the week before *DruidSynge* opened at the Lincoln Center Festival, Hynes explained that the experience of producing Synge's *Playboy* in 1982 fuelled in her 'an ambition to present Synge whole, as a radically modern writer – look at how he shaped Beckett, for instance'.[47] Randy Gener's 'Front and Center' piece in *American Theatre*, entitled 'Synge Our Contemporary', also emphasized that Hynes's 'landmark staging of Synge's complete works ... seeks to restore the writer's essential modernity'.[48] While a number of reviewers echoed these sentiments and the name of Beckett was often invoked, Synge's modernity was not, by and large, foregrounded in the press reports. The production's 'earthiness' was much commented upon, given that Francis O'Connor's set featured 'a damp dirt floor as gritty as Synge's characters'.[49] David Cote thought that Synge's lyricism conveyed 'more texture than sense', but nevertheless found *DruidSynge* impressive 'for letting New Yorkers walk around in Synge country for a day. You may even find yourself looking down to see if you've got peat on your soles'.[50]

Often what critics chose to focus upon read as a litany of the usual Irish stereotypes. For Toby Zinman, all the plays revolved around the same issues: 'Lonesome people search for love; the beauties of the natural world are praised; the Catholic Church fails to provide; poverty is the general condition; drunkenness is the frequent condition; and violence is the normal recourse'.[51] *The Washington Times* saw 'murders, betrayals, unfortunate accidents, beatings, drunken brawls, raging thunderstorms and other assorted bad luck and mayhem'.[52] The greater part of the critical responses to Druid's 2006 US tour of the Synge cycle appeared to confirm Patrick Lonergan's contention that the majority of contemporary theatre-goers do not wish to be unduly challenged, but rather seek confirmation of what they think they already know. *DruidSynge* in America revealed at least as much about American presuppositions about Irishness as it did about Druid's interpretation of the plays of J.M. Synge.

---

[1] The six plays were *Riders to the Sea, The Shadow of the Glen, The Tinker's Wedding, The Well of the Saints, The Playboy of the Western World*, and *Deirdre of the Sorrows*. Synge's early play *When the Moon Has Set* did not feature.

[2] Karen Fricker, 'Expanding the Cottage Walls', *Irish Theatre Magazine* 5.24 (Autumn 2005) (22-24): 22. The subsequent page reference is included in the text.

[3] 'Pre-Lincoln Center DruidSynge Hits St Paul's Guthrie 6/27', *BroadwayWorld*, 22 June 2006.

[4] Karen Fricker, 'Druid Company Sings Synge Song', *Variety* 399.9 (25-31 July 2005): 54.

[5] Deirdre Falvey, 'Druid Returns to its Spiritual Home', *The Irish Times*, 28 March 2009, Weekend: 8.

[6] Quoted in Lorna Siggins, 'Druid Performs Three Plays in Three Time Zones', *The Irish Times*, 13 November 2009: 2.

[7] Patrick Lonergan, *Theatre and Globalization: Irish Drama in the Celtic Tiger Era* (Basingstoke and New York: Palgrave Macmillan, 2009): 28.

[8] John P. Harrington, 'The Abbey in America: The Real Thing', *Irish Theatre on Tour*, eds. Chris Morash and Nicholas Grene (Dublin: Carysfort, 2005): 37.

[9] Patrick Lonergan, 'Druid Theatre's *Leenane Trilogy* on Tour: 1996-2001', *Irish Theatre on Tour*: 210.

[10] Lonergan, *Theatre and Globalization*, 86.

[11] Melissa Sihra, 'Marina Carr in the US: Perception, Conflict and Culture in Irish Theatre Abroad', *Irish Theatre on Tour*: 180.

[12] Toby Zinman, 'Tragedy, Comedy, Repetition in Synge Marathon', *The Philadelphia Inquirer* 12 July 2006: C3.

[13] Charles Isherwood, 'Nasty, Brutish and Gloriously Long', *The New York Times*, 28 August 2005, Section 2: 1.

[14] Charles Isherwood, 'Why Not Take All of Synge?' , *The New York Times*, 12 July 2006: E1.

[15] Fintan O'Toole, 'In the Theatre, the Audience Makes the Play', *The Irish Times*, 31 October 2009, Weekend: 9.

[16] John Simon, Review of *DruidSynge* (Lincoln Center), Bloomberg, 14 July 2006

[17] Joe Dziemianowicz, 'Something to Synge About', *The New York Daily News*, 12 July 2006: 35.

[18] Denis Staunton, 'US Finds Synge Worth the Strain', *The Irish Times*, 15 July 2006, Weekend: 7.

[19] 'Synge-ing Joy, but Mostly the Blues', *The Washington Times*, 7 July 2006

[20] Ed Huyck, 'New Guthrie Sets New Course, Honors Tradition', *BackStage*, 12 July 2006

[21] Zinman, C3.

[22] Michael Feingold, 'Synge, Synge, Synge', *The Village Voice*, 19-25 July 2006: 45.

[23] Frank Scheck, 'Fluid Druid at Fest', *The New York Post*, 12 July 2006: 60.

[24] Terry Teachout, 'All Synge, All the Time', *The Wall Street Journal*, 14 July 2006: W5.

[25] Barbara Hoffmann, 'Playing an Extended Run', *The New York Post*, 12 July 2006: 60.

[26] Scheck, 60.

[27] Jeremy McCarter, 'Blackboard Jungle '06', *The New York Magazine*, 24 July 2006.

[28] Feingold, 45.

[29] Lonergan, *Theatre and Globalization*, 69.

[30] David Finkle, Review of *DruidSynge* (Lincoln Center), *Theatermania*, 11 July 2006.

[31] 'Synge-ing Joy', n.p.

[32] Dziemianowicz, 35.

[33] Zinman, C3.

[34] Michael Kuchwara, ' "DruidSynge" a 9-Hour Celebration', *The Washington Post*, 11 July 2006

[35] Dziemianowicz, 35.

[36] Celia McGee, 'An Irish Director Arrives With 8½ Hours of Her Countryman', *The New York Times*, 2 July 2006, Section 2: 4.

[37] Simon, n.p. The subsequent quotation is from the same article.

[38] Fricker, 'Expanding the Cottage Walls', 24.

[39] Fintan O'Toole, 'A Gallous Story and a Dirty Deed: Druid's Synge', *Synge: A Celebration*, ed. Colm Tóibín (Dublin: Carysfort, 2005): 34.

40 Colm Tóibín, cover text, *Synge: A Celebration.*

41 'Synge-ing Joy', n.p.

42 Feingold, 45.

43 Brooke Allen, 'Summer Offerings (New York Theater)', *New Criterion*, 25.1 (1 September 2006): 89.

44 Teachout, W5.

45 Charles Isherwood, 'Theater; Waking Up the Rock Musical and Other triumphs', *The New York Times*, 24 December 2006, Section 2: 4.

46 David Cote, Review of *DruidSynge* (Lincoln Center), *TimeOut* (New York) , 564 (20-26 July 2006)

47 McGee, 4.

48 Randy Gener, 'Synge Our Contemporary', *American Theatre*, 23.6 (July-August 2006): 23.

49 Dziemianowicz, 35.

50 Cote, n.p.

51 Zinman, C3.

52 'Synge-ing Joy', n.p.

4 | Abbey Tours to London after 1990

Richard Cave

In the early 1900s, the Abbey Theatre was the only Irish company touring regularly to England.[1] That position, as sole carrier of the Irish theatrical flame into England, went largely unchallenged until the formation of the Gate Theatre in the late 1920s.[2] Even then, the amount of Irish drama performed exclusively by Irish actors in productions originating in Ireland accounted for a small fraction of the fare being offered annually in metropolitan theatres. By the 1990s, the situation had changed significantly. The Abbey is now but one of many Irish companies coming to tour in London. In part, this is because of the great proliferation of alternative or fringe companies throughout Ireland, which matches that in England since the 1970s. This certainly fulfils Yeats's dream of a vibrant theatrical culture, fuelled by fine playwriting; but it is a situation that has to some extent marginalized in English perceptions the theatre that he helped to found. In the period 1990-2006, a total of 585 productions of plays by Irish dramatists have been performed in London.[3] Of these only sixty (10.25%) were toured to England by major Irish repertory companies (the Abbey, the Gate, Druid, Field Day, Rough Magic); exactly half of that number were the work of the Gate, where some 19 productions made up the Beckett Festival promoted by BITE at the Barbican Theatre in 1999, seven of which were revived for the Beckett Centenary Season also at the Barbican in 2006. Abbey Theatre productions in London over this period number 13 if one counts only Irish plays (or 15 if one includes stagings of plays by Ibsen and Euripides[4]). What impresses is the increasing number of smaller, less established companies coming to fringe venues in London in these years.[5] What surprises is the vastly increased number of English productions of Irish plays: The Royal National Theatre (25), the Royal Shakespeare Company (17), Royal Court (25), Tricycle (33), Bush (15), Almeida (10), Orange Tree (16), Hampstead (7), and Young Vic (5) account for a total of 153 productions (26.17% of the total number of productions monitored over the period).[6] Noticeable in this list is the high proportion of theatres in receipt of major state funding.

One can only speculate about what these figures might indicate. One might interpret them as suggesting an appropriation of the Irish theatrical heritage by English practitioners; as implying a concern to cater for a substantial minority but vocal social group within the fabric of cosmopolitan 'English' society; as an attempt in the context of the peace process for Northern Ireland, which struggled into existence over this same period, to come to terms with the inherited consequences of the historical process of colonialism and to understand the Irish situation more precisely through an engagement with its cultural expressions; or it may involve a recognition of a vibrancy and urgent energy and a brilliance of linguistic usage in Irish playwriting felt to be lacking in English dramaturgy. These reflections are the product of studying the reception of many of these productions (Irish and English) in the press reviews, where critics find a need to explain the surge in new Irish writing and revivals of so-called 'classics'. A crucial touchstone in such speculations is the indisputable success of Nicholas Kent as Artistic Director of The Tricycle Theatre in Kilburn which aims its work consistently at the interests of the local community (a mix of spectators with Irish or Caribbean roots and cultural affiliations) but has steadily attracted audiences from a far wider demographic through the sheer quality and challenge of its stagings.[7]

Where the Abbey once sustained a solo position in terms of touring in England, the theatre is now but one voice amongst many and its status as Ireland's *national* theatre is scarcely mentioned in reviews unless, ironically, critics are writing adversely about the particular production on offer. The rest of this essay engages with the complex reception of Abbey productions by English reviewers. To facilitate an in-depth analysis, four productions only have been chosen for close examination; the choice has been influenced by the fact that the four can be readily viewed in pairs, a situation occasioned by the productions in each pairing being staged in London only weeks apart. In one pairing (Frank McGuinness's *Observe the Sons of Ulster Marching Towards the Somme* and Marina Carr's *Portia Coughlan* in 1996 at the Barbican Theatre and the Royal Court respectively) a known, if relatively new play by an established writer is undergoing a major revival, while the other is an instance of an emerging voice. In the other pairing a decade later (O'Casey's *The Plough and the Stars* and Dion Boucicault's *The Shaughraun* in 2005 at the Barbican and at the Albery in the West End respectively), two revivals from the Irish dramatic heritage were offered as part of the Abbey's centenary celebrations. What do the productions reveal to English critics about the Abbey's sense of an identity in this period, particularly when the company's work and repertoire may be viewed against a far wider spectrum of Irish, English, and international theatrical endeavour than had previously been the case?

Observe the Sons of Ulster Marching Towards the Somme had been staged by Michael Attenborough at London's Hampstead Theatre some seventeen months after its initial production at the Peacock in February 1985. Its worth, aesthetic, social, and political, had been immediately apparent, winning McGuinness the Evening Standard Drama Award that season for Most Promising Playwright and seven further prizes. In the ten years between the initial Hampstead production and that visiting from the Abbey in 1996, McGuinness had sustained a regular presence on English stages. Twelve productions of his work included two revivals of *Carthaginians*; two premieres (*Mary and Lizzie* in 1989, commissioned by the Royal Shakespeare Company, and *Someone to Watch Over Me* in 1992, which transferred to the West End at the Vaudeville after a short run at the Hampstead Theatre); three adaptations of established classics, of which two were touring Irish productions (Chekhov's *The Three Sisters* for the Gate Theatre came to the Royal Court in 1990; and *Uncle Vanya* for Field Day which came to the Tricycle in 1995) and one (Ibsen's *Peer Gynt*) a commission from the Royal Shakespeare Company for a production in 1994 designed to tour internationally and be staged by the renowned Japanese director, Ninagawa; there were productions of earlier plays (*Baglady, Factory Girls* and *Innocence*). Already in the pipeline were commissions for an adaptation of Sophocles' *Electra* (1997) and for a new work, *Mutabilitie* (to be staged at the Royal National Theatre the same year by its then Artistic Director Trevor Nunn). This is a prodigious record of achievement and proof that by 1996 McGuinness had an enviable stature within the English theatrical scene to be rivalled only by Friel amongst living Irish dramatists.[8]

This contextualizing is necessary to explain the tone of near-reverence that obtains throughout most of the reviews of the Abbey revival of *Observe the Sons of Ulster*. Critics saw it as a contemporary play in terms of its composition and performance but one of recognized and proven worth that was the foundation stone of McGuinness's career in England. Moreover, it was a play with a stage history, allowing critics an approach akin to how they might view a revival of a work by O'Casey or Synge. Many of the reviewers had previously commented on the earlier Hampstead production, so they had a personal history in relation to the play: consequently they had secure grounds for effecting comparisons and for confirming the appropriateness of their original praise (the tenor and subject of the play, however, militated against overt self-satisfaction at formerly witnessing the birth of a masterpiece, though most were quick to claim the play as such).[9] A greater focus than perhaps would usually occur in critiques of new plays was therefore given to Joe Vanek's design (starkly simple to allow for atmospheric lighting), to Patrick Mason's direction ('an outstanding revival of an outstanding play'[10]), and to the subtle discriminations evident in the acting. If attention was paid to McGuinness's dramaturgy it was to comment on 'the beauty of [his] bleak poetry'[11]; the 'series of slightly surreal rituals and ceremonies, in which Ulster soldiers discover the bonds that bind them'[12]; the powerful dominant irony of Pyper, 'a sceptical, self-destructive spirit', alone surviving 'to carry the message of no surrender on into the 1980s'[13]; the marrying of 'humour [...] with growing fear and despair as the moment of reckoning draws near'[14]; the 'sharp dialogue, fierce dramatic rituals and rich cross-currents of feeling'[15]; and above all the 'heroic feat of empathy'[16] involved in a Donegal playwright exploring Orange iconography, inherited myths and political commitment with such a rare degree of insight ('Inside the patriots are men, and inside the men are feelings that transcend any sectarian divide. What could be more obvious? What could be harder to acknowledge?'[17]), compassion ('McGuinness hates the sins but loves the sinners'[18]) and 'a profound understanding of how such appalling circumstances [as life in the trenches of the Somme offensive] bound even the most incompatible of men together'.[19]

An unexpected political irony, not lost on these critics, coloured English spectators' reactions to the production. Patrick Mason had conceived his revival in 1995 as a celebration of the IRA ceasefire that seemed to offer a large step forwards for the Peace Process and power-sharing initiatives in Northern Ireland and it was in such a spirit that the production was taken in the summer of that year to the Edinburgh Festival and an international tour planned. The opening in London coincided with a resumption of IRA bombing with the inevitable reprisals. If one traces the reviews collected into *Theatre Record* back to their originating newspapers, one finds them situated amidst pages of analysis of the political situation: the enduring timeliness of the play ('its resonance ... amplified by external events'[20]) could not have been more finely demonstrated. Ian Shuttleworth, for one, confessed to finding the performance 'ineffably moving' as a 'Northern Irish protestant reviewer'. Six of the twelve reviewers whose columns are collected into *Theatre Record* took occasion to comment how circumstance had brought a poignant and disturbing immediacy to their engagement with the action and McGuinness's representation of the complexities of the Orange psyche and the fears and loyalties that bring individuals from widely diverse backgrounds into a fierce union quite *other* than their quotidian selves. Benedict Nightingale in *The Times* went so far as to ask whether McGuinness's artistry in this play achieves a cathartic potential of considerable social significance, though he hedges his claim with careful reservations, which indicates a deep unease at where his instincts are urging his thinking to progress: ' ... though I would be mad to make any claims for the power of drama to touch the intransigent, I must still ask what more constructive and humane example could be set to either Prod or Pape'.[21] The syntactical construction here (that strange balancing of 'though I would ...' with 'I must still ...') is revealing of an intricate motivation, but the performance moved him to write one of the longest and most detailed of the twelve reviews, setting the play in clearly defined social, historical and theatrical contexts while subtly commenting on the director's sensitivity to the dramaturgy and the uniformly fine characterization of the actors.

There were two dissenting voices amidst the general praise for the production: an anonymous review in the *Daily Express* (dated 24 March 1996)[22] and Robert Butler writing for the *Independent on Sunday*. Perhaps this is an unfair comment on the reviewer for the *Daily Express*, who recognized the social timeliness of play and production ('As relevant as ever, alas') and the poignancy and pathos of many of the sequences in the action, but like Butler he or she found fault with the playwright's dramaturgy: 'McGuinness deals here in types rather than characters'. Given that the writer goes on to praise Peter Gowen's 'ferociously impassioned performance as the young Pyper', the strong casting and Mason's 'sombrely beautiful production', the adverse comment is the more remarkable. It is as if the reviewer were discomfited by the power of the piece to impress emotionally and psychologically, and needed to find some means of establishing a distance from the experience by asserting that the subject and its representation were somehow predictable but redeemed by excellent staging (the assertion is not substantiated by any attempt at analysis, however brief). One might argue (as the other critics discussed consistently do) that the disconcerting power of the play as written is that McGuinness establishes the eight men as recognisable types only to reveal depths of individualising emotion behind the public selves they project onto their world. Perhaps the reviewer needed to resist that recognition?

Butler's opening paragraph in the *Independent on Sunday* (dated 10 March 1996) immediately states his doubts about the play's 'classic status' and much of the ensuing review is taken up with substantiating this view. Again the issue is with McGuinness's dramaturgy, which Butler implies is overly contrived (he writes of what he terms the dramatist's 'essay-plan', a too conscious thesis he wishes to promote, which 'in Patrick Mason's fraught production ... feels stiff and inert', while the structuring of the section entitled 'pairing' he dismisses as 'emblematic writing [which] has a stark predictable quality'). The play is at its best in Butler's view when McGuinness relaxes his tense intellectual hold on events and characters and allows a seeming spontaneity to take over, and he gives as a 'superb' instance of this the mock re-enactment of the Battle of Scarva: 'In these unbuttoned moments McGuinness achieves a real lightness and depth'. What Butler and to a less reasoned extent the critic of the *Daily Express* seem to be asking for here is a different mode of realism, a monochromatic style, one more closely following the patterns of English dramatic usage in this period, which observes chronology, eschews devices of heightening, avoids imagistic intensity, intrusions of verse and song, and the technique of mixing styles and genres which is to some degree McGuinness's *forte*.[23] One could defend McGuinness as writing firmly within the Abbey tradition of poetic realism (one that clearly, from his enduring popularity on the English stage, continues to find favour with a high percentage of English theatregoers). The creative links with O'Casey and Synge are palpable in such techniques as those listed above and in the sudden intrusions of verbal flamboyance. The textural richness would appear to be anathema to Butler, showing McGuinness's want of stylistic decorum. It demands of spectators a flexibility of engagement with the play in performance, an ability to make imaginative leaps and connections by lateral thinking. Butler would appear to be resisting such a requirement.

Portia Coughlan, which toured to the Royal Court's main stage, opening in May 1996, was a new play by an unknown writer; there was no suggestion that reviewers were seeing an established classic, so cultural reverence was on none of their agendas. *Theatre Record* carries fifteen reviews from a range of newspapers and journals, showing critics trying to write in a balanced way with varying degrees of success.[24] Some were outright hostile, pouring scorn on the perceived links with Shakespeare's *Merchant of Venice* ('the relationship ... is nominally clear but otherwise impenetrable'[25]); seeing parallels with *Cold Comfort Farm*, Stella Gibbons' satire on the preposterous aspects of the popular rural novel (Sheridan Morley recalled Aunt Ada Doom's constant expectation of finding 'something nasty in the woodshed'; and Sarah Hemming opined that everyone on stage as in the novel needed 'a good slap'[26]); while some five critics expressed exasperation with the authentic dialect as rendering the characters unintelligible and the dialogue obscure ('deserving as [Portia's] case is, it is easy to lose sympathy and become tired of the highly wrought poetic language with which she expresses herself'[27]). Others, seeking to give their readers a way into the unchartered territory of Carr's vision and dramaturgy, in a more kindly spirit invoked Albee and his portraits of 'marriages inexorably heading for nasty rocks' (Nicholas de Jongh), O'Neill 'at his most relentless' (Benedict Nightingale), Pinter's *Moonlight* where too 'the dead are present in the living' (Michael Billington) and Henry James's 'secretive, conspiratorial siblings in *The Turn of the Screw*' (Michael Coveney).[28] What impresses is that none of these comparisons seems forced or detrimental to Carr's achievement but emerges as genuinely illuminating.

Seven of the critics chose to comment on the play's structure and particularly Carr's decision to place the conclusion to the action (Portia's suicide, the winching of her body out of the River Belmont and the ensuing wake) in the second act rather than the third. Sheridan Morley in a generally negative review sees this as 'a twist typical of Marina Carr's obscurantist writing' in wanton defiance of traditional dramatic logic, but de Jongh considered this a brilliant strategy 'so dramatic irony works its painful effect' as one observes the implacable drive in Portia's psyche towards her demise and he admired in this 'how artfully Carr plays with time'.[29] Jane Edwardes took issue with the pacing of incidents, by which she presumably means the discovery that Portia's parents were unknowingly committing incest, that Portia's incestuous activity with her twin brother dates from their childhood, and that his suicide was motivated by seeing his sister sexually involved with another man. Edwardes argues that 'the revelations flow rather too fast for comfort (too fast for credibility too)', implying that there is more than a touch of the novice about Carr's dramaturgy; but she is alone in voicing such a critique.[30]

Views were divided too about Garry Hynes's direction. Where most considered her control over the play unrelenting, exact and exacting ('stark', 'simple', 'lucid', 'unfussy', 'intense' 'burning but precise' are recurring epithets with the more evocative description, 'moody, sepulchral', coming from Sarah Hemming), Nicholas de Jongh demurred, considering the staging 'second-rate, without any sense of place or atmosphere – despite the poetic vividness of Carr's language'[31]. He partly lays the blame for this with the designer, Kandis Cook: de Jongh comments on the remarkable specificity of the setting intimated through Carr's stage directions with its three precise venues (Portia's home, the local bar, and the riverbank), whereas Cook in his view 'uselessly sets the play in a void with only table and chairs, and a shimmering backcloth to suggest the river'.[32] Billington also uses the adjective 'shimmering' and couples it with 'translucent' to evoke the set, while Sarah Hemming carries the visual intimations of these terms into the psychological in referring to the 'surreal, glittering background' as 'represent[ing] the water that lures Portia on'; the continual, seen presence of the curtains seemingly defined for her both the limits of the stage and, in the poetic domain, the limits of Portia's life, a mesmeric image of the fate that lures her to drown herself. The curtains made the same impression on Jane Edwardes: 'Cook's watery drapes are a permanent reminder of the pull of the Belmont river', whereas Benedict Nightingale found them more disturbing, since he saw a 'backcloth which, Rorschach-style, teems with trees, spectral faces or both'.[33] But this image did not resonate with all reviewers who commented on Cook's design: to Charles Spencer, the 'set, with a backdrop of what looks like black bin-liners, is a shoddy, unevocative disgrace'[34]. That only a third of the critics chose to comment on the design elements suggests that for the rest the setting adequately fulfilled its requirements, creating an acceptable playing space.

Where the fifteen reviewers were unanimous, was in praise of the acting (the production boasted in Coveney's view 'some of Ireland's finest actors').[35] Donald Hutera perhaps offers the most sensitively judged account:

> Each performance is such a model of nuance and energy that they all deserve mention ... Sliding and soaring through Carr's heart-quickening text and Hynes' unfussy staging, these actors do the kind of work that sticks in the memory.[36]

Irving Wardle considered 'there were amazing moments when, without taking a breath, the characters switch into broad comedy'.[37] Hutera too admired how the actors negotiated the 'troubling, often blisteringly comic poetry' that Carr creates out of despair, and Coveney praised how they handled the complexities of Carr's writing, which he described as 'a poetic repository of natural speech aerated with swingeing idiom, vigorous scatology and heavily aspirated consonantal patterns'.[38] The play was generally viewed as a superb demonstration of ensemble playing, necessary to offset the excellence of Derbhle Crotty's performance as Portia. Here the superlatives abound: 'spellbinding', 'riveting', 'ethereal and savage', 'a triumph', 'fierce', 'striking', 'remarkable' 'a tempestuous yet utterly controlled performance', 'great, rhapsodic', 'the performance of a lifetime'. Surprisingly, however, a recurring stress is on the meticulously judged physicality of Crotty's interpretation. Sarah Hemming

commented on how 'with her pliant body language' she 'looked like a
rag doll that has been carelessly hurled away'; for Nicholas de Jongh,
'everything about her droops, from listless voice to slumping body';
for Michael Billington, 'Crotty captures all of Portia's death-wish and
unease in her own body'; and for Nightingale, 'Crotty, her pale, bony
face gleaming, cuts a huddled, quaking figure most of the time – and
a fierce, feral one when Portia's internal demons run amok'.[39] From
its earliest years under Frank Fay's direction, the acting style of the
Abbey company had been focused on delivery of the text with
movement kept to a stylized minimum (except in the performance of
Yeats's dance plays). This had been greeted in the 1900s by English
critics as captivating because different from the grandly mannered
business that characterized the English style. Little in the intervening
decades, when that English style had changed beyond recognition,
had come from Ireland to challenge the prevailing opinion of Irish
style.[40] Playwrights such as Tom Mac Intyre or Thomas Kilroy are
not generally known to English audiences, not having been widely
toured[41]; and physicality was not, significantly, an aspect of Mason's
production of McGuinness's play that excited comment.[42] Hynes's
staging, like most of her work with Druid and with the Abbey,
attended markedly to *embodying* the text; but this, her characteristic
style of directing, has only recently gained international, as distinct
from Irish recognition, chiefly through her work with the Synge
canon.[43] In that sense, *Portia Coughlan* with its focus on the
heroine's body (graphically displayed when winched aloft from the
riverbed at the start of Act Two) was a revelation, inviting a wholesale
revision of conventional English attitudes to the Abbey Theatre.

Though the Abbey celebrated its centenary in 2004, it was not
until the following year that productions from that celebratory
season reached London. O'Casey's *The Plough and the Stars* came to
a Barbican much changed from its previous visits: the Royal
Shakespeare Company had departed and the theatre season now
comprised visiting companies, chiefly from abroad. Language was in
most cases less the medium of communication now than the visual
dimension.[44] Interestingly reviews of *Plough* (once they had
commented on the signature status of the play in the Abbey's
repertoire, given its history) focused on the actors' physicalization of
their characters and on Francis O'Connor's setting. This severely
limited the playing space by surrounding the stage on all sides with
mounds of domestic rubbish (broken furniture, sandbags, doors,
prams and the like) so the action was played out within this frame.
Paul Taylor in the *Independent* thought this created 'a literal gulf'
between stage and audience that it was difficult for the actors to
bridge, while Susannah Clapp in the *Observer* felt this distancing
effect caused the performers to over-act and 'caper like comic cut-

outs'; Charles Spencer considered it 'dwarfed the actors'; others just found the set 'excessively untidy' or 'clumsy'.[45] The general response was more positive, seeing it as a powerful expressionist evocation of both the effects of the Rising and, within the larger international scene, of the trenches of the Great War. The sense of humanity caught inexorably in a universal decline into mud was disturbing, locating the play (as Michael Billington observed) closer to *The Silver Tassie* in O'Casey's canon than to *Juno and the Paycock*.[46] This symbolism defined precisely the social context of the play's action and reviewers felt there were gains and losses in this. Billington thought Ben Barnes as director deliberately chose with this setting to play down the drama's 'comic gusto', but he continued like others to praise the 'persuasive' stress placed on the inhabitants of the tenement as 'the victims of war', on O'Casey's 'artful interweaving of domestic and political themes', as 'public events shadow private lives'.[47] The recurring concern of reviewers is with O'Casey's continual redefinitions of heroism, finding it in unconventional places and revealing it 'in all its contradictions'.[48] An over-riding preoccupation was whether the production sustained most critics' opinion that *Plough* rates 'as maybe the 20th-century's greatest play'.[49] Barnes' choice to bring his production to London as the representative work in the Abbey's hundred-year endeavour was judged generally to be exemplary on these grounds.[50]

No review of the plays so far discussed mentioned the Abbey as Ireland's National Theatre in terms of what might be considered a suitable repertory for such an institution. This was not the case with the other centenary production: Boucicault's *The Shaughraun* which came to the Albery in the West End in June 2005. Of seventeen reviews, three invoked Yeats and Lady Gregory with reference to their known distaste for Boucicault's plays and one the Abbey's *national* status.[51] The Abbey had previously toured Boucicault's melodrama to London in 1968 (Hugh Hunt's production starred Cyril Cusack); and on that occasion there was general praise for the vigour of the acting and the developed sense of an ensemble.[52] More recently in 1988 the English National Theatre had staged an acclaimed revival of the play as a vehicle for Stephen Rea. Comparisons were inevitable and to the detriment of John McColgan as director. There were three admirers of the venture and three lukewarm appraisals, but the general response was scathing. Direction, design (Francis O'Connor again), and acting style were relentlessly dissected; worse, the production posed for critics serious questions about the taste of Abbey audiences in lauding it and of London audiences prepared 'to pay £40 for flapdoodle'. Attendance was extremely low.[53]

Reviewers found themselves in an unusual cultural time-warp: if Yeats dismissed Boucicault's plays as caricaturing Irish peasantry to pander to the patronizing taste of English audiences, this production by an Irish company a century on shocked English critics for playing what they (the English) deemed a superior play as over-the-top caricature.[54] Was this Irish company deliberately sending up themselves and their theatrical heritage? Postcolonial-inspired cultural cringing on the part of most critics was paramount. The sets looked tacky and fake (or worse, Disneyfied); the direction owed more to *Riverdance* than any other tradition, historical or contemporary; and the acting inspired many critics to comparisons with the *Carry On* films for 'playing cutesy Oirish clichés to the hilt without any visible irony'.[55] Theoretically disposed critics clearly hoped they would find grounds for interpreting the experience as consciously postmodernist *kitsch*, but were frustrated in the attempt. Admired actors such as Stephen Brennan (Kinchela) or Anita Reeves (Conn's mother) fell from favour and the overall want of taste of the enterprise was viewed contemptuously in comparison with the subtleties of production, design, and acting in Friel's *The Home Place*, which had as recently as May that year transferred into the West End from the Gate in Dublin.

These four productions demonstrate a marked shift in English responses to the Abbey. A century past, critics in London delighted in playwrights' verbal artistry and (by comparison with the current English style) the restrained style of acting; design was generally serviceable, functional, but not notable.[56] Played in the final years of the twentieth century to audiences now well-versed in the dynamic variety of international modes of staging and design, Abbey stagings continued to excite comment on playwrights' dramaturgy, but there is a developing close observation of the organic relation of stage setting and chosen acting style with dramatic artistry in all four productions discussed here. It is the integration, the coherence of the presentations (whether revivals of known plays or mountings of new drama) that is the locus of critical attention. Anglo-Irish political relations hovered to varying degrees over critical responses to Mason's production of *Observe the Sons of Ulster* in calculating its timeliness and relevance; but the responses to *Plough* did not engage with specific politics (despite the subject matter of the play) so much as with the horrors of poverty amongst the working class and the repercussions on private life of the Rising and the Great War (this more generalized reaction was prompted particularly by the setting and by the situating of the production in a season specializing in the work of major European directors). Cultural politics came (almost comically) into play with McColgan's staging of *The Shaughraun* in a manner that illuminated the changing ways in which Irish and

English audiences were prepared to respond to issues of representation. *Portia Coughlan* provoked some stereotypical anti-Irish biases in a few befuddled critics, but Carr was generally praised as a welcome new dramaturgical voice of notable power. Can one generalize from this selection of toured productions? Not with any confidence, perhaps. Most noticeable, however, is how Irish drama is increasingly viewed as no longer 'special' or 'other', but is situated, whether for praise or blame, within critics' and audiences' extended, global awareness of the possibilities of theatre. For that we have to thank the upsurge of Irish plays in performance on English stages since 1990 and the touring to England by so many more companies than the Abbey.

---

[1] At the time of its initial visit in May 1903, the company was still going under the name of The Irish National Theatre Society.

[2] Tours by the Gate to London began in the 1930s. After the dividing of the ways between Edwards and MacLiammóir on the one hand and the Longfords on the other when two independent companies were established, the Edwards/ MacLiammóir company in particular became regular visitors to London into the 1960s.

[3] In creating the following statistics, I have taken as my guide Peter James Harris's 'Chronological Table of Irish Plays Produced in London (1920-2006)'. This invaluable research tool was published by Harris in Richard Cave and Ben Levitas (eds.), *Irish Theatre in England*, Irish Theatrical Diaspora Series: 2 (Dublin: Carysfort Press, 2007). The computations are entirely mine and mine consequently any inaccuracies involved.

[4] These were *A Doll's House* and *Medea*, which both starred Fiona Shaw.

[5] These amount to well over sixty productions where the originating companies can be verified as coming from Ireland, but the number may be substantially more.

[6] These figures relate only to in-house productions and not to productions touring to these theatres from Ireland.

[7] Mustapha Matura's *The Playboy of the West Indies* (a Trinidadian rewriting of Synge's satirical comedy) has appropriately become a kind of signature play for Kent's ethos at the Tricycle. It has seen regular revivals.

[8] Again for these details I am deeply indebted to Harris's 'Chronological Table', though the interpretation I have put upon the facts is wholly mine.

[9] These generalizations are culled from a reading of the twelve reviews of Mason's production collected into *Theatre Record*, 26 February – 10 March 1996: 303-305. The comments of individual critics who are quoted in the following sentences are symptomatic of general patterns of response recurring throughout the reviews. I have chosen what seemed to me the best expressed of particular ideas. The dates of the

various reviews are given as recorded in the headings used in *Theatre Record.*

10 John Gross, *Sunday Telegraph*, 10 March 1996.

11 Sheridan Morley, *Spectator*, 16 March 1996.

12 Nicholas de Jongh, *Evening Standard*, 7 March 1996.

13 Benedict Nightingale, *The Times*, 8 March 1996.

14 Ian Shuttleworth, *Financial Times*, 12 March 1996.

15 John Gross, *Sunday Telegraph*, 10 March 1996.

16 Gross, 10 March 1996.

17 Benedict Nightingale, *The Times*, 8 March 1996.

18 Ian Shuttleworth, *Financial Times*, 12 March 1996.

19 Jane Edwardes, *Time Out*, 13 March 1996.

20 Ian Shuttleworth, *Financial Times*, 12 March 1996.

21 Benedict Nightingale, *The Times*, 8 March 1996.

22 That this paper proffered a review is in itself of interest, since the *Daily Express* rarely reviews what one might term serious drama and especially not that with an Irish interest or origin (there are no *Daily Express* reviews collected by *Theatre Record* for any of the other three productions considered in this essay).

23 Interestingly, Robert Butler gets to the heart of what I am analyzing here in his review of Carr's *Portia Coughlan* later in the year, which opened in the same week as Simon Gray's *Simply Disconnected*, when he drew a precise distinction between 'covert English irony and raw Irish emotionalism' (*Independent on Sunday*, 19 May 1996, reproduced in *Theatre Record*, 6-19 May 1996: 611). When starkly confronted by the juxtaposition in one week's reviewing between the predictability of the preferred English style and the challenging dynamism of Carr's new voice, Butler on this occasion chose to favour the Irish dramatist.

24 See *Theatre Record*, 6-19 May 1996: 608-612. Dates for individual reviews are as assigned in this collection.

25 David Nathan, *Jewish Chronicle*, 24 May 1996.

26 Sheridan Morley, *Spectator*, 25 May 1996, and Sarah Hemming in the *Financial Times* 16 May 1996.

27 Jane Edwardes, *Time Out*, 22 May 1996. A cruder expression of distaste for the language was expressed by Charles Spencer in the *Daily Telegraph*, 16 May 1996: 'the Irish brogue is sometimes so thick you lose the meaning' but he had the grace to admit the play undeniably possessed 'a raw, draining power'.

28 See Nicholas de Jongh, *Evening Standard*, 15 May 1996; Benedict Nightingale, *The Times*, 16 May 1996); Michael Billington, *Guardian*, 18 May 1996, and Michael Coveney, *Observer*, 19 May 1996.

29 Sheridan Morley, *Spectator*, 25 May 1996 and Nicholas de Jongh, *Evening Standard*, 15 May 1996. Billington in the *Guardian*, 18 May 1996 also sounded an adverse note (the sole negative criticism in his review) when he opined that he found Carr's 'narrative structure

clumsy', remarking how 'the story of Portia's life is interrupted, half-way through, by a gratuitous vision of her eventual death'.

30 Jane Edwardes, *Time Out*, 22 May 1996.

31 Nicholas de Jongh, *Evening Standard*, 15 May 1996.

32 De Jongh, 15 May 1996.

33 Michael Billington, *Guardian*, 18 May 1996; Sarah Hemming, *Financial Times*, 16 May 1996; Jane Edwardes, *Time Out*, 22 May 1996; and Benedict Nightingale, *The Times*, 16 May 1996.

34 Charles Spencer, *Daily Telegraph*, 22 May 1996.

35 Michael Coveney , *Observer*, 19 May 1996.

36 Donald Hutera, *What's On*, 22 May 1996.

37 Irving Wardle, *Sunday Telegraph*, 19 May 1996. John Peter, *Sunday Times*, 19 May 1996, agreed with this view: 'Carr's writing is brutally funny and ruthlessly observant, hallucinatory and haunted'. Charles Spencer (*Daily Telegraph*, 22 May 1996) linked this technique with the tradition of Irish playwriting: 'Like many fine Irish writers (one thinks particularly of O'Casey), Carr has a knack of combining piercing pain with shafts of outrageous humour.'

38 Donald Hutera , *What's On*, 22 May 1996 and Benedict Nightingale, *The Times*, 16 May 1996.

39 Sarah Hemming , *Financial Times*, 16 May 1996; Nicholas de Jongh, *Evening Standard*, 15 May 1996; Michael Billington, *Guardian*, 18 May 1996; and Benedict Nightingale, *The Times,* 16 May 1996.

40 A notable exception had been the expressionist plays of Denis Johnston but they had long since fallen out of memory and moreover they were staged by the Gate Theatre rather than the Abbey.

41 Kilroy's *The Secret Fall of Constance Wilde* was not a conspicuous success when it toured to the Barbican Theatre in September 2000, though it made extensive use of mime and puppetry. Better known in England are certain practitioners such as Olwen Fouéré or Tom Hickey, notable for their highly physicalized performing styles, but they have tended to appear in London in English productions until recently.

42 This was remarkable, since much of the play's exploration of the distinctions between the homosocial and the homosexual was subtly defined in the production by physical means.

43 Druid has in recent years started a policy of widescale international touring and in England has formed a special relation with the Oxford Playhouse to receive productions of classic Irish texts. Oxford is then seen as a base from which an English tour might operate, as was the case in 2009 with *The Playboy of the Western World* and in 2010 with *The Silver Tassie.*

44 Surtitles are often available but these do not offer the same experience to audiences as engaging with a playwright's words. Much subtlety is lost.

45 Paul Taylor, *Independent*, 24 January 2005; Susannah Clapp, *Observer*, 23 January 2005; Charles Spencer, *Daily Telegraph*, 22 January 2005; Quentin Letts, *Daily Mail*, 21 January 2005; and Joe Cushley, *What's On*, 26 January 2005. These and subsequent reviews that are cited here are drawn from the collection (amounting to thirteen critiques overall) in *Theatre Record*, 1-28 January 2005: 64-67. The dates assigned to individual reviews are again as given in *Theatre Record*.

46 Michael Billington, *Guardian*, 21 January 2005.

47 Ibid., Dominic Maxwell, *Time Out London*, 26 January 2005; Nicholas de Jongh, *Evening Standard*, 20 January 2005; and Billington in Ibid.

48 Benedict Nightingale, *The Times*, 21 January 2005.

49 Nightingale, 21 January 2005.

50 Only Paul Taylor, *Independent*, 24 January 2005 and Susannah Clapp, *Observer*, 23 January 2005 disagreed. Taylor, alone amongst reviewers, referred to the dispute between Barnes, as artistic director, and the Abbey board that marred the celebrations of the centennial year and thought the production demonstrated a loss of confidence in the vitality of the repertoire, while Clapp opined that the staging was 'not so much a revival as an act of taxidermy'.

51 The reviews are to be found in *Theatre Record*, 4-17 June 2005: 796-800. Because it was deemed a 'West End' show, more newspapers sent critics to this production by the Abbey than had been the case with the three previous productions discussed.

52 For a more detailed discussion of this production as viewed in London, where it appeared in 1968 as part of Peter Daubney's World Theatre Season at the Aldwych, see my essay, 'The Abbey Tours in England' in Nicholas Grene and Chris Morash (eds.), *Irish Theatre on Tour*, Irish Theatrical Diaspora Series: 1 (Dublin: Carysfort Press, 2005): 21.

53 Susannah Clapp, *Observer*, 12 June 2005.

54 Superior in quality as written, that is, to the play as here performed. A finer play seemed to be trying to emerge than the production would allow.

55 McColgan, of course, had directed *Riverdance* and it was his River Production company that funded the production coming to London. Both productions in the reviews were seen as in Nick Curtis's words, flogging 'crude stereotypes of Irish culture to the world', *Evening Standard*, 9 June 2005. The final quotation above is from Kate Bassett's review, *Independent on Sunday*, 12 June 2005. Other critics concurred in finding the repetitive gags, mannerisms and stage business, the continual (literal) winking at the audience, the repeated injunctions by voiceover to spectators to 'hiss and boo the villains' cloying at first, grating on the nerves later, and ultimately a bore.

56 I am thinking here of critical comments in the early 1900s on the Irish Players at the Abbey from the likes of C.E. Montague, Max Beerbohm,

and James Agate. For a discussion of Yeats's ideas on acting style, see his essays in *Samhain* and *Beltaine,* and especially 'The Reform of the Theatre' in W.B. Yeats (ed.) *Samhain,* September 1903: 9-12 and 'The Play, the Player and the Scene' in W.B. Yeats (ed.) *Samhain,* December 1904: 24-33. For a fuller discussion of design at the Abbey in those early years, see my essay, 'On the siting of doors and windows: aesthetics, ideology and Irish stage design' in Shaun Richards (ed.) *The Cambridge Companion to Twentieth-Century Irish Drama* (Cambridge: Cambridge University Press, 2004): 93-108. The only designers at the Abbey whose work excited particular comment in those early years were Robert Gregory and Charles Ricketts; Edward Gordon Craig had designed for two of Yeats's plays but had stipulated that the settings should not be toured out of Ireland until he had patented his system of screens.

5 | Ireland Onstage at the Birmingham Repertory Theatre

James Moran

This essay describes the ways in which Irishness has appeared onstage at one of England's best-known provincial playhouses, the Birmingham Repertory Theatre. The venue, which celebrates its centenary year in 2013, was initially established as a kind of English version of Dublin's Abbey theatre, and staged some notable Irish productions during the twentieth century. However, the bombing campaign waged in England by the IRA during 1974 had a long-lasting effect on the Birmingham playhouse, and meant that different iterations of Irishness then appeared in response to the changing fortunes of the local Irish community.

The Birmingham Repertory Theatre is currently housed in Centenary Square, a reasonably high-profile location in the city, with the playhouse positioned next door to a multi-million pound concert venue and an international sports arena. The Repertory Theatre itself consists of two stages: a main auditorium modelled on a Greek amphitheatre, seating almost 900 spectators, and a smaller, more flexible studio space that seats between 140 and 190 people. Between 2011 and 2013 the building is closed to the public in order to build a third stage – a 300-seat arena – as part of the city's library redevelopment.[1]

The theatre is a producing house and stages about twenty productions each year, but the name may be somewhat misleading: the playhouse has never truly been a 'repertory' theatre in the sense of, say, a venue like Shakespeare's Globe, with Birmingham creating no equivalent to the way that the Lord Chamberlain's Men rotated work from a specified repertoire. Nevertheless, the Birmingham theatre has a significant place in the history of the British stage, having produced a number of impressive if uncommercial works during the first half of the twentieth century, including the 1923 British premiere of Shaw's *Back to Methuselah*, and the famous 1925 modern-dress production of *Hamlet*, nicknamed 'Hamlet in plus fours'.[2] During the mid-twentieth century, the young prodigy Peter Brook launched his directorial career at the theatre, with a landmark production of *King John* in 1945 starring Paul Scofield.[3] Scofield himself was only one of a number of famous actors who gained early acting opportunities at the Birmingham playhouse, and the Repertory Theatre's hall of fame also boasts the young Laurence Olivier, Albert Finney, John Gielgud, Peggy Ashcroft, and Derek Jacobi.[4]

However, a less well-known part of the theatre's history is the role played by Irish drama in the playhouse's original formation.[5] At the start of the twentieth century, before the Birmingham company found a home in the Repertory Theatre, the group was known as the Pilgrim Players, a group of amateur actors who formed an acting company and were strongly influenced by the success of the Abbey in Dublin. Indeed, one of the co-founders of the Abbey, Willie Fay, who came to work at the Birmingham Repertory Theatre after the First World War, correctly observed that the English playhouse had developed after the Birmingham actors had been inspired by seeing an Abbey tour to the city in 1907; and in the New York Public Library there exists some fascinating correspondence between Yeats and those who were establishing the Birmingham theatre group in the early twentieth century.[6] The Birmingham company had originally performed in an assortment of local church halls and local homes, with the small but enthusiastic audiences sitting very close to the actors. They contacted Yeats after seeing the Abbey players in Birmingham, and Yeats himself replied positively. After all, he had his own views about the value of small, intimate, and uncommercial theatre ventures, whose players might perform for invited audiences. He had seen his Abbey theatre develop from performances at the ninety-six seat Molesworth hall, where audiences and actors faced one another at eye level, and initially seems to have felt a strong affinity with the similar situation of the Birmingham players.

The Birmingham acting troupe saw themselves as part of a movement to take important theatre events away from London, and specifically aligned themselves with the Abbey in their founding document, declaring that 'Dublin has made a distinct and valuable contribution to the modern stage with its National Irish Theatre'.[7] Yeats in turn praised the verse written in Birmingham by one member of the company, the Georgian poet John Drinkwater.[8] Yeats travelled to Birmingham to watch the players, explaining afterwards how much he had enjoyed his stay and the production of *Measure for*

Measure that he had seen.[9] Yeats also told the Birmingham company that 'I shall be delighted if you revive *The Hour Glass,* for you gave a most excellent performance of it. May I make one suggestion: not to correct anything you have done, but to ask you to hide my errors'.[10]

Yeats also invited the Birmingham players to perform in collaboration with the Abbey company, but his enthusiasm soon cooled when he returned to Dublin, where Lady Gregory dissuaded him from working with the Birmingham amateurs. He wrote to the Repertory Theatre to explain that 'I have just heard from Lady Gregory, she thinks it will be better for your Company to play by itself.'[11] Lady Gregory's intervention may explain the slightly schizophrenic aspect to this correspondence: despite Yeats's early enthusiasm for the Birmingham company, he later sent messages to the English midlands to tell the actors that their performance of *The Countess Cathleen* was a 'disaster', that the performances lacked 'vitality, movement, [and] external life', and that none of the women in the Birmingham company would be good enough to act in his play *Deirdre.*[12]

Nevertheless, although Yeats apparently withdrew his initial support, the Birmingham players continued to perform Abbey Theatre plays. When these Birmingham actors toured to Liverpool in April 1912, they enjoyed such critical success with a production of Yeats's *Deirdre* that they founded a new permanent theatre building, a 464-seat building at the back of New Street Station, which was England's first purpose-built repertory playhouse when it opened in 1913. By 1914, the Abbey players themselves arrived at the theatre to perform *Cathleen ni Houlihan,* and in the first four years of the new Birmingham venue, local audiences could have watched thirteen productions of plays by Synge, Yeats, and Gregory.[13] So closely did the Birmingham theatre mirror the Abbey that the Repertory Theatre had its own riot in response to a Synge play in 1917, when an audience protested over a version of *The Tinker's Wedding,* directed by and starring Maire O'Neill, during which the Birmingham poet John Drinkwater decided to impersonate Yeats by ineffectually haranguing the audience from the stage.[14] Once the fuss had died down, one of the future productions at the Repertory Theatre offered a wry comment on this riot. Just as the real-life Birmingham protests of 1917 had seen an Irish Catholic group hurling abuse and projectiles in objection to Synge's fictional clergyman, so the 1949 production of Paul Vincent Carroll's *Shadow and Substance* depicted an Irish Catholic mob assaulting and throwing stones at the (appropriately named) O'Flingsley, the author of an anti-clerical book.[15]

According to Sean O'Casey, the founder of the Birmingham Repertory Theatre rejected *The Silver Tassie* even before Yeats did.[16] And by the late 1920s the city seemed to have lost its enthusiasm for

Irish plays. The *Birmingham Post* condemned a 1927 version of Synge's *The Well of the Saints* by saying 'A good deal of water has flowed down the Thames, the Liffey and the Rea since this play was new ... At the Repertory Theatre they try to delude us not by bringing the period up to 1927, but by taking us back to 1427'.[17] Similarly, a 1928 production of *John Bull's Other Island* inspired the *Post* to comment that the play was written 'a long time ago' in a period of 'ancient history'.[18] And a dull version of *Playboy* in 1930 inspired the same newspaper to ask incredulously, 'Was this the play that cleft a thousand skulls?'[19]

But although the Birmingham Repertory Theatre never engaged so closely again with the work of the Abbey's founders, the playhouse did stage frequent productions by Oscar Wilde and – most notably – G.B. Shaw, who was coaxed into co-founding the nearby Malvern drama festival because of his connection to the Birmingham Repertory Theatre.

The Birmingham playhouse also staged newer Irish plays that met with a generally positive critical response.[20] Most notably, in November 1933, the Repertory Theatre gave the British premiere of Denis Johnston's *The Moon in the Yellow River*, a work that had been produced by the Abbey in April 1931 and by the Theatre Guild of New York in 1932. The play describes a charismatic IRA man who decides to destroy a new, German-made power plant, and although he is shot by an old comrade who is now a commandant in the Free State army, by the end of the piece the power plant is destroyed in a comic accident. As Christopher Murray explains, this play proved topical when first produced in Ireland, as the Shannon power scheme had recently been completed by the German firm of Siemens Schuckert.[21] But when staged in the heart of industrial Birmingham, the rebel's persuasively articulated desire for arcadia had a newfound resonance. After all, wealthier members of the audience travelled in from the outlying suburbs, where – as shown by Solihull's '*urbs in rure*' motto – residents had an anxiety about industrial encroachment. Indeed, the best-known literary expression of this anxiety is found in the work of J.R.R. Tolkien, whose time in King's Heath during the early years of the twentieth century inspired the contrasting locations of his Middle Earth.[22] And Johnston's play articulated these concerns, with his rebel declaring:

> Listen to the noise of your turbines and then come back and give me any adequate reason for it all. The rest of the world may be crazy, but there's one corner of it yet, thank God, where you and your ludicrous machinery haven't turned us all into a race of pimps and beggars.[23]

This play risked putting the well-heeled English audience members in sympathy with the IRA man, even though the real-life members of the IRA would shortly emulate their fictional counterparts by beginning the 1939 bombing campaign in Birmingham with an abortive attempt to put Hams Hall power plant out of action, followed by assaults on electricity pylons around the city. The fact that this campaign concluded with the death of five shoppers in a notorious IRA bombing at nearby Coventry in August 1939 meant that when the play was revived by the theatre, in May 1954, the audience may have been markedly less sympathetic towards the IRA man's aims and methods.

Nonetheless, the Repertory Theatre staged other Irish plays with a potentially revolutionary connection in the post-war period. In September 1956, the playhouse staged *Happy as Larry* by Donagh MacDonagh, the son of one of the leaders of the 1916 uprising. Those who knew MacDonagh's famous family background may have enjoyed the autobiographical elements in this play about death and widowhood, as well as the way that he toyed with the ideas of sacrifice associated with his father:

> ... 'Promise,' says he
> 'That you'll remember John that died for you'.
> And so I promised, though I still can't see
> How stuffing shellfish down his throat was love![24]

Perhaps, then, a revisionist impulse existed even within the families of 1916.

From the mid-1940s, the Birmingham theatre engaged more explicitly with Irish revolutionary politics. In a 1945 production of *Juno and the Paycock*, the Birmingham Repertory Theatre brought armed irregulars onto the stage, and showed the brutal consequences of Civil War; in Joseph O'Conor's *The Iron Harp* (1957) the playhouse depicted British Black and Tan soldiers as sadistic and thuggish, as well as showing the ruthlessness of those IRA commanders who could commit cold-blooded murder during the Anglo-Irish War; and, in a 1964 production of Brendan Behan's *The Quare Fellow*, they presented a version of prison life as remembered by a one-time IRA bomber.[25]

Just as Johnston's *The Moon in the Yellow River* had done, so in November 1950 a production of George Shiels's *The New Gossoon* at the Repertory Theatre again contrasted rural Ireland with the world of industrial modernity. In this play a young man (the 'gossoon' of the title) buys a motorbike, something that signals a dangerous intrusion in the Irish farmland where he lives, with the other characters worrying that his machine will attract a 'town hussy' rather than an honest country woman, and with the motorbike itself becoming a rather suggestive prop:

> **LUKE.** (*Angrily*) Who's touching my machine?
> **SALLY.** 'Twas me, Luke. I only touched the horn.
> **LUKE.** Well, leave it alone! What do you know about a machine?
> **SALLY.** Good Lord, it doesn't need a mechanical genius to blow the horn![26]

Thus town life, and its associated mechanical paraphernalia, is associated with all of those sexually loose and dangerous impulses that might threaten the Catholic ethos of mid-century rural Ireland. And away from the playhouse, in an era of post-war emigration, this contrast between the town and the country was indeed becoming a predominant concern for many Irish families. Indeed, Shiels's play refers directly to migration, with one of the characters worrying that if her son leaves Ireland for Scotland "Twould more likely make him a corner boy. Then he'd come back to me and bring a dirty wife and child with him'.[27]

Certainly, the post-war period saw a major shift in Birmingham's demography. Official census records show that the city's Irish-born population leapt from 6,470 in 1931, to 36,349 in 1951 and then 58,961 in 1961, or from 0.65 percent to 5.31 percent of the city's population in thirty years. The city's economic adaptability and the rise of 'clean' industries in the English midlands meant that large inflows of migrants travelled to the area and, as a result, between 1951 and 1961, 22,000 people arrived in Birmingham from Ireland, alongside smaller but significant groups from the West Indies and India-Pakistan.[28] As a result, Birmingham became the second largest conurbation in England during the twentieth century, and by the mid-1960s, one in every six births in the city was to a couple consisting of at least one Irish parent, with the *Birmingham Mail* giving the reasonable estimation that every tenth person in Birmingham could claim Irish identity by birth or extraction.[29] As Claire Cochrane has pointed out in her study of the Birmingham Repertory Theatre, the city had become 'a complex construct of diverse communities of interest' and from the 1960s the Birmingham Repertory Theatre would attempt to 'appeal more directly to those different communities'.[30]

The theatre was undoubtedly assisted in its ability to appeal to minority communities by a shift in venue. When the company moved to the current building in 1971, it became possible to stage less profitable shows in its studio space, away from the necessity of selling almost 500 tickets to achieve a full house, which had been a feature of the original playhouse. One of the first plays to inaugurate the smaller of the two stages was therefore the premiere of David Edgar's *Death Story*. This work has now largely been forgotten, but at the time of its original staging in 1972 the script offered a response from an English playwright to the deteriorating situation in the North of Ireland. *Death Story* is scarcely the most subtle of works: the play is a modernized *Romeo and Juliet* in which the Montagues and Capulets are mapped onto the Catholic and Protestants of Ulster. From today's perspective, we might sigh with exasperation here, as the idea of seeing 'the Troubles' in terms of the Romeo and Juliet story has become a familiar one. Indeed, Joe Cleary has written recently that:

> Adapted to the contemporary Northern Irish situation, the effect of this device is to depict the Catholic and Protestant communities generally as symmetrical tribal and atavistic entities, and the two young lovers then come to represent a more modern-minded, liberal minority, struggling heroically to overcome the entrenched sectarian attitudes associated with the opposing factions.[31]

But although Edgar's *Death Story* does contain some of the features that Cleary criticizes, and can appear passé to us today, the work may have had a rather different and potentially more troubling implication when originally staged in Birmingham. After all, this production occurred only a few months after Bloody Sunday, and for any English members of the audience, Edgar sought to disturb the kind of lazy thinking that Cleary describes, by showing the external army that attempts to separate Montague from Capulet is in fact one of the major villains of the piece. In Edgar's play it is not only the Montagues and Capulets who are bloodthirsty and malevolent, but also the intervening army, which an audience in 1972 would inevitably have read as the British forces in the north of Ireland. Rather than presenting the good-hearted Tommies of *Oh What a Lovely War*, Edgar presents an army intelligence officer who deliberately provokes carnage and mayhem in order to clamp down on the civilian population.[32]

Of course, the Repertory Theatre could afford to stage such provocative work in the small studio space, whilst productions with more 'mainstream' appeal took place on the main stage. In 1973, the Repertory Theatre staged its next Irish play, but this time the production occurred in the nearly 900-seat auditorium and so there was nothing to hint at Edgar's suggestion that the British Army might be responsible for the deteriorating situation in the north of Ireland. Instead, in May and June 1973, the theatre dealt with Ireland in music-hall mode when staging Brendan Behan's *The Hostage*. The knockabout action of this performance did not, as Edgar's work had done, encourage the audience to consider the complexities and culpabilities of the current situation, but instead offered a reassuringly escapist vision, which highlighted the drunkenness and folly of Irish Republicans. According to the *County Express*, audiences saw the 'Comic soldiers of the IRA', those 'daft Irish characters' who 'rush around yelling, screaming, swilling Guinness, shooting off guns and occasionally roaring out pointless comments on patriotism, religion, love and life'.[33] The critic for the *Birmingham Post* confirmed that the production 'romps along with a fine sense for farcical timing', whilst the *Walsall Observer* praised the production under the headline 'Begorrah, it's a broth of a show'.[34] Nevertheless, despite the slapstick presentation of the Irish characters onstage, the theatre was genuinely attempting to appeal to the large Irish minority in the city (most of whom were Catholics from the South), with the theatre programme describing Northern Ireland as a 'colonial' problem, and giving fulsome biographies of Eamon de Valera and Michael Collins.

However, dealing with Irish republicanism onstage became a great deal more problematic a few weeks after the production of *The Hostage*, when the real-life IRA began a bombing campaign in the English midlands. This campaign began on 29 August 1973 and reached a bloody climax on the evening of 21 November 1974, when bombs detonated in two of Birmingham's busiest city centre pubs, only ten minutes' walk from the Birmingham Repertory Theatre. This most devastating attack of the IRA's Birmingham campaign injured 162 people and killed twenty-one, the worst death toll as a result of any operation planned by the IRA.[35] The killings were obviously a personal tragedy for many local people, but they also had a devastating effect on Irish cultural events in the city, forcing the Irish community to go to ground, cancelling their high-profile St Patrick's Day parade for twenty-two years, and being subjected to a similar kind of racism and prejudice to that which Britain's Islamic community have now become accustomed. Even though four of those who died in the bombing had been Irish citizens, a number of revenge assaults on local Irish people took place, as well as firebomb attacks on the Birmingham Irish Centre, local Catholic churches and schools, as well as pubs associated with the Irish community.[36]

The IRA attack marked a decisive halt to Irish productions at the Repertory Theatre, which had continued to stage Irish work after difficult earlier periods such as the Anglo-Irish War of 1921 and the IRA bombing of neighbouring Coventry in 1939. But the scale of the Birmingham attack, and the fact that it took place on the doorstep of the Repertory Theatre, meant that that tradition of staging Irish work was now interrupted. Birmingham city council now began to give a number of ominous hints about potential cuts to the arts budget.

With the threat of austerity measures, the Birmingham Repertory Theatre opted against sticking its head above the parapet, and avoided potentially controversial Irish material that might focus the attention of conservative councillors on the matter of the playhouse's subsidy.[37]

It took more than a decade for an Irish-themed drama to appear at the Birmingham Repertory Theatre, and when the playhouse did decide to stage an Irish work, the 1986 premiere of Stewart Parker's play about Dion Boucicault, *Heavenly Bodies*, it was a play that explored the life of the Victorian playwright but also at times seemed to offer a bleak commentary on the 1980s. For example, at one point in *Heavenly Bodies*, Parker included a description of an 'Irish Singing Clown' who tries to reconcile Orange and Green by singing a special song, but whose attempt ends in disaster:

> **BOUCICAULT.** Permit me to speculate – abuse hurled from both sides, faction fights ensuing, Patterson set upon by both camps simultaneously.
>
> **JESSIE.** It just says there was a riot, he was trying to save the circus equipment from the mob, and was struck on the head by an iron bar.[38]

By staging such sentiments at the Repertory Theatre, it may have seemed to some in the audience that the bombings witnessed in the city were simply part of an atavistic and inexplicably violent conflict which had simmered in similar form for many years, and anyone who felt that the conflict could be resolved might well suffer the fate of that unfortunate singing clown. Indeed, when this play was premiered in 1986 the pub bombings were still widely, and bitterly, remembered in Birmingham, particularly as an assortment of campaigns had been launched to help free the unjustly imprisoned and abused Birmingham Six, including a high-profile 'World in Action' television exposé in October 1985. Such campaigns continued to draw local attention to the emotive events of the bombing and its aftermath. Indeed, the play Parker wrote after *Heavenly Bodies* was *Pentecost*, in which a Northern Irish character called Peter has moved to Birmingham in the months before the pub bombings of 1974 in the hope of escaping the conflict at home. And there are some terrible ironies in that play as Peter tries to convince his old friends in the North that Birmingham is a place where people are concerned about other matters.

> **PETER.** You do realise – the rest of the world has crossed the street, long since, passed on by – on account of having fully-grown twentieth-century problems to be getting on with – the continued existence of the planet, say, or the survival of the

species?
LARRY. So is that what they fight about in Birmingham?[39]

Any audience member with knowledge of the recent situation in Birmingham realized that, although Peter so confidently attempts to put sectarianism behind him, the violence of the Troubles would indeed erupt in Birmingham later in 1974, making people like Peter afraid to speak with their own Irish accents.

Nevertheless, the fact that the innocence of the Birmingham Six was becoming increasingly apparent during the late 1980s meant that the atmosphere began to change in Birmingham, encouraging a more sympathetic view of the Irish in the area. As part of this reassessment, in 1989 the Repertory Theatre staged a work called *Heartlanders* that, in contrast to *Heavenly Bodies*, displayed a more positive attitude towards Irish integration. *Heartlanders* was scripted by the Belfast-born playwright Anne Devlin together with Stephen Bill and David Edgar (who had earlier written that Romeo and Juliet play *Death Story*), as part of the celebrations to mark Birmingham's first hundred years as a city. And the city being celebrated by the play was a self-consciously inclusive and diverse one: 300 amateur actors took part in the production, which revolved around a character from Ireland who meets and befriends various characters from a wide variety of cultures and ethnic groups.[40] As if to illustrate this theme of reconciliation in real life, the first day of that production also saw the release of three of the Guildford Four, who on the day of their release straightaway joined the chorus of voices demanding the freedom of the Birmingham Six.[41]

Following *Heartlanders*, the Birmingham Repertory Theatre decided to stage another work that might reflect Irish reconciliation, and produced a successful version of *Translations* in 1991. This play has been described by Marilynn Richtarik as 'a fairly balanced portrayal of the various tensions between the Irish and English characters that result from mutual misunderstanding and arrogance', and such notions appealed to the management of the Birmingham Repertory Theatre in the year that the Birmingham Six were freed.[42] After all, as Richtarik notes:

> In Derry, where the world premiere took place [in 1980], the impact of *Translations* appeared to derive as much from the fact that it was produced in the city and was the result of a co-operative effort among people of many political persuasions as from the script itself ... reviewers for the nationalist *Derry Journal* and the unionists *Londonderry Sentinel* were equally enthusiastic about the play.[43]

In the decade since that premiere, *Translations* had become widely known as one of the most significant works of the twentieth-century Irish stage, and after staging a Birmingham version, the Repertory Theatre management saw that they might fill the playhouse by staging other Irish 'classics'. Hence in February 1993 the playhouse gave the British premiere of John B. Keane's 1969 play *Big Maggie*, and then staged Synge's *The Playboy of the Western World* in 1993, both on the theatre's main stage.[44] However, whilst *Playboy* and *Big Maggie* might have had a certain shock value when they were first written, that could scarcely be the case in Birmingham in the 1990s, the decade during which the British stage saw Mark Ravenhill's *Shopping and Fucking* (1996), Sarah Kane's *Blasted* (1995), and other 'in-yer-face' productions. And the Birmingham Repertory Theatre instead opted to stage a number of more challenging works in the studio space that might question and probe difficult ideas and assumptions about Ireland.

In February 1999 the theatre premiered Declan Croghan's *Paddy Irishman*, a play that echoes the plot of Sean O'Casey's *The Shadow of a Gunman*, but which updates the action so that a hard-line IRA man who objects to the Good Friday Agreement leaves a bomb with two unknowing Irish immigrants in a London bed-sit. In some ways this play was soon eclipsed by Martin McDonagh's *The Lieutenant of Inishmore*, which was premiered two years later, a few miles away at the Other Place in Stratford. Like the better-known work of McDonagh, Croghan's play sought to find humour in the actions and attitudes of a republican hardliner in the endgame era, and where McDonagh included the discomforting sight of 'bodies' being dismembered onstage, Croghan included descriptions of death and killing that were given an added air of horror by being delivered so close to the site of the 1974 attacks. At one point in *Paddy Irishman* for example, one of the flatmates realizes that 'There has been a big shoot out down in the pub ... Your mate from fuckin Monaghan ... (*drinking the whiskey by the neck*) He storms in and wipes out the whole lot of them'.[45] Such descriptions of an IRA pub massacre conjured up disturbing memories for members of an audience in Birmingham, particularly when, a few moments later, the same flatmate realizes that he has been left with a bomb and sarcastically contemplates whether to 'plant the bomb and then we will phone up and give them a warning'.[46] Croghan thus presented the audience with a kind of warped and distorted version of the 1974 attack, with his combination of visceral horror and expletive-filled humour providing a precursor to the play that McDonagh would soon premiere in the English midlands.

The year after Croghan's work, the Repertory Theatre premiered *Belonging* by Kaite O'Reilly, a second-generation Irish writer, whose work also asked provocative questions about the pub bombings, and did so in a more specific way than Croghan's had done. During the play a first-generation immigrant argues with her daughter, who is Birmingham-born but heavily involved in 'Irish Studies'. The mother angrily declares:

> I'll tell you what it was like to be spat at in the street, having names hurled after you if you so much as opened your mouth and they heard the accent. Made guilty by association. They tried to lynch a fella at the car factory where your father worked ... I'm going [back to Ireland]. But first I'm going to walk through this city with my head held high. And if anyone shouts at me to get off the road, I'll tell them your father built the road; that we own the fucking road.[47]

After a twenty-two year hiatus, the Birmingham St Patrick's Day parade had resumed in 1996, and this secular version of the pre-1974 religious parade was now attracting up to 100,000 local people and being heralded by local Irish groups and the city council alike as a symbol of how the city could host peaceful multicultural festivities that transcended the troubles of the past. However, Kaite O'Reilly's play reveals that for the Irish families of Birmingham such assertions of national identity might in fact conjure up a series of bitter memories. In *Belonging*, the second-generation Irish members of the household may be able to transcend the bitterness and racism of the 1970s, but the first-generation are forever marked by it, and cannot participate in the drunken, multi-cultural jamboree of St Patrick's Day in the same way as their children. However, members of the second generation have their own problems in trying to orientate themselves: they may not feel fully English but, as one of them complains, they are scarcely fully Irish either: 'I have the parentage, citizenship – bank account. I know my history, culture – I'm even learning the bloody language – but I'm still Plastic Paddy, hand-crafted in Digbeth'.[48] And by the end of *Belonging*, because of the chicanery of a corrupt friend, the old family property in Ireland has been lost in any case, leaving the entire family stuck in Birmingham, no matter where they feel they 'really' belong.

In 2005, the Birmingham Repertory Theatre chose to premiere another play about Ireland in the small studio space, Billy Cowan's *Smilin' Through*, which again looked back to the earlier kind of violence that had marked the period of 'the Troubles'. However, in Cowan's tongue-in-cheek play, the terrorist atrocities of the past now recur in a camp form, as the play features a terrorist from the 'Irish Queer Liberation Army':

> **KYLE.** You actually kill people then?
> **TERRORIST.** I don't know many terrorist groups who only shout abuse, do you?
> **KYLE.** I don't know many terrorist groups who wear combats

as a fashion statement either.

TERRORIST. We wear them because they're practical for the kind of work we do.

KYLE. You wear them because you think it makes you look good, admit it?[49]

Despite such comedy, Cowan's play makes a serious point, showing that the problems of the past might not be as easily escaped as some of the contemporary talk about 'peace and reconciliation' might suggest. In the words of his terrorist character, it is now the time for another minority group in the North to start 'fighting for our right to be treated the same'.

In February 2010 the Birmingham Repertory Theatre staged a relatively conservative version of Brian Friel's *Dancing at Lughnasa*, but returned to more controversial fare in November, when Richard Bean's new play *The Big Fellah* toured to the venue. Bean's earlier play, *England People Very Nice*, had caused the first ever onstage protest at the Royal National Theatre in London during the previous year, in part because of Bean's provocative depictions of Ireland's emigrants. In 2010, *The Big Fellah* revisited this theme, by giving an unflattering portrayal of the Irish in New York, and depicting the activities of an IRA cell in the city from the 1970s to 2001. Bean's play argues that the terrorist atrocities which occurred in the UK and Ireland during that period often originated in dysfunctional hatreds and vanities of such groups in the USA, and ultimately attempts to show millennial al-Qaeda as inheriting the mantle of the IRA of the 1970s and 1980s.

What I think is noteworthy, then, is that between 1999 and 2010, the plays dealing with Ireland at the Birmingham Repertory Theatre often pick up and elaborate the ideas and resonances of the earlier pub bombings. Those devastating explosions, which took place so close to the playhouse, stifled discussion of Irishness on the stage of the Repertory Theatre during the final quarter of the twentieth century, but by the start of the twenty-first century the legacy of the bombings had actually been embraced by the Birmingham playhouse. The theatre was now, as it had been at the time of its foundation almost a century earlier, willing to ask difficult questions about Irishness and to engage with Irish politics.

Such a programming policy is, however, fraught with difficulty. If a playhouse like the Birmingham Repertory Theatre opts to produce deliberately 'edgy' work that deals with the city's ethnic minorities, then there exists the potential to offend and alienate members of those communities. In recent years this has not happened when such provocative work has been staged about the increasingly wealthy and well-integrated Irish community at Birmingham's studio space, but it has happened when the Repertory Theatre has used that same stage to deal with other minority groups. Most famously, the playhouse saw riots and worldwide media attention when attempting to produce the 2004 production of Gurpreet Kaur Bhatti's *Behzti*, which deals with the issue of clerical abuse in a Sikh temple. Shortly afterwards, a smaller press controversy broke out when the studio was used to stage a play about a Muslim brothel, Yasmin Whittaker Khan's *Bells*.[50] We now wait to see whether, following the increased sensitivity about minorities at the theatre that the *Behzti* scandal has brought about – as well as the fact that the demise of the Celtic Tiger means that members of the large Irish diaspora in Birmingham may not necessarily enjoy the kind of cultural and economic cachet that they experienced in recent years – the Birmingham Repertory Theatre may now take a more conservative approach to putting Irishness onstage.

---

[1] Birmingham Repertory Theatre, 'Library of Birmingham', <http://www.birmingham-rep.co.uk/about/library-of-birmingham/> [accessed 23 March 2009].

[2] Robert Hapgood, 'Introduction', in William Shakespeare, *Hamlet*. Edited by Robert Hapgood (Cambridge: Cambridge University Press, 1999) (1-97): 63.

[3] J.C. Trewin, *The Birmingham Repertory Theatre: 1913-1963* (London: Barrie and Rockliff, 1963): 136-39.

[4] See Claire Cochrane, *Shakespeare and the Birmingham Repertory Theatre 1913-1929* (London: Society for Theatre Research, 1993): 1.

[5] See also James Moran, *Irish Birmingham: A History* (Liverpool: Liverpool University Press, 2010).

[6] W.G. Fay and Catherine Carswell, *The Fays of the Abbey Theatre: An Autobiographical Record* (London: Rich and Cowan, 1935): 226; Trewin, 11.

[7] '"The Pilgrim Players": New Birmingham Society', *Birmingham Post*, 16 December 1907: 4.

[8] Yeats, New York Public Library [henceforth NYPL], Berg Collection, folder 940410, letter of 27 February 1909. Material from Yeats's letters reproduced by permission of Oxford University Press, and the Henry W. and Albert A. Berg Collection of English and American Literature, The New York Public Library Astor, Lenox and Tilden Foundations.

[9] Yeats, NYPL, folder 940411, letter of 28 April 1910.

[10] Yeats, NYPL, folder 940413, undated letter.

[11] Yeats, NYPL, folder 940411, letter of 28 April 1910.

[12] Yeats, NYPL, folder 940412, letter of October 1913; folder 940411, letter of 3 December 1911; and folder 940412, letter of 3 May 1912.

[13] Information about performances in 'Performing Arts', *Arts and Humanities Data Service* <http://ahds.ac.uk/ahdscollections/docroot/birminghamrep/birminghamrepsearch.jsp> [accessed 22 May 2008].

[14] 'Trouble at the Birmingham Repertory Theatre', *Birmingham Mail*, 16 May 1917: 3.

[15] Carroll, Birmingham Central Library [Henceforth BCL], Birmingham Repertory Theatre Collection, *Shadow and Substance* Prompt Book.

[16] Sean O'Casey, *Autobiographies,* 2 vols (London: Macmillan, 1963): II, 271.

[17] 'The Repertory Theatre', *Birmingham Post*, 1 February 1927: 5.

[18] 'The Repertory Theatre', *Birmingham Post*, 2 April 1928: 6.

[19] 'Synge's Comedy at the Repertory', *Birmingham Post*, 17 November 1930: 11.

[20] The *Birmingham Post* praised *The Moon in the Yellow River* as 'one of the finest of modern Irish plays', whilst J.C. Trewin said that Joseph O'Conor's *The Iron Harp* was a play to please 'anyone with faith in the English stage'. 'An Irish Play at the Repertory Theatre', *Birmingham Post*, 27 November 1933: 4. J.C. Trewin, "The Iron Harp' at the Repertory Theatre', *Birmingham Post*, 2 October 1957: 11.

[21] Christopher Murray, *Twentieth-Century Irish Drama: Mirror up to Nation* (Manchester: Manchester University Press, 1997): 125.

[22] For more on Tolkien and King's Heath see Joseph Pearce, *Tolkien: Man and Myth* (San Francisco: Ignatius Press, 1998): 18.

[23] Denis Johnston, *The Moon in the Yellow River*, in *Three Irish Plays*, ed. by E. Martin Brown (Harmondsworth: Penguin, 1959) (9-98): 57.

[24] Donagh MacDonagh, BCL, Birmingham Repertory Theatre Collection, *Happy As Larry* Prompt Book: 5. The fact that *Happy as Larry* was written in verse and features a mysterious time-travelling chorus also perhaps connected it with the writer's similar radio play about the 1916 Rising, *Easter Christening*. Donagh MacDonagh, National Library of Ireland, *Easter Christening*, MS 33,720.

[25] Sean O'Casey, *Juno and the Paycock*, in *Three Dublin Plays*. Edited by Christopher Murray (London: Faber, 1998)(63-148): 143-44. Joseph O'Conor, *The Iron Harp*, in *Three Irish Plays*. Edited by E. Martin Browne (Harmondsworth: Penguin, 1959)(99-164):135, 163.

[26] George Shiels, *Selected Plays of George Shiels*, selected and introduced by Christopher Murray (Gerrards Cross: Colin Smythe, 2008), p.144.

[27] Shiels, p.187

[28] Gordon E. Cherry, Birmingham: A Study in Geography, History and Planning (Chichester: Wiley, 1994): 204.

[29] Corporate Statistician, Birmingham Central Library, Ethnic Origins of Birmingham Children 1966-81, Birmingham Central Statistical Office, LF 40-1. Martin Davies, 'The Flow is Slowing Down', *Birmingham Mail*, 27 October 1965: 10.

30 Cochrane, 2.

31 Joe Cleary, Outrageous Fortune: Capital and Culture in Modern Ireland (Dublin: Field Day, 2007): 254-55.

32 Birmingham Central Library, Shakespeare Collection, Death Story, S345.92F, fol.3, fol.43.

33 A.J.W., 'Comic Soldiers of the IRA', *County Express*, 11 May 1973: 11.

34 Birmingham Repertory Theatre Collection, Birmingham Central Library, in first of three cuttings from May 1973-Sept 1974.

35 Gareth Parry, 'Bombs Hit Two Pubs', *Guardian*, 22 November 1974: 1.

36 'It Feels Bad to be Irish in Birmingham', *Observer*, 24 November 1974: 5. Wendy Hughes, 'Backlash Hampering Police – Warning', *Birmingham Post*, 25 November 1974: 5.

37 Cochrane, 212-15. 'CBSO and Rep Warned: Axe your Budget', *Birmingham Mail*, 3 April 1974: 9.

38 Stewart Parker, *Plays 2* (London: Methuen, 2000): 88.

39 Parker, 200.

40 Stephen Bill, Anne Devlin, David Edgar, *Heartlanders* (London: Hern, 1989).

41 Chris Mullin, *Error of Judgement: The Truth About the Birmingham Bombings*. Fourth edition (Dublin: Poolbeg, 1997): 367.

42 Marilyn Richtarik, Acting Between the Lines: The Field Day Theatre Company and Irish Cultural Politics 1980-1984 (Oxford: Clarendon Press, 1994): 29.

43 Richtarik, 51.

44 Birmingham Central Library, Birmingham Repertory Theatre Archive, Programme for *Big Maggie* and Programme for *The Playboy of the Western World*.

45 Declan Croghan, Paddy Irishman, Paddy Englishman, and Paddy...? (London: Faber, 1999): 55.

46 Croghan: 60.

47 Kaite O'Reilly, *Belonging* (London: Faber, 2000): 76-77.

48 O'Reilly, 88.

49 I am grateful to Billy Cowan for the script of *Smilin' Through*.

50 See Dalya Alberge, 'After Sikh Riot, Theatre Stages Muslim Brothel', *The Times*, 22 March 2005.

6 | Contemporary Irish Theatre in German-Speaking Countries[1]

Werner Huber

1. The 'World Stage Vienna' Project

> [I]n area Ireland is not colossal, but neither is she microscopic.
> Mr. Shaw has spoken of her as a 'cabbage patch at the back of
> beyond.' On this kind of description Rome might be called a
> hen-run and Greece a back yard. The sober fact is that Ireland
> has a larger geographical area than many an independent and
> prosperous European kingdom, and for all human and social
> needs she is a fairly big country, and is beautiful and fertile to
> boot. She could be made worth knowing if goodwill and trust are
> available for the task.[2]

Even more than ninety years after James Stephens's plea for Ireland
to take its place among the nations of Europe, the question remains
to what degree Continental Europe is taking note of cultural products
such as Irish theatre and drama and thereby confirming the implicit
value of Irish drama as world literature. If indeed the correct spelling
of a contemporary Irish dramatist's name 'in itself is fame, on the
continent' – to adapt Oscar Wilde's famous quip[3] – a cynic's
adequate response would have to be: 'but does it go beyond that?'

The present essay comes out of a larger research project based at
the University of Vienna, whose full title is '*Weltbühne Wien*: The
Reception of Anglophone Plays on Viennese Stages of the Twentieth
Century.' Its contributors come from a variety of disciplines and
departments: English Literature, Comparative Literature, Theatre
and Media Studies, Translation Studies.[4] As the title suggests, this
research group has been exploring processes of cultural transfer,
adaptation, reception, and interculturality with regard to English-

language plays and their Viennese productions. In the words of the *Weltbühne Wien* website: 'the project will focus on questions relating to cultures in contact and cultural transfer, to circulation and blockage of (foreign) cultural elements, to play selection and censorship, to the role of national stereotypes within the reception process ... .'[5] Detailed studies have been investigating the history of individual Viennese theatres and their directors, impresarios, dramaturges, reviewers, translators, and other cultural 'agents'. The period chosen also provides structural paradigms, as transfer processes were quite dramatically determined by the sequence of politico-historical events and the corresponding changes in the ideological climate in Austria: the Habsburg monarchy 1900-1918, the First Austrian Republic 1918-1938, 'Anschluss' (Austria and Nazi Germany) 1938-1945, allied occupation 1945-1955, the Second Austrian Republic 1955 to present. Thus, for example, censorship, re-education, and the privileging of one theatre tradition over another are the prevailing issues of the post-World War II theatre scene.[6]

The present author's contribution will be largely concerned with contemporary Irish theatre, as the more 'international' Irish dramatists – Oscar Wilde, George Bernard Shaw, and Samuel Beckett – are being considered in separate subsidiary projects. Irish authors featured in the *Weltbühne Wien* database (with a total of 1767 productions, as of 1 May 2010) include Brendan Behan, Brian Friel, Martin McDonagh, James Joyce, Conor McPherson, Sean O'Casey, Mark O'Rowe, Enda Walsh, and a few less well known namesf.

Before this essay moves on to a discussion of specific cases and aspects of the reception of Irish drama in German-speaking theatres and in Vienna in particular, a few general remarks may be in order. These concern the main resources and collections of theatre history data as would appear essential for any study of the reception of Irish dramatists in German-language theatres. It is also important to remind oneself of the larger (global) literary-historical contexts and frames of expectations (*Erwartungshorizonte*, to adapt Jauss's famous term) within which the Irish play translated into a foreign language and (a) foreign culture(s) is produced.

2. General Aspects (Tools and Contexts)

In the wider context of the Irish Theatrical Diaspora project and the particular issues of reception via translation addressed here, it may be useful to point out some of the resources for such reception-oriented studies pertaining to German-speaking countries. It should not be forgotten that at best the sources mentioned here are transnational and cover theatres in Germany, Austria, Switzerland, and the Southern Tyrol.

The *Deutsche Bühnenverein* [Federal Association of Theatres and Orchestras] issues annual reports (*Wer spielte was?* [Who Did What?]) on the productions (title and basic facts) of every theatre (479 theatres during the 2007/08 season) in the categories of drama, dance, opera, musical. In addition, there is a yearbook series (*Theaterstatistik* [Theatre Statistics]) which details statistics regarding economic issues such as incomes, subsidies, attendance, and personnel. For details of individual authors, translations, and German-language premieres the database administered by *VDB: Verband Deutscher Bühnen- und Medienverlage* [Association of German Theatre Publishers] is the most convenient avenue of access, as it provides concise information on copyright, translators, plot summary, genre, English and German premieres, and the availability of stage manuscripts and editions (www.theatertexte.de/data). The comprehensive history of theatre productions in Austria since 1945 has been recorded by *THEADOK*, a database created under the aegis of the Vienna Society for Theatre Research and the Department of Theatre, Film and Media Studies at the University of Vienna (currently listing 26,000 productions). Three periodicals, which are positioned somewhere between academic journals and popular monthlies, take stock of the latest trends, new plays, translations, and premieres of foreign-language plays: *Theater heute*, *Die Deutsche Bühne*, and *Theater der Zeit*. These monthlies are extremely useful for their indexes of new dramatic writing and regular (annual) surveys among theatre critics. Established publishing houses quite often have subsidiary divisions which promote contemporary (Irish) drama in German translation. Their respective websites provide theatre professionals with basic information on playwrights, playscripts and their availability from such publishers as Hartmann & Stauffacher Verlag, S. Fischer Verlag Theater & Medien, Rowohlt Theaterverlag, Suhrkamp Theaterverlag.[7]

Contemporary Irish drama in the German-speaking theatre world is – as we shall see later – more often than not (and more often than is legitimate) subsumed under the general rubric of 'British/English Theatre'. *Briten-Schocker* [British shocker of a play][8] probably must pass as the most common stereotypical designation of plays associated with a period of theatre history that was initiated by Sarah Kane (*Blasted*, 1995) and Mark Ravenhill (*Shopping and Fucking*, 1996) and that Alex Sierz has surveyed under the label of 'In-Yer-Face' theatre.[9] It would be an exaggeration to say that Irish playwrights feature prominently in Sierz's history; nevertheless, in the public eye, such playwrights as Martin McDonagh, Enda Walsh, Conor McPherson, and Mark O'Rowe also are assumed to belong to this 'school' or 'movement'. In fact, performance and production statistics for plays by McDonagh, McPherson, and Walsh, according to *Wer spielte was?,* point to the high degree of popularity which Irish drama enjoyed in the German-speaking theatre scene in the years between 1998 and 2002. Martin McDonagh had thirty-two productions and 469 performances; Conor McPherson fifty-one productions and 519 performances; Enda Walsh fifty-nine productions and 684 performances. Walsh's *Disco Pigs* (1996) has undoubtedly been the darling of German-speaking theatre directors and dramaturges, with forty-two different productions between 1998 and 2001 – in terms of production numbers thus rivalled only by Patrick Marber's *Closer* (1997).[10] The play's potential for easy adaptation to different settings marked by local accents and dialects may be one of the obvious reasons for its 'intercultural' popularity. These statistics help to confirm an impression verbalized in countless reviews: that the intensive reception of Irish plays constitutes something like a second phase or wave of 'In-Yer-Face' theatre.[11]

There are other markers beyond mere statistics with which to highlight the 'cultural capital', marketing value, and 'public importance' of a play in the processes of translation and cultural transfer. Three Irish plays were recently voted 'play of the year' following annual surveys of theatre critics organized and published by the prestigious (west) German monthly *Theater heute.* Martin McDonagh's *The Pillowman* (Royal National Theatre, London, 2003; *Der Kissenmann*) with its rival premieres (on 20 November 2003) at Berlin's Deutsches Theater and Vienna's Akademietheater was designated 'best foreign play' of the 2003/04 season, while Enda Walsh's *bedbound* and *New Electric Ballroom* were awarded this title for the 2001/02 and the 2004/05 season respectively. It may further help to explain Walsh's immense popularity on the continent to realize that he has been firmly associated with the high-profile Munich theatre Kammerspiele – both *bedbound* (2001) and *Chatroom* (2005) received their German-language premiere there. *New Electric Ballroom* was actually commissioned by Kammerspiele, and its Munich premiere (30 September 2004) preceded the English-language version by four years (it premiered at Druid Lane Theatre, Galway, on 14 July 2008). Likewise, Walsh's latest play, *Penelope,* was 'commissioned' in the context of the *European Capital of Culture Ruhr 2010* project and first staged at Theater Oberhausen on 27 February 2010, well before its English-language premiere in Galway (Druid Lane Theatre, 13 July 2010).

3. Case Studies: Irish Plays in Vienna

These notes refer to a project that sets out to explore the reception and reception history of Irish authors and their plays in Viennese theatres. Three notable exceptions have to be made at the outset: as has been mentioned above, Oscar Wilde, George Bernard Shaw, and Samuel Beckett as more trans-national or inter-national dramatists have been given special consideration in other *Weltbühne Wien* projects. It is important to understand, however, that making these exceptions already highlights the special nature of the definition of what constitutes an Irish play – even (or especially) when the focus is on contemporary Irish theatre.

Irish drama and theatre has traditionally defined itself as being committed to Irish subjects, themes, motifs, characters, locales, and so on – in other words as expressing, if not branding outright, Irishness as a cultural commodity. In the age of the Celtic Tiger and its twilight, globalization and the idea of a worldwide Irish diaspora strongly militate against such self-centredness and self-reflexivity. In a 2000 essay on Irish theatre and identity, the playwright Declan Hughes delivered a broadside on the backwardness of Irish theatre today:

> I'd like to see Irish theatre embrace the profound change that has occurred: that we are barely a country any more, never have been and never will be that most nineteenth century of dreams, a nation once again; that our identity is floating, not fixed. I could live a long and happy life without seeing another play set in a Connemara kitchen, or a country pub.[12]

This problematic issue is all the more virulent when an Irish play is translated/transplanted/translocated and produced in a 'foreign' cultural context. What are the expectations regarding the play's 'Irishness' with regard to theme, content, and mode?[13]

The focal point of this work in progress will be the various ways in which images of Ireland and Irishness condition the reception of Irish plays in Vienna. The methodology will be cultural-studies oriented with special reference to 'imagology' (the study of national images and stereotypes). As Joep Leerssen has defined it, 'the nationality represented (the *spected*) is silhouetted in the per-spectival context of the representing text or discourse (the *spectant*).' Imagology explores 'the dynamics between those images which characterize the Other (*hetero-images*) and those which characterize one's own, domestic identity (*self-images* or *auto-images*).'[14] It is expected that the results of this research will contribute to the current debate on the global versus the local and probe into the valorization of trans-national, if not universal, subjects and thematics through processes of acculturation and inter-cultural exchange.

It is believed that the analysis should first be directed towards mechanisms that precede the actual reception process. Before documenting audience reactions it is imperative to study the various strategies employed (on the part of authors, directors, dramaturges, literary managers, impresarios, and so on) to alert audiences to the cultural Other implied by the respective play, thus re-affirming preconceptions and evoking hetero-stereotypes of the *spected*. Accordingly, at this stage ancillary material in the shape of paratexts (in a Genettian sense) needs to be privileged over theatre reviews as documents of reception. Such paratexts or allographic epitexts may consist of editorial material, advertisements, posters, press releases, directorial statements, visuals aids, and so on. A brief sample relating to Viennese productions of recent Irish plays is introduced here.

Conor McPherson's *The Good Thief* (1994) was first produced as *Der gute Dieb* by Guerilla Gorillas at Vienna's Theater Drachengasse in 2008 and directed by Holger Schober and Dana Csapo. The epitext comprises a programme note-cum-advertisement-cum-summary-cum-poster. On the poster, the anonymous protagonist is seen brandishing a bottle of whisky: Scotch and of the classy variety. The storyline is described as *insane* ('irrwitzig') and *full of dry humour as good as Irish whiskey*.[15] To summarize the goings-on as a bloodbath, a hostage-taking, and a vendetta involving half of Dublin's underworld and describe it as quite a normal day in the life of an Irishman is an indication of the exoticism that is assigned to the play, despite the obvious gestures of hyperbole necessitated by marketing strategies.

In the theatre programme for the Austrian premiere of Mark O'Rowe's 1999 drama *Howie the Rookie/Blutige Anfänger* (directed by Georg Staudacher, Theater Drachengasse, Vienna, 2001) the play is characterized as a bizarre *bad-boys story situated between farce and tragedy*. It is highly revealing that the apodictic reference to the play's country of origin is apparently considered a self-fulfilling mechanism, as we are informed that *in the best Irish tradition, Death is wearing the comedian's masque.*

Martin McDonagh's 2001 play *The Lieutenant of Inishmore / Der Leutnant von Inishmore* received its Austrian premiere in January 2002 at the Akademietheater, Vienna, which is part of the national theatre (Burgtheater) complex and thus endowed with higher prestige and higher value as cultural capital than the experimental Theater Drachengasse. This version (directed by Bulgarian director Dimiter Gotscheff) was seen by the majority of critics as a kind of 'Reservoir Cats' and 'trash comedy'[16] which dealt with the issue of terrorism in an irresponsible manner. In the Burgtheater's own bimonthly magazine *Vorspiel* (April/Mai 2003), McDonagh is credited with turning the *bitter tragedy* of a troubled country into a farce, a *grotesque comedy on old-style terrorism* (that is, terrorism from the period before 11 September 2001). Without explicitly mentioning Synge, the discrepancy between 'a gallous story and a dirty deed' is put forward as a *topos* of Irish literature.[17] In a newspaper article announcing the premiere of the play, reference is made to McDonagh's black humour, which is thought to reduce *the nostalgia for a patriotic, ur-Gaelic grand gesture for folk and fatherland to a petty quarrel.*[18]

To judge by its title, another apparently Irish play, *Die Blinden von Kilcrobally/The Blind People of Kilcrobally*, received its premiere at the Akademietheater in June 1998. The play, set on the 'west coast' of Ireland (time: the present) had all the trappings of a contemporary Irish drama, with heavy McDonaghesque overtones, and at times employing an artificial, synthetic dialect which is as much different from standard High German as the stage language of Synge and O'Casey is from standard Hiberno-English. While the church is burning down, the fire brigade are drinking excessively and watching porn movies in an isolated barn; the priest (*pace* Father Welsh/Walsh) could not care less, as he is most disillusioned with his profession, the hypocritical behaviour of his flock, and Catholicism in general; to him, the church has become a heap of petrified lies. The secret of confession is no longer honoured, and it emerges that the blind people in Kilcrobally are victims of the publican's methylated spirits.[19] The author of the play at its first printing and in theatre programmes was given as 'George O'Darkney'; in reality the man behind this pseudonym is the German scriptwriter and dramatist Jörg Graser.[20] Whatever his motives may have been for indulging in such acts of mimicry and the exploitation of stereotypes, the play, as its wider reception has shown, was not necessarily and not immediately treated as a theatrical hoax. A South Tyrolean amateur drama group seriously considered the play a critical-topical comment on the relationship between church and society.[21] And, according to reviews of the Berlin production directed by Johanna Schall (Kammerspiele, Deutsches Theater Berlin, 1999), the suggestion there was that the play's 'Irishness' functioned as a defamiliarization technique: that is, that the conflict between religion and society could easily be negotiated in a quaint and exotic West of Ireland setting, but definitely not in the secularized and united Germany of the 1990s.[22] When we consider this play as an acid test of Irishness in drama, the experiment failed, and, at least according to one reviewer of the Vienna production, audiences were not fooled by the inferior quality of this play, *because the label 'British' means success guaranteed and nobody could imagine that a British author could ever come up with such puffed-up nonsense.*[23] It is interesting to note how through the double ironic twist (the opposition of fake Irish play vs. authentic Irish play; the blurring of the distinctions between 'British' and 'Irish') stereotypes are left to perpetuate themselves.

4. Conclusion

The tracing or even the chasing of stereotypes may be a trivial pursuit, but some heuristic value adheres to the intrinsic nature of stereotypes, as they facilitate the ordering and categorizing of a new cultural experience. The obvious needs to be stated, but it is important to see this as a question of varying degrees of emphasis, as these examples of Viennese productions of contemporary Irish plays demonstrate. When we analyze how the Irish and Irishness as 'the spected' are represented, three basic stereotypes recur: (1) Violence (in the forms of terrorism as well as urban violence) is foregrounded as a national stereotype, which in turn is seconded by general references to Ireland's 'troubled history'. (2) Alcohol and the (excessive) consumption thereof are constantly cited as markers of national identity – the ubiquity of drinking paraphernalia as stage props are iconographic proof of this. (3) A penchant for black humour and the grotesque to be localized in character, author, and genre is often perceived as denoting Irishness.

All these themes and motifs contribute to reinforce the most basic and the most crude (but nevertheless the most persistent) stereotype that the peoples of the German tongue have in their repertoire: 'Irland' is 'Irrland' [Mad Ireland]. This homophonic pun is based on a folk etymology and equates *irre* ('mad', derived from the Indo-European root *er[ə]s as in Latin *errare*, Old High German *irri*, Old English *ierre*) with *Irrland* ('Ireland' in eighteenth-century German orthography).[24] The perception of Ireland's history as complicated and troubled would certainly be one of the main factors contributing to this stereotypical view.

As regards the reception of Irish drama proper and its place in the writing of literary histories, it has to be noted that from a continental (that is, a Central European) perspective, the distinctions between 'British' and 'Irish' are often blurred, if not confused and obliterated outright. This does not only apply to general (non-academic) usage, but also to a large section of agents in the cultural field of theatre (dramaturges, PR managers, press officers, reviewers, and critics). Eventually, this leads to problems of interference and misrepresentation. Thus, from around 1998 onward, much of contemporary Irish drama abroad is subsumed under the 'in-yer-face' label (*Briten-Schocker*). What the public is consequently taught to expect is a type of latter-day kitchen-sink realism (as associated with post-1956 British/English drama) rather than farce, tragicomedy and eccentricity (as associated with the Irish theatrical tradition).

---

[1] I am extremely grateful to Dr Sandra Mayer, Ms. Barbara Schwarzenbacher, MA, and Dr. Lilien Halada for valuable suggestions and references.

[2] James Stephens, Foreword, *The Insurrection in Dublin* [1916], intro. John A. Murphy (Gerrards Cross: Colin Smythe, 1978): xxxi.

[3] Oscar Wilde, *An Ideal Husband*, *The Complete Works of Oscar Wilde* (London and Glasgow: Collins, 1966): 485.

[4] To date, the project has among other things generated two essay collections. For more generally and theoretically oriented papers, see *Weltbühne Wien/World Stage Vienna, Vol. 1: Approaches to Cultural Transfer*, eds. Ewald Mengel, Ludwig Schnauder, Rudolf Weiss (Trier: WVT Wissenschaftlicher Verlag Trier, 2010).

[5] See <http://www.univie.ac.at/weltbuehne_wien>.

[6] Such case studies and studies of the reception of individual authors (e.g. Shakespeare, Shaw, Wilde, Beckett, Pinter, Osborne, Barker) can be found in *Weltbühne Wien/World Stage Vienna, Vol. 2: Die Rezeption anglophoner Dramen auf Wiener Bühnen des 20. Jahrhunderts*, eds. Ewald Mengel, Ludwig Schnauder, Rudolf Weiss (Trier: WVT Wissenschaftlicher Verlag Trier, 2010); see especially the papers by Sandra Mayer (on Oscar Wilde), Barbara Pfeifer (on G.B. Shaw), and Ewald Mengel (on Beckett and Pinter).

[7] On general aspects of the reception of contemporary theatre and drama in German-speaking countries, see also the activities of *The German Society for Contemporary Theatre and Drama in English* (CDE) <http://fb14.uni-mainz.de/projects/cde> as well as the information portals <http://www.theaterportal.de> and <http://www.theaterforschung.de>.

[8] Sabine Oppolzer, 'Noch ein mißverstandener Briten-Schocker', *Die Presse* 17 March 1999: 32.

[9] Aleks Sierz, *In-Yer-Face Theatre: British Drama Today* (London: Faber, 2001); see also the accompanying website: <http://www.inyerface-theatre.com>.

[10] Michael Raab, 'The End of a Wave: New British and Irish Plays in the German-Speaking Theatre', *(Dis)Continuities: Trends and Traditions in Contemporary Theatre and Drama in English*, eds. Margarete Rubik and Elke Mettinger-Schartmann, CDE 9 (Trier: WVT Wissenschaftlicher Verlag Trier, 2002): 45.

[11] See Holger Zimmer, 'Irinnen im Aufwind', *Theater der Zeit* (February 2001): 34; Aleks Sierz, 'Still In-Yer-Face? Towards a Critique and a Summation', *New Theatre Quarterly* (69) 18.1 (2002): 23; Raab, 39.

[12] Declan Hughes, 'Who the Hell Do We Think We Are? Reflections On Irish Theatre and Identity', *Theatre Stuff: Critical Essays on*

Contemporary Irish Theatre, ed. Eamonn Jordan (Dublin: Carysfort Press, 2000): 13. Fintan O'Toole in e.g. *Tom Murphy: The Politics of Magic* (Dublin: New Island Books; London: Nick Hern Books, 1994): 22, reports a similar determination on the part of Tom Murphy and his friend Noel O'Donoghue that, whatever they wrote, "One thing is fucking sure – it's not going to be set in a kitchen."'

[13] The playwright Martin McDonagh quite interestingly emblematizes the aporias and dilemmas of cultural transfer in his œuvre. In *The Pillowman* (Royal National Theatre, London, 2003; Akademietheater, Vienna, 2003), McDonagh had for the first time given up the familiar settings of his earlier plays – the 'True West' of Ireland– for a vaguely Central or Eastern European context and the theme of a writer in a totalitarian state, thereby abandoning the successful formula implied by a pastiche of the Irish peasant play or Irish kitchen-sink drama, as, for example, in his *The Beauty Queen of Leenane* (Town Hall Theatre, Galway, 1996; Theater Drachengasse, Vienna, 1997), *The Lonesome West* (Town Hall Theatre, Galway, 1997; Theater Drachengasse, 1999), or *The Lieutenant of Inishmore* (Royal Shakespeare Company, The Other Place, Stratford, 2001; Burgtheater, Vienna, 2001). On McDonagh's reception in Vienna, see Barbara Schwarzenbacher, 'The Reception of Martin McDonagh's Plays on Viennese Stages', MA thesis University of Vienna, 2009, and Lilien Halada, 'McDonagh auf der Bühne, 1996 bis 2008: Eine Dokumentation irischer und österreichischer Inszenierungen der Stücke Martin McDonaghs', PhD thesis University of Vienna, 2010; Halada provides extremely rich and valuable, if somewhat unsystematic, documentation of the reception history of McDonagh's plays in Vienna and elsewhere.

[14] Joep Leerssen, 'Imagology: History and Method', *Imagology: The Cultural Construction and Literary Representation of National Characters: A Critical Survey*, eds. Manfred Beller and Joep Leerssen (Amsterdam: Rodopi, 2007): 27. Leerssen adds the important caveat: 'Both *spected* and *spectant* are usually categorized in national terms, but in both cases the scholar will be wary of seeing in this appellation a straightforward reflection of empirical real-world collectives.' See also Leerssen's imagology website: <http://cf.hum.uva.nl/images>.

[15] In the following I have italicized my translations/paraphrases of key passages from the German epitexts.

[16] See, for example, Hans Haider, 'Irische Clowns auf der Kleie', Review of *Der Leutnant von Inishmore*, by Martin McDonagh, *Die Presse,*28 Jan 2002.

[17] *Vorspiel: Magazin des Burgtheaters*, 19 (April/May 2003).

[18] Ingrid Noll, 'Bombengeschäfte', *Die Presse* 25 Jan 2002: Supplement.

[19] For summary information on the play, see <http://users.south-tyrolean.net/Pustertaler-Theatergemeinschaft/Blinden.htm>.

[20] George O'Darkney, *Die Blinden von Kilcrobally, Spectaculum* 67 (1998): 175-210.

[21] See the homepage of Pustertaler Theatergemeinschaft.

[22] See Gerhard Ebert, *Neues Deutschland* 13 April 1999, and Ijoma Mangold, *Berliner Zeitung* 12 April 1999.

[23] Claudia Voigt, 'Schreib ein Stück!', *Der Spiegel* 28 (1998): 162-164.

[24] See, for example, Werner Krause, who relies on both folk etymology and a pun on one of Ludwig Wittgenstein's most famous apothegms ('the world is all that is the case/bang') for the title of his review: 'Irrland oder Die Welt ist, was der Knall ist', Review of *Der Leutnant von Inishmore*, by Martin McDonagh, *Kleine Zeitung* 27 Jan 2002.

7 | Blue Raincoat Theatre Company and its Influences

Rhona Trench

> Not everyone knows how I killed old Mathers, smashing his jaw in with my spade. [pause]. But first, it is better to speak of my friendship with John Divney, for it was he who first knocked old Mathers down, by giving him a great blow on the neck with a special bicycle pump which he had manufactured himself out of a hollowed iron bar.[1]

As the lights come up, the audience can see in shadow a man facing them, drawing them into a monologue of murder, betrayal, and intrigue.[2] The light rises and the protagonist, known as Man and played by Sandra O Malley, is shown standing at the centre of a giant open book, literally positioned within its narrative. For more than seven minutes Man charts his tale of entrapment. The sequence ends in darkness with the sounds of bicycle chains and pedals, the movement of wheels, an eerie whistling, the noise of ticking clocks, and the blowing of a wind, interrupted by a man calling out: 'Who's there? Who's there? Who's there?'[3] Then silence.

So begins Blue Raincoat Theatre Company's production of *The Third Policeman*, an adaptation by Jocelyn Clarke of the novel by Flann O'Brien, which was first performed at the company's home theatre The Factory, Sligo in October 2007. In the production, spoken narrative is important for the telling of the story, but the physical body – choreographed and energized – is central to the production. This essay examines the significance of the text in Blue Raincoat's production of *The Third Policeman*, but also points out the importance of the visual features of the production, arguing that Blue Raincoat's innovations stem from their long history of negotiation with the conventions of Irish theatre. Those negotiations involve a variety of issues: acting styles, dramaturgical influences, directorial lines, the representation of the west of Ireland, and something that Anthony Roche has described as 'the principle of creative contradiction, of speaking against received narratives', which 'ensures the ongoing vitality of Irish drama.' [4]

Figure 3: *The Third Policeman*, produced by Blue Raincoat Theatre Company (Photograph by Joe Hunt)

Blue Raincoat was founded in 1991 by Malcolm Hamilton, who became the company's Writer-in-Residence, and Niall Henry, who became Artistic Director. Henry recalls how 'Malcolm asked me to start the theatre. He specifically came to Paris ... not to study what I was doing for five years at mime school in Paris, but to ask me to start the company and to come back with him' to Ireland.[5] Without knowing Henry well, Hamilton believed that he would want to pursue (with no financial backing and against reason) the ideal of staging work in new ways, placing the body as central to the making of meaning. Furthermore, Hamilton believed that Henry might be attracted to the idea of founding the first professional theatre company in his hometown of Sligo.

In June 1993, the company moved into the refurbished Factory Space, which was officially opened by Marcel Marceau, with the then Minister for Arts Michael D. Higgins as guest of honour. As an artistic hub of Sligo's community, the Factory provides a venue for workshops, exhibitions, music, and poetry recitals.

The Factory has a history of being associated with blood and death. Used as a slaughterhouse in the 1980s, it remains a place where things are dismembered and re-processed into something else. This notion of the performance space as abattoir represents figuratively Blue Raincoat's rejection of the theatrical style that dominated Irish theatre in the 1980s and 1990s – plays which, in Eamonn Jordan's words, represent, 'a surrender to and sundering of ... pastoral idylls'.[6] The rejection of that approach was based on the company's dedication to physical theatre. That approach had local and international contexts.

The local context is worth emphasising. The activities of Blue Raincoat were based firmly on a number of theatrical forces particular to the northwest of Ireland: a fully-charged political environment, a diversity of approaches to theatrical practice, a vibrant tradition of community theatre. As was the national experience, emigration from the northwest was also a key feature in the day-to-day lives of its people. Eamonn Jordan reminds us that 'at a time heavily dominated by the Catholic Church, Ireland was in part a world of suspicion and little compromise'[7], while Christopher Murray writes of the 1980s that 'The country was beset by changes of government, ever-rising unemployment, a new wave of emigration and a strong sense of entropy.'[8] Blue Raincoat emerged from that environment, and its continued existence owes something to its founders' determination to overcome some of the limitations mentioned by Jordan and Murray. Hence, the founding of Blue Raincoat began as a struggle against multiple challenges: the cultural construction of the west of Ireland, audience expectation, the dominance within Irish theatre of plays that employ linear and realistic representations of action and characterization, the dominance of text-based approach to Irish theatre, a resistance to European influences, and the difficult economic and social circumstances of the time.

Blue Raincoat's early role models were other Irish companies with a strong local emphasis: Druid Theatre Company, founded in 1975 in Galway, and Red Kettle Theatre Company, founded in 1986 in Waterford. Druid has always placed great importance on the idea of ensemble, because it originally involved a core group of theatre-makers and actors, who trained together and developed their style over several years. Druid believes that individual artistic careers achieve meaning through long-term commitment to an evolving company of peers. Indeed, in 1991, Niall Henry phoned Garry Hynes to ask her advice on Druid's pioneering work as an independent theatre company in the west of Ireland.

Red Kettle was originally founded on the idea of an 'Arts for All Movement', whereby community theatre would embrace all ages and all kinds of arts, including poetry, painting, sculpture, plays and writing.[9] Blue Raincoat was influenced by this idea, and now plays a key role in the development of community access to and participation in the arts in Sligo, providing a broad range of professional arts-related support for community and cultural programming within its immediate region.

Moving from the local to the international context, Blue Raincoat's interest in corporeal mime offers a particularly useful example of the kinds of influences that the company has absorbed from overseas. Its practice is derived from the work of Jacques Copeau, Marcel Marceau, and Étienne Decroux. The central principles and philosophies of those men are observable in Blue Raincoat productions in many ways: physical agility, mask work, ensemble acting, mime, the ways in which thought shapes movement, and many other methods of thinking about the expressive possibilities of the human body.

The work of these practitioners is worth exploring in some detail. Jacques Copeau, founder of the Théâtre du Vieux-Colombier in 1913, was an influential French theatre director, critic, producer, actor, and dramatist, who despised what he saw as the crude commercialism of the stage of his day. His fascination with the actor inclined him towards the possibilities of actor-training, his approach to which was based on the hope that the actor could be encouraged to return to instinctive artistic creation. His approach demanded that actors commit to strict timetables of rigorous daily exercise including athletics, dance, games, movement, improvisation, and silence. Importantly, actors were challenged with exercising in slow movement. Copeau believed that this technique was more sincere, allowing actors to access a simplicity of movement where external action is matched by state of mind.

Decroux recalls the demands on the actor at Copeau's school, 'where students were stripped of costumes, props, of text, their faces veiled statements, allowing no doubt in the audience's mind as to what the character was thinking or feeling.'[10] Thomas Leabhart notes: 'From this central idea [of covering the actor's face, and an awareness of] the importance of the core of the actor rather than his extremities, modern mime was born.'[11] This peeling back of all of the theatrical elements except those absolutely necessary to the performance allowed the actors to achieve a greater productivity and effectiveness.

Copeau's repositioning of the actor to the instinctual core essential for acting was carried forward into the work of Decroux, whereby the actor is essential to the definition of theatre and vital to the stage. In moments of silence between words, it is the actor who develops the play's meaning. For Decroux, mime was not a performing art form that serviced the spoken theatre, but an end in itself: 'Theatre is the actor's art' [*l'art d'ácteur*], he stated, placing all other dramatic elements extraneous to it: 'Music, dance and song are but occasional visitors [to the stage].'[12]

But while Copeau abhorred stage scenery unless it was minimal and symbolic, Decroux believed that scenery, lighting and sound could be used, even if they were not essential to the theatre. In 'My Definition of Theatre' he reiterates the idea that the actor holds the power. All scenery and props were banned from Decroux's first ten years of actor training because he felt that the actor could give the impression of (for example) staircases through using the body, creating the illusion of being on a different level from other actors 'when in reality they are side by side.'[13]

For Marceau, however, the illusion is seen in the object rather than in the actor. Marceau's mime radically shifted away from Decroux's teaching, tending more towards styles of pantomime, which he developed through his 'Bip sketches'; he also dedicated more attention to performances rather than teaching or writing. These differences saw Decroux and Marceau go their separate ways.

While Marceau officially opened the Factory for Blue Raincoat in 1993, he is the least influential of these three practitioners in terms of the company's movement style. Yet it must be acknowledged that Marceau's fame raised the profile of mime on an international scale, making pathways for Decroux's teaching to reach a worldwide audience, as well as raising the profile of codified movements of the body.

Developing Practice

Drawing on these practitioners' work, Blue Raincoat came to be known as a 'physical theatre' company from the mid-1990s. The 'physical theatre' Blue Raincoat was making in 1991 attempted to embrace movement and visual design, but was inspired and driven by Henry's training: he trained at L'École Internationale de Mimodrame de Paris Marcel Marceau from 1984 to 1987. Max Decroux, Étienne Decroux's son, taught Henry for one of those years. There, he met another significant teacher, Corinne Soum, who had studied mime with Étienne Decroux, and who became Decroux's assistant, sharing in his research, teaching, and creations. She was the professor of Corporeal Mime at the École de Mimodrame Marcel Marceau for seven years, travelling the world as an invited lecturer and writer on Decroux and corporeal mime. After Henry completed his training at the École de Mimodrame in 1987, he spent two years at Corinne Soum and Steve Wasson's Theatre de l'Ange Fou and the International School of Corporeal Mime in Paris.

In the early 1990s, Blue Raincoat's notion of 'physical theatre' involved a certain kind of political intervention. Henry states that 'in Irish theatre, representations of the body have fallen short.'[14] His aim was to incorporate mime and movement into the shape of his productions – an aim that was directly related to his training in Paris. Blue Raincoat's choice of plays in the company's earliest days reveals Hamilton and Henry's sense of the need to (re)present familiar theatre in new ways. Thomas Kilroy's 1986 play *Double Cross* was their first production, being staged in 1991. That was followed in 1993 by Dario Fo's *Accidental Death of an Anarchist* (1970), Tom Murphy's *A Whistle in the Dark* (1961), and Martin Sherman's *Bent* (1979); Synge's *Playboy of the Western World* (1907) was staged in 1994. The company's productions of well-known plays deliberately flouted conventional approaches to such work, exploring those plays' treatment of communal experience, and refusing to present them as representative of the 'real world'. In general, however, the early productions remained heavily dependent on text, because the notion of mime and movement as central to making meaning was a one-person project – Niall Henry's – which could not be fully realized. At that time, the company performers had not been trained, though all would do so at different stages and for different durations at the Theatre de l'Ange Fou and the International School of Corporeal Mime in London or Paris.[15]

Blue Raincoat initially promoted a peculiar kind of anarchy in their approach to costume, sound, and lighting. Class and sexual politics as represented through the body became the primary modes of experience and presentation. There was a sense in the early productions of an urgency and impatience that bordered on the reckless. *Double Cross*, for instance, is a history play set during the Second World War, which concerns loyalty, treason, and deception, with a sense of theatricality interwoven into the text. The notion of 'the double' and of 'doubling' calls attention to the inherent performativity of the play. Henry's objective with this production was to stage it as a form of resistance to typical representations of how the body communicates in Irish theatre. The betrayal in the work – the 'double cross' of the title – was presented as the body's power to communicate betrayal before cognitive issues of psychology and language.

Political identity accentuated the importance of the body in Blue Raincoat productions. The ideas of conflicting expressions of betrayal, killing, and loyalty present in *Double Cross* were extended in the company's subsequent work, in such productions as *Westport*

Murders, written by Brendan Ellis and staged in 1995. The play was set against the background of rapid social changes wrought by the first phases of the Celtic Tiger period. The story was dramatized around issues of brutality, and was planned as a political and historical drama that aimed to have an impact on the conscience of the audience, who were asked to consider their sense of moral responsibility.

In 1996, the company staged a production of *Hamlet*, which dramatized the protagonist's moral integrity by contrasting it with his struggle for vengeance. Blue Raincoat's political approach to power and corruption involved the use of colour-coded fabric costumes to emphasize characterization, and the construction of a ten-foot high metal scaffolding grid around the stage. This increased the level of energy, anger, and conflict in their production.

Authenticity was and still is a key component of Blue Raincoat's practice, based around the idea of identity. Bernadette Sweeney points out that 'Irish authenticity has become an economic tool in creating a market for things Irish, a means of ironic self-reflection, and a seemingly limitless source of artistic inspiration, acted upon or reacted against but ever present.'[16] The authentic body allows for a freedom to express the multi-layered nature of human possibilities. For Charles Taylor, authenticity involves the individual's own created or discovered (not by imposition) understanding of the self. Taylor believes that true authenticity also involves recognition of and openness to what he calls 'horizons of significance' — certain larger contexts within which humans exist.[17] Paradoxically, the individual self can only be understood in relation to others who provide a sense of personal connection with a larger political, social, or religious source of meaning. Taylor's exploration of 'the politics of identity' is bound up with ideas of dignity, recognition, and authenticity. With this in mind, Blue Raincoat's geographical location on the northwestern edge of Connaught, Ireland, and Europe means that there is a certain kind of marginality intrinsic to the company's identity. At a unique position in relation to the rest of the world, Blue Raincoat could perform new and well-known texts in different, innovative, and authentic ways.

The authentic body also had implications for the performance processes, which are based on the notion of ensemble. 'Ensemble' for Blue Raincoat has come to mean an attempt to rid themselves of the ancient division of labour between directors, actors, designers, technicians, and other practitioners. Although all company performers trained in the physical discipline of corporeal mime, they all have different levels of skill and talent (as would be true in any group of people). Henry allows ideas to unfold, and his decisions about which ideas will remain determine the overall shape of the production.

For Henry, then, the actor is central to the rehearsal process, in terms of how the body can tell the story. The company also executes a strict and self-disciplined daily routine, involving a physical and vocal warm up before rehearsal. Warm-ups typically depend on the choice of production being staged. In the case of *The Third Policeman*, that play is text-heavy and involves a range of movement, so there was a balance between the physical and the vocal for that production, with the warm-up lasting at least one hour before rehearsals began. The warm-up can be carried out individually or as a group, depending on which aspect of the production the performers are working on.

However, the company's use of the actor is not its only method of creating meaning in performance. The *mise en scène* of Blue Raincoat productions demonstrates how important design is as an expressive element of the stage. Yet the actors must draw on their own resources first, in an attempt to reach the audience. In order to achieve this goal, few props or stage scenery are used in the early stages of rehearsal. Unlike Decroux, Henry then incorporates set, lights, sound, and music into the rehearsal process. Together with the production manager Peter Davey, the designers are also usually present for most of the rehearsals. They attend rehearsals at the beginning of the process when much of the discussions and workshops take place, but their design realizations (sound/lighting/projection) begin to emerge collaboratively with the performers' work later in the process.

Improvisation, part of the training at the mime schools, is central to the rehearsal process of all Blue Raincoat productions. Performers respond to one another in the context of the visual tapestry of the performance, and do not specifically react to the story or the portrayal of characters themselves. The use of improvisation, based on small but significant parts of the text, frees the actors from being tied into specifics and allows them to work with a *feeling* or *idea* and not a literary aspect of the text.

Sometimes, the justification for a physical movement is not found straightaway; rather, it comes from a sense, a broad notion or a moment in the text that is improvised and work-shopped. From this process, Henry selects and challenges a physical movement or phrase that corresponds to the purpose inspired by the text. However, such direction is not always easy to communicate, because, as actor Kellie Hughes points out, 'to articulate a system of direction in language loses a lot of how and what actually takes place in the rehearsal process.'[18]

The ensemble company retains five productions in repertoire. These are performed and toured nationally and internationally while the group develops new works. All members work out of the Factory on an annual basis, making their living from the company. The actors' formal training in corporeal mime means that they strive to express abstract and universal ideas and emotions through codified movements of the entire body, especially the trunk. The primary feature of Blue Raincoat's performance ensemble means that, as a permanent group, their practice stems from a shared language and aesthetic. The group has performed together over a long period, using the same production crew for most of their shows.[19] As a regularly funded ensemble theatre company, their performance style is constantly evolving, shaped by the group from within – while from outside, external factors such as the economy, society, and technology significantly affect the operation and role of the ensemble.[20] Thus, Blue Raincoat's education programme, which aims to teach, train, and influence others in the company's corporeal style of acting, has also become a necessary part of its remit, especially in terms of generating an income, given that the Arts Council has significantly cut Blue Raincoat's funding since 2002.[21]

While Blue Raincoat is aware of what being an ensemble theatre company in Ireland means, it is also aware of what it is not. Critics, academics, practitioners and students have a tendency to refer to work as 'physical theatre' when it does not fit into a category of literary dramatic theatre or contemporary dance.[22] The difficulty in defining such work comes from the multiplicity of its origins, such as puppetry, clowning, mime, contemporary dance, corporeal mime, and commedia dell'arte. As Dympna Callery notes, 'many current practitioners resent the way their work is categorized as physical theatre,'[23] placing very different kinds of physical work for performance into one category. Yet, what can be argued is that physical theatre pursues the realization of theatre primarily through the physical body; the actor is placed as a significant creator of meaning with his/her body as the text. What Marceau refers to as 'body miming, gestures and attitudes', was a way to give theatre its own art form which had previously been located in dance.[24] Practitioners and their companies might be classified as 'mime', 'physical', 'physically based', 'movement-based' or 'visual theatre' – all labels which cannot account for styles that blur or cross the lines between some or all of these forms of practice. Franc Chamberlain's term 'post-physical theatre', as a way of catching the diversity of what is happening in the performance world in the wake of the physical theatre adventure, comes closer to describing the move away from the physical in the generic sense. As Chamberlain notes, post-physical theatre can 'go beyond the binary of physical/non-physical', yet it offers a way of escaping the confines of the physical.[25] He adds that there is 'no fundamental rejection of the dramatic in either physical or post physical performance.'[26]

Blue Raincoat's idea of mime and movement has multiple angles and directions – spillages and crossovers, connections which allow for theatre companies like them, branded as they have been for various reasons as 'physical theatre', to process new evolutions of their style. Certainly Decroux's principles of training as developed by Corinne Soum have had long-term influences on Blue Raincoat's orientation.

The Third Policeman

Figure 4: Sandra O Malley in *The Third Policeman*.
(Photo by Joe Hunt)

In the company's 2007 production of *The Third Policeman*, Sandra O Malley's act of donning a hat and pursuing the opening monologue as a 'grotesque clown-like figure' helped Henry and Clarke see that the protagonist was trapped in the narrative.[27] This, they felt, was the primary tangible action that emerged from the company's visit to Annaghmakerrig, the artists' retreat in Co. Monaghan, where four members of the cast went with Henry and Clarke for one week to work on *The Third Policeman*. Following this insight, the improvisation of bicycle movements helped in the exploration of rhythm, sound, and visuals within the text, pushing the performers to work with each other and to align their idiosyncratic movement choices to the overall pattern of the performance. If aspects of characters emerged, they were filed away or put aside initially in favour of the shape of the performance.

Using the bicycle movement, Henry presented Decroux's three elements at the actor's disposal, as the means of dramatic expression – the design, the intensity, and the rhythm of a movement or movements in bringing shape to the ideas of the visual form. The design of the movement allows the actor to create an image in space and to position his or her body into what Anne Dennis calls a 'stage picture', communicating specific ideas to the audience.[28] The intensity of movement seeks to focus the audience on what is important, while the rhythm controls the level at which the audience will take in the action.

Figure 5: *The Third Policeman* **(Photo by Joe Hunt)**

As adapted for the stage by Jocelyn Clarke, *The Third Policeman* tells the story of Man, the narrator, who charts his tale of entrapment in a never-ending 'hell' caused by his part in the murder of Phillip Mathers. John Divney, Man's accomplice, inveigles his way into Man's home after Man's parents disappear. Divney prolongs his stay by promising that he will reveal the whereabouts of Mathers' cash box. Established at the start as a somewhat 'normal' world, the environment of the play soon becomes remote. An unusual village police force is entangled in the story, with depictions of bicycles as half-humans and humans as half-bicycles being added. This hellish world has no rules or laws; linear order is abandoned and language is destabilized as the tale unfolds.

In a scene in which Man calls to the police station in search of his American gold watch (a watch he pretends to own because he thinks it will help him find out when he will find the Black Box) he meets Policeman Pluck (Ciarán McCauley) who is in conversation with Gilaney (Fiona McGeown) about finding Gilaney's missing bicycle. Man is asked to partake in the search and dutifully assists. All three either 'cycle' on their bicycles or walk on a 'journey' round the 'village' where clues of the missing bicycle are found. The oversized book centre-stage offers the actors a route around and over which to travel. One of Pluck's conversations on this journey informs Man of the 'Atomic Theory', reminding the audience of the half-human half-bicycle hypothesis.

> **PLUCK.** Did you ever study Atomics when you were a lad?
> **MAN.** No.
> **PLUCK.** That is a very serious defalcation but all the same I will tell you the size of it. Everything is composed of small particles of itself and they are flying around in concentric circles and arcs and segments and innumerable other geometrical figures too numerous to mention collectively, never standing still or resting but spinning away and darting hither and thither and back again all the time on the go. These diminutive gentlemen are called atoms. Do you follow me intelligently?[29]

The movement of atoms described by Pluck is used as a metaphor for the actors' movements on stage. Following Decroux's intensity of movement, the cyclical nature of the world of *The Third Policeman* and the sometimes haphazard movement of atoms, reflected by the bicycle movements, are repeatedly experienced through different levels of tension, directing the audience's attention to the nightmarish world of entrapment. The rhythm of the bicycle movements alternates between a slow and fast pace, presented at times fleetingly and at other times in a long and focussed way, controlling the level at which the audience will take in the action.

The production's set designer Jamie Varten matched the verbal extravagance and movement with a visual opulence. Varten's vision of the surreal, which he associated with the original novel, was supported by Michael Cummins's lighting design: tiny streams of light poured through the many holes in the back wall, creating a starry effect and shining towards the audience. The back wall also contained a moon-dial, a window high up on the right, a barred door somewhat like a jail door, and high up on the left of the back wall, hung a bicycle. Joe Hunt created an original musical score for the production, using various noises of bicycle chains and pedals, the movement of wheels, eerie whistling, ticking clocks, and the blowing of a wind as the machine-age and technology pronounced the onslaught of communal identity and raised issues of alienation and estrangement. The overall design took on the qualities and manner of the unstable universe of the play, showing the audience that humankind does not know its world, and revealing the ways in which science competes with the imagination in order to explore the mysteries of existence. The black box space in the Factory allowed the designers to emphasize the actor in the environment of the play, highlighting the tentative reality of the world alongside questions about fiction in the narrative. The large book underscores this notion and allowed for many different compositional arrangements to be presented on the stage. Henry directed the action in different planes, staging action in front of the book, behind it, beside it, and on top of it.

Man's opening monologue beside the book sets the story of how Mathers was killed and the narrative follows the convoluted search for Mathers' wealth, hidden in a black box under his house. Ironically, the monologue emphasizes the importance of the words on stage and introduces the significance of Man as the storyteller throughout. The content of the spoken word is literally reflected in the positioning of the book centre stage. It also represents Man's unfinished 'de Selby' book, the philosophies of which O'Brien painstakingly inserted in footnotes throughout the novel. Man's stand-up narrative in particular is without the physical virtuosity that is typically associated with movement theatre. Henry, in dialogue with Clarke, did not cut the length of sentences (despite opposition from O Malley due to the length of her lines) nor did he shy away from the soaring images in the work, embracing the long sentences, tirades, and words.

Decroux's corporeal language, often misunderstood as seeing movement as a replacement for speech, dealt with the pre-verbal, post-verbal and non-verbal, but also the verbal. Henry became absorbed in the non-real world, placing the language of the visual beside the language of the word throughout the production. Mime and movement in *The Third Policeman* demonstrate Leabhart's statement:

> they are not some precious and separate disciplines outside of mainstream theatre, but, rather ... they are again, as they used to be, multifaceted forms of expression which is at the heart of theatre – a theatre of the creative actor who determines the synthesis of movement, text, music, lighting and décor. Mime and movement are the cradle of theatre.[30]

The relationship of Blue Raincoat with European practitioners involves complex cultural transitions that are never linear. Today, the company continues to blend the Irish with the international, perpetuating and resisting, disrupting and reworking familiar, non-naturalistic, and new works. Yet their work contributes to strategies for physical/ movement/visual performance in and of Ireland, calling on the ensemble to create work using text, audience, space, performers, designers, and cultural context. Their work continues to develop strategies for performance and new ways of practice in Irish theatre.

------

[1] Jocelyn Clarke's adaptation of Flann O'Brien's *The Third Policeman*, performed at The Factory in October 2007, Sligo. Unpublished.

[2] The opening monologue runs for almost ten minutes, with few interruptions.

[3] The voice of 'Old Mathers' in Jocelyn Clarke's *The Third Policeman*, DVD archive, The Factory, Sligo.

[4] Anthony Roche, *Contemporary Irish Drama*, Second Edition, (Basingtoke: Palgrave Macmillan, 2009): 12.

[5] Rhona Trench, Interview with Niall Henry, 26 November 2008.

[6] Eamonn Jordan, *Dissident Dramaturgies: Contemporary Irish Theatre*, (Dublin: Irish Academic Press, 2009): 116.

[7] Eamonn Jordan (ed.), *Theatre Stuff: Essays on Contemporary Irish Theatre* (Dublin: Carysfort Press, 2000): xvii.

[8] Christopher Murray, *Twentieth-Century Irish Drama: Mirror up to Nation* (Manchester University Press, 1997): 223.

[9] Interview with Noreen Hennessy, one of the original founding members of Red Kettle Theatre Company, 27 September 2009.

[10] Anne Dennis, 'Étienne Decroux – An Actor, A Teacher of Actors, An Actor's Director' in *Mime Journal* (Pomona, CA)1993/1994: 20. I think this is the correct way of citing an article in a journal where the place of publication might be obscure.

[11] Thomas Leabhart, *Modern and Post Modern Mime*, (London: Macmillan, 1989): 75.

[12] Étienne Decroux, *Words on Mime*, Trans. Mark Piper, *Mime Journal* 1985.

[13] Decroux, *Words on Mime*: 26.

[14] Niall Henry Interview.

[15] Blue Raincoat actors studied at The Theatre de l'Ange Fou and the International School of Corporeal Mime in London or Paris as follows: John Carty (founding member of the company since 1991 who trained at the mime school in 1994); Ciaran McCauley (core member since 1991 who trained at the mime school in 1994); Fiona McGeown (joined the company in 1995 after training at the Gaiety School of Acting, Dublin and the mime school in 2004); Sandra O Malley (joined in 1997 after training at the mime school that year); and Kellie

Hughes (joined in 2004 immediately after her three years training at the mime school).

16 Bernadette Sweeney, *Performing the Body in Irish Theatre,* (Basingstoke: Palgrave Macmillan, 2008): 10.

17 Charles Taylor, *The Ethics of Authenticity,* (Cambridge: Harvard University Press, 1991): 66.

18 Rhona Trench, Interview with Kellie Hughes, 26 March 2009.

19 The most recent addition to the ensemble, Kellie Hughes, joined the company in 2004 and most of the other actors have been with the company for at least ten years. On occasion, the company has invited other theatre artists to work on shows. For example, Jocelyn Clarke has adapted novels to stage plays and has acted as dramaturg for them since 1993. Other significant contributors are Jamie Varten, set designer since 2005; Ruth Lehane, actor since 2006; and Mikel Murfi, actor since 2006. The inclusion of such practitioners broadens the appeal of Blue Raincoat's work and exposes the company members to other talents and approaches.

20 Some of their other training includes annual intensive voice workshops at the internationally recognized Roy Hart Theatre School in Marlargues near Marseille, France, facilitated by David Goldsworthy, and workshops facilitated by Anne Bogart of SITI Company (Saratoga International Theater Institute) and additional SITI company workshops in Ireland facilitated by SITI's actors and tutors Barney O'Hanlon and Leon Ingulsrud, at The Factory, Sligo.

21 See Blue Raincoat's Arts Council Funding Applications for 2002, 2003, 2004, 2005, 2006, 2007, 2008 and 2009 available at The Factory, Sligo or on the Arts Council of Ireland website http://www.artscouncil.ie. (In 2009 Blue Raincoat Theatre Company received €320, 000 and in 2010 they received €250,000.)

22 See Dympna Callery, in 'Gesturing towards post physical performance' in John Keefe and Simon Murray (eds.*), Physical Theatres: A Critical Reader* (London: Routledge, 2007): 120.

23 Ibid.

24 Marcel Marceau in *Mime Journal,* 1983: 9.

25 Franc Chamberlain, *Physical Theatres: A Critical Reader* (London: Routledge, 2007): 121.

26 Ibid.

27 Rhona Trench, Interview with Jocelyn Clarke, 10 October 2009.

28 Anne Dennis, 'The Articulate Body; The Physical Training of the Actor', in Keefe and Murray: 184-186.

29 Jocelyn Clarke's *The Third Policeman,* DVD archive, Blue Raincoat Theatre Company Production, The Factory, 2007.

30 Leabhart: 16.

8 | Beyond the Passion Machine: The Adigun-Doyle *Playboy* and Multiculturalism

Christopher Murray

In recent times, the question of immigrants in Ireland has pressed itself forward as a sociological and ethical issue deserving public debate and changes in Irish law. An issue of the Jesuit quarterly *Studies* was devoted to the topic in 2007, and the editorial concluded: 'Immigration is inevitable. It has changed Ireland very dramatically in a very short time'.[1] The word 'dramatically' here has nothing to do with the theatre, however, and nowhere in this interesting issue of *Studies* is the literary representation of immigrants addressed, which, broadly speaking, is the context of this essay.

The specific object is to advance the recently successful Abbey Theatre version of *The Playboy of the Western World* as a means of exploring the arrival of multiculturalism at the Irish national theatre, and to consider what this might mean. The Adigun-Doyle *Playboy* opened at the Abbey on 29 September 2007 and ran to packed houses for two months; the following year it was revived, this time during the Christmas period, running from 16 December 2008 to 31 January 2009. It could readily be described as a major hit. Secondly, I want to view the style of this new version of the *Playboy* as in some measure derived from Passion Machine, a company founded in 1984 dedicated to attracting young people to a theatre occupied mainly with working-class Dublin experience, and thereby to question how far and in what idiom in this specific instance the local and the universal are conversing with each other via the medium of re-interpretation of a classic Irish play.

By way of introducing the first part it is necessary to say a few words about the recent relationship between Irish drama and multiculturalism. Such a relationship was not on the agenda until Donal O'Kelly put it there in 1994 with his play *Asylum! Asylum!*, first staged in the Peacock Theatre (within the Abbey) in that year. Besides being an inventive actor and writer, O'Kelly was co-founder of Calypso, 'a Glasgow-Dublin production company specializing in dramas dealing with human rights issues'.[2] *Asylum! Asylum!* is an issue play, concerning a fictional Ugandan, Joseph Omara, seeking asylum in Ireland, who falls foul of the EU legislation then being imposed. Having fallen in love with his free legal aid lawyer, Mary Gaughran, Joseph decides to make a run for it when the immigration officers arrive to remove him forcibly from the country. At first Mary tries laughingly to dissuade Joseph, who thinks he and she can simply disappear together in Ireland: 'Who'll ever think to look at us twice!? Joseph! You're black! ... You can't hide here!' (160). Then she goes with him. Thus the ending denotes the reverse of the ending of Synge's *Playboy*, where the outsider is driven off at the close. In that regard it is an optimistic though subversive problem play. Reviewing its first production Fintan O'Toole said *Asylum! Asylum!* 'not only deals bravely and passionately with an important public issue, it also challenges, in a way that a national theatre should do, some basic aspects of our self-perception as a people'. [3]

Its seriousness has not been matched in the Irish theatre since 1994, even though the play is now dated, since the legal procedures dealing with asylum seekers and naturalization have been modified. *Asylum! Asylum!* has been followed mainly by comic explorations of the multicultural issue, as in Jim O'Hanlon's *The Buddhist of Castleknock* (2003), which 'explores the tensions which rise to the surface during a traditional Christmas get-together',[4] when a young man brings home his Kenyan girlfriend from London and shocks his conservative Irish family by announcing his conversion to Buddhism. The title is a clear reference to the best-selling novel by Hanif Kureishi, *The Buddha of Suburbia* (1990), but as the play is written by a young Irish playwright who has written for British soaps such as *Coronation Street*, it is no surprise that *The Buddhist of Castleknock* was aimed at the general ear of Dublin middle-class theatre: aimed and hit the target, one may say, since the comedy proved very successful. There have, however, also been quite serious if tentative new ventures on RTÉ radio and the Dublin stage by ethnic companies struggling to air problems faced by African immigrants in Ireland (of which, more will be said below). But these have tended to be occasional and to date have made little or no impact. The Abbey's multicultural version of Synge's *Playboy* may therefore be viewed as a belated effort to address this vacuum in the professional Irish theatre.

The Adigun-Doyle version was commissioned by Arambe Productions, founded in Dublin in 2003 by Bisi Adigun, a Nigerian immigrant, and officially launched by Roddy Doyle in February 2004. The main aim of the company is 'to afford members of Ireland's African communities the unique opportunity to express themselves through the art of theatre,' and the means of doing this is to be 'by producing classic and contemporary plays in the Irish canon'.5 Apart from the *Playboy* project the only other Irish play to be 'reinterpreted' by Arambe so far has been Jimmy Murphy's *The Kings of the Kilburn Road*, a play about Irish immigrants in London, newly staged with an all-African cast in Dublin in 2006, and again at Notre Dame University (Indiana) for a conference on 'Race and Immigration in Ireland' in October 2007. A more recent production by Arambe was a modernization by Bisi Adigun of Wole Soyinka's 1963 play, *The Trials of Brother Jero*, staged at the Samuel Beckett Theatre, Trinity College Dublin, in February 2009, directed by Adigun himself. As one reviewer put it, the production was 'daubed with playful local [Irish] and contemporary references', including making Soyinka's Brother Jeroboam a banker.6 But even that detail indicates how Adigun's imagination inclines towards the recycling of a classic.

Leaving aside a controversy which has arisen over the revival of this Abbey version of the *Playboy*, related to author's rights (excluding Synge's in this case),7 the main significance of the jointly authored adaptation by Adigun and Doyle is that the hero or anti-hero and his father are both Nigerian. Adigun insists that this idea was his alone. Some grounds for the claim may be derived from an article he published in 2004, 'An Irish Joke, a Nigerian Laughter'.8 Having arrived in Ireland from Nigeria in 1996, Adigun found himself unable to appreciate Irish humour, and consequently Irish comic drama. They were literally foreign to him, and little wonder: as O'Casey's Seumas Shields says, in *The Shadow of a Gunman* (1923), 'That's the Irish People all over — they treat a joke as a serious thing and a serious thing as a joke'.9 It takes getting used to. Adigun did nothing to help himself by viewing, in succession, Murphy's *Bailegangaire* (1985) and McDonagh's *The Beauty Queen of Leenane* (1996), as he could not understand why Irish audiences found them funny. Then he saw a student production of Synge's *Playboy* around the year 2002 and he found that it 'resonated with me on an entirely different emotional level as an outsider trying to come to terms with Irish culture'. Indeed Adigun saw Christy Mahon as 'the epitome of a majority of immigrants constantly searching for who they are in a foreign land' (81-2). As one among some 30,000

Nigerians living in the Irish Republic at this time, Adigun felt compelled to see 'a parallel between Christy's circumstances and the prevailing issue of asylum seekers and refugees in Ireland'. He concludes: 'That is why I see *The Playboy of the Western World* as more of a prophecy than a comedy' (82). He became all the more interested in this theme after he saw O'Hanlon's *The Buddhist of Castleknock* and could not understand the audience's laughter at the fate of a black woman whom a suburban son brings home from London to Castleknock for Christmas. Dermot Bolger's programme note, however, helped him to observe 'the thin veneer of unconscious racism within [Irish] people whose outwardly comfortable lives allowed them the luxury of never having to confront such prejudices before' (cited Adigun, 84). But it was only when he saw Marie Jones's *A Night in November* (1994) around the same time that Adigun understood that he need not, as he put it, 'feel like an outsider watching an Irish play' (86). He was now ready for the first time to insert a version of his own experience into an Irish text. By 2004 he had met Roddy Doyle, who had seen and admired the Nigerian play *The Gods Are Not to Blame*. At this point Adigun was already dreaming of a production of the *Playboy* with Christy to be played by the Nigerian actor Kunle Animasaun.[10]

For his part, Roddy Doyle had become fascinated by Synge's *Playboy* while teaching it for many years to teenagers before he became a full-time writer. He found that to his pupils, living in a deprived area of Dublin's north-side, reading the *Playboy* aloud in class came as a delight. It was for them a 'play about people on the edge of the rules, and the kids I taught knew that place ... They knew [also] the power and fun of language; language was one of the things they owned'.[11] It only remained for Doyle to develop an interest in foreign nationals, beyond the outrageous cry in *The Commitments* (1988) that 'the Irish are the niggers of Europe, lads' to a more serious consideration of the race issue.[12] He admired the start made by two Nigerian journalists living in Ireland who started a multicultural newspaper in April 2000 called *Metro Eireann*; Doyle met one of them and volunteered to write a story in instalments, subsequently published in his collection *The Deportees* (2007). Entitled 'Guess Who's Coming to the Dinner?', with a nod towards the famous 1967 film starring Sidney Poitier, it concerned bringing a sophisticated Nigerian into a suburban working-class Irish home, where the joke lies in the very disjunction between the ignorance of the father-figure and the sophistication of the Nigerian accountant. As this is the very aporia Adigun had experienced himself in watching McDonagh's *The Beauty Queen* and O'Hanlon's *The Buddhist of Castleknock*, it is to be expected that it must reappear in the collaboration with Doyle over Synge's *Playboy*. Yet there is a knowing line in Doyle's story where an echo of Synge anticipates the style of the adaptation. The narrator says at one point, as the Nigerian eats a piece of cake eased onto his plate by his girlfriend and her mother in defiance of her ignorant father, 'there in front of his nose, *two fine women fought to the death*' on his – the Nigerian's – behalf.[13] Meantime, Doyle re-configured *Guess Who's Coming to the Dinner?* as a successful play for the Dublin Theatre Festival, staged by Calypso.[14]

The text of the *Playboy* collaboration, the main focus point for this essay, is both modernized in setting and inflected with a contemporary racial issue. The setting is a public bar in Dublin's drug-land, light years away from Synge's shebeen in rural Mayo. Michael James Flaherty is into drugs and crime, while Philly O'Cullen and Jimmy Farrell his two minders, still comic, though in a key different from Synge, hint a certain menace behind the drunken joviality. Pegeen is a tough and rather foul-mouthed manager of the bar and the Widow Quin did not, in this version, kill her man, who was instead shot down by Michael James's gang in a drugs dispute. For his part, Christopher — as he is called throughout — wins his heroic spurs not in any pastoral sporting contests but as security man by fighting off the leader of a rival gang rejoicing under the name of The Rattler. The young girls capture Christopher's bravery on their mobile phones for admiration on-stage, in lieu of his reported prowess at sport in Synge's original. Appropriately, in the final scenes of the adaptation Michael James has plans for Philly and Jimmy to drive both Christopher and his father up the Dublin mountains to dump their bodies, after they have been shot, of course. The modernization is accompanied by up-to-date Dublin speech, including the regulation obscenities used by all except the two strangers. There may also be a joyous sense of retrieval here of Synge's play from the clutches of Druid, for that company had recently virtually stamped all of Synge's plays as 'made in Galway'.[15] The *Playboy*, of course, was written for the Abbey Theatre.

The racial issue reflects the reverse discrimination one would expect from Adigun as Nigerian exponent of the rights of black people in a white society. This concern results in a certain amount of overload. Christopher Malomo is introduced as a bourgeois figure, well educated, with an MBA and a cultivated, if slightly stilted way of speaking. Yet the loneliness of Synge's character is well replicated, for example in the lines in Act II when he is about to go away thinking his story is in the newspapers:

PEGEEN. Are the jails nice in Nigeria, Christopher?
CHRISTOPHER. You've made your point. (*Finding his shoes; putting them on*) If I am not safe here, then it would be best if I continue my wandering. Like Cain. 'Cursed be thou by the earth

which has opened its mouth and drunk the blood of thy brother'.
PEGEEN (*beginning to play with him*). Jesus, did you kill your
brother as well?
CHRISTOPHER (*looking up as he ties his shoes*). You can
laugh? This is amusement for you? (*Showing her a shoe;
holding it up*) Look. I have walked hundreds of kilometres. See?
I thought it was over, but now I must start again. (*Puts his foot
in the shoe; it's obviously uncomfortable*)
PEGEEN. Where are you going?
CHRISTOPHER (*packing as he talks*). I pray it never happens
to you. Looking over your shoulder all the time. Only desperate
strangers as your companions — a lonely and terrible
experience. Crossing the desert, for days, burnt, scorched,
dehydrated and famished. Guarding your neck and your wallet.
Agony is the word. You cannot believe how I felt when I finally
got on the plane. I slept throughout. And to this city, where
everybody stares at me but, truly, I do not exist. I have become
simply a feeling. Sheer and utter loneliness.[16]

When Christopher's father (always called Malomo in the play)
arrives, he too is characterized as notably dignified. Far from Synge's
representation of a grotesque wreck, an alcoholic madman, this is a
polished, ennobled figure who when pressed to have a drink calls for
a glass of Merlot. According to the stage direction, '*He wears a
traditional attire; agbada (flowing gown), complete with cap. There
is a pair of reading glasses around his neck. He carries a small
business case, and holds a diary. He also has a walking stick. He
speaks with an educated Nigerian accent*' (42). Widow Quin is vastly
amused at his appearance, and finds it easy to get him to set off on a
false trail to find the Belfast train (rather than across the sands to
Belmullet!), on which he will probably travel first-class. Malomo and
his son stand out in the play in contrast to the skittish and deceitful
Irish. Assuming that Doyle wrote the dialogue for the Irish, for it is in
his style, it is interesting that his introduction of racial matters is
always provocative. For example, in the interrogation when
Christopher first enters the pub we hear this line of questioning,
strikingly different from Synge's text:

MICHAEL. So, you're some sort of a refugee or asylum seeker,
yeah?
SEAN. Mr Flaherty?
MICHAEL. Yeah?
SEAN. He can't be a refugee. He just arrived, like.
MICHAEL. What?
SEAN. He has to go through the asylum process first, like. And
if he is granted, then he can —
MICHAEL. Good man, Sean. (*To* **CHRISTOPHER**) So.

You're an asylum seeker. Am I technically correct there, Sean?
SEAN. Yeah.
MICHAEL. Great. That's established, so. You're an asylum seeker.
CHRISTOPHER. You may say so, sir.
MICHAEL. I may say so, sir? Are you messing with me, son?
CHRISTOPHER. No, sir.
JIMMY. I think he is, Michael.
PEGEEN. Leave him alone.
MICHAEL. Look it, so. Stop acting the bollix. Just tell us.
CHRISTOPHER. I am here to seek refuge, in Ireland ... My life isn't safe at home. (11)

The interrogation continues, as Michael and the others in the pub suggest various reasons why it might not be safe in Nigeria at present: tribal warfare, a young woman, religious strife, persecution ... none of their suggestions meets with Christopher's agreement. Then Michael asks ignorantly if it might not be 'the genital mutilation'. Pegeen points out that Christopher is male. This allows the punch-line, 'Oh, is that right? Did no one ever get a kick in the balls in Nigeria?' (11). Crude though the joke is (to cover Michael's own absurdity) it does at least introduce a topical and controversial issue related to asylum seekers in Ireland. [17]

Although the race question is not explored in any detail in the play, nor is a debate initiated by the issue; this is because Synge's form and conventions are conservatively retained. The spirit in which they are retained is that of the Passion Machine production style, as inherited by Roddy Doyle from his early days as a writer. Passion Machine was founded in 1984 by Paul Mercier and others with a specific agenda in mind, to create new work related primarily to the experience of young, mainly working-class lives. It was community theatre in the sense that it was located specifically on Dublin's north-side, with the SFX Centre in Sherrard Street as venue, but it did not interest itself in overtly political issues. Indeed John Sutton, then producer for Passion Machine, former Community Enterprise Worker, and latterly Roddy Doyle's agent, stated: 'we actually abhor didactic or agit-prop work. We believe that you must entertain first and make your point second'.[18] This says little about the Passion Machine style which was characterized by on the one hand high-energy movement, virtually non-stop action, and on the other by demotic Dublin speech larded with the usual post-Behan obscenities. Mercier's own plays of the 1980s, *Drowning* (1984), *Wasters* (1985), *Studs* (1986, then filmed in 2006) set the pattern. Doyle saw these, admired the work enormously and wrote two plays for Passion Machine as a result, *Brownbread* (1987) and *War* (1989), one concerned with the kidnapping of a bishop by young fellows with no clear motive in mind, and the other a play about pub quizzes.[19] Both were major successes, transferring to the downtown Olympia Theatre to prove it. The actor Brendan Gleeson, at this time a member of the company, also wrote and directed a play called *Breaking Up* (1988), a rite-of-passage play about teenagers celebrating the end of their school years. The opening stage direction perhaps says it all: 'Lads all around bursting themselves laughing drunkenly'.[20]

Yet it has to be said that even if Doyle carried with him lessons in holding a young audience learned from his days with Passion Machine — as he certainly did — the version of the *Playboy* at the Abbey both falls short of that style and transcends it. It falls short in that the Abbey space is not the SFX Centre, a bit of a barn of a place and a venue for rock bands, so that Christopher's offstage fight with the Rattler, the gangland figure, is made to stand in for the antics a Passion Machine production would probably have choreographed to make Christy's physical derring-do the highlight of the play. Passion Machine was largely a counterpart to the Dublin Youth Theatre; many of the actors came from that source, whereas the Abbey, of course, has quite a different remit. [21] In this instance, Jimmy Fay, who was first director of the Dublin Fringe Festival in 1995-96, was actually acting Literary Director of the Abbey when this Adigun-Doyle version of the *Playboy* was accepted and Fay directed it. Indebted to the Passion Machine though it was for its outrageousness, Fay's production was never naïve.

On the other hand, the addition of the race issue would never have been part of the Passion Machine agenda. It was always the local issues and never the universal with Passion Machine.[22] It may be tentative rather than radical, but the race issue is certainly and obviously rendered part of the discourse in the Adigun-Doyle modernization of the *Playboy*. Significantly, the roles of Christopher and his father were played by black actors, Giels Terera and Chuk Iwuji from London playing Christopher in 2007 and 2008, Olu Jacobs and George Seremba, from Nigeria and Uganda respectively, playing Malomo (i.e., Old Mahon). The younger actors playing Christopher did not in their biographies in the Abbey programme indicate a country of origin, but both of the older actors determinedly did and the difference is of interest. It may be that for the younger black actors, more secure of their place in the English theatre, the issues of national identity and history are less important. In contrast, Olu Jacobs described himself in the Abbey programme as 'one of Nigeria's foremost actors', having worked with the National Theatre of Nigeria. He had also, however, worked in Dublin in the 1970s, appearing in Conor Cruise O'Brien's *Murderous Angels* (a play about the Congo), in the Dublin Theatre Festival in 1971; in the posthumous premiere of Brendan Behan's *Richard's Cork Leg*, compiled by Alan

Simpson out of Behan's papers, at the Peacock in 1972; and in Desmond Forristal's *Black Man's Country*, set in the Nigerian missions 1967-70, which premiered at the Gate Theatre in 1974.[23] Behan's play apart, these were early multicultural Irish plays, and Jacobs provides a valuable link between them and the current use of Nigerians in the *Playboy*.

George Seremba, who played Malomo on the 2008 revival, is a Ugandan-Canadian actor, who stated in his programme bio that he was forced to flee from Obote's military regime in 1980, moved to Kenya to write and thence to Toronto, where he had a successful career in the theatre before he arrived in Dublin. Here he has made a name as playwright and actor, especially in Athol Fugard's *Master Harold and the Boys* (2004), another fine Calypso production. In 2008, Seremba appeared as narrator in Jimmy Fay's magnificent production of *The Resistible Rise of Arturo Ui* at the Abbey.

With talent like that of Seremba and Jacobs, one can conclude that director and authors of the *Playboy* adaptation were serious about the casting of black actors for the show. Indeed, the seriousness threatened at times to overbalance the farcical qualities of this glib and street-wise Dublin relocation, what one might call the Passion Machine element of the production.

That said, the ending of the Adigun-Doyle *Playboy* nevertheless makes its critique neatly enough. When the resurrected Malomo re-enters towards the close of Act III to ask why his son is tied up, Christopher replies: 'They are going to kill me, because I killed you'. Malomo asks, 'Jungle justice?' and Christopher replies, 'On the ball, Dad'. Then, as he makes his exit it is the 'villainy of Ireland' (66) and not just Synge's 'villainy of Mayo'[24] that Malomo finally denounces. To which one can only add, '*touché*'. Ireland has taught the Nigerian Christopher an important lesson in achieving modernity: 'You have transformed me into a *hard* man. From now and forever more, I am master of my own destiny' (66-7, surprising emphasis in original). Pegeen's sobs as the lights go down, after she has told her father to 'fuck off' when he promises to set up the match with Sean again, might be contemporary Ireland feminized and debased coming to consciousness of its racism, and recognizing the loss incurred in adhering to parochial values.[25]

If this is so, it is clear that the *Playboy*, always a subversive play arising from Synge's detestation of Irish moral complacency, has now been successfully restyled to show up the contemporary faultlines between Irish self-deception over ethnicity and Nigerian migrants' deeper understanding of the ethical and sociological issues involved in upholding identity in a foreign land. In a contribution to the issue of *Studies* on immigration referred to above, Theophilus Ejorh points out that 'a new African Diaspora has emerged in Ireland', and argues that 'it is mostly individuals from affluent and middle class backgrounds who can afford the high costs of international migrations compared to those in the lowest rungs of society'.[26] This means that Christopher Malomo represents the new Nigerian immigrant, who is less a threat than many Irish nationals may think. The irony lies in a former missionary culture's being represented as so incapable of rising to embrace the products of its historical missionary success that it drives them away in disillusionment. The comic tone of the adaptation of the *Playboy* probably threatens to overwhelm this irony; the vehicle may be too light to carry the weight of its collaborators' political sensibility. It may now be time to take such issues away from adaptations of classics and into new forms of drama to initiate afresh the debate on multiculturalism, still but an embryo within the Irish theatre.

---

[1] Fergus O'Donoghue, 'Editorial', *Studies*, 96 (Spring 2007): 6.

[2] *New Plays From the Abbey Theatre 1993-1995*, eds. Christopher Fitz-Simon and Sanford Sternlicht (Syracuse: Syracuse UP, 1996): xviii. O'Kelly's *Asylum! Asylum!* is published in this volume. Unhappily, Calypso went into liquidation in 2009. See Suzanne Lynch, 'Final curtain falls for theatre group as liquidator appointed', *The Irish Times* 13 August 2009: 3.

[3] Fintan O'Toole, *Critical Moments: Fintan O'Toole on Modern Irish Theatre*, eds. Julia Furay and Redmond O'Hanlon (Dublin: Carysfort Press, 2003): 127.

[4] Jim O'Hanlon, *The Buddhist of Castleknock* (Dublin: New Island, 2007): summary on back cover. This play premiered in Dublin in 2003 as a Fishamble production.

[5] 'Arambe Productions: Shedding Light on Africans,' advertisement page in programme for the *Playboy of the Western World*, in a new version by Bisi Adigun and Roddy Doyle (revival), Abbey Theatre, 16 December 2008.

[6] Peter Crawley, '*The Trials of Brother Jero*: Samuel Beckett Theatre, Dublin', *The Irish Times*, 27 February 2009: 18.

[7] See Mary Carolan, 'Copyright breach claim over modern production of "Playboy" at Abbey'. *The Irish Times*, 18 May 2010; and Fintan O'Toole, 'Theatre Has Nothing to Declare but an Innate Uncertainty' in *The Irish Times*, 22 May 2010.

[8] In *The Power of Laughter: Comedy and Contemporary Irish Theatre*, ed. Eric Weitz (Dublin: Carysfort Press, 2004): 76-86. Subsequent quotations will be indicated by page numbers given in parenthesis in the text.

[9] Sean O'Casey, *Three Dublin Plays* (London: Faber and Faber, 1998): 9.

[10] Bisi Adigun, 'In Living Colour', *Irish Theatre Magazine*, 19 (summer 2004): 31.

[11] Roddy Doyle, 'Wild and Perfect: Teaching *The Playboy of the Western World*,' in *Synge: A Celebration*, ed. Colm Tóibín (Dublin: Carysfort Press, 2005) (139-44): 142-3.

[12] Roddy Doyle, *The Barrytown Trilogy* (London: Minerva, 1993): 13.

[13] Roddy Doyle, *The Deportees* (London: Vintage, 2008): 24, emphasis added to identify Synge's line at the end of act 1, *The Playboy of the Western World*. Here see also Maureen T. Reddy, 'Reading and Writing Race in Ireland: Roddy Doyle and *Metro Eireann*', *Irish University Review*, 35 (autumn/winter 2005): 374-88.

[14] Although Doyle's *Guess Who's Coming for the Dinner?* remains unpublished, an excerpt can be found in *Irish Theatre Magazine*, 2.9 (summer 2001): 64-66.

[15] See my 'Unlocking Synge Today', in *A Companion to Modern British and Irish Drama 1880-2005*, ed. Mary Luckhurst (Oxford: Blackwell, 2006): 110-24.

[16] Bisi Adigun and Roddy Doyle, 'The Playboy of the Western World' typescript: 38. I am grateful to Roddy Doyle for access to the typescript, which is dated 2006 and the basis for both the 2007 and 2008 productions. Acknowledgement is hereby made to both authors for permission to quote from the script. Subsequent quotations from the typescript are referenced in the text by numbers in parenthesis.

[17] In December 2008, Roddy Doyle wrote to the Minister for Justice, Dermot Ahern, supporting Pamela Izevbekhai in her bid to resist deportation to Nigeria, where her two daughters, she feared, would risk being subjected to genital mutilation. Bisi Adigun also came out in support of Ms Izevbekhai in an article published in *The Irish Times* on 2 April 2009.

[18] John Sutton, 'City Centre Buzz,' *Theatre Ireland*, 12 (1987): 67.

[19] 'I hadn't been to many plays. I'd been to none more than once. I went to *Wasters* four times, *Studs* five, and the next one, *Spacers*, four times. I'd never seen anything like them. They were brilliant'. Roddy Doyle, Introduction, *Brownbread and War* (London: Minerva, 1993): 2.

[20] Brendan Gleeson, *Breaking Up* (Dublin: Passion Machine, 1989): 1.

[21] John Sutton, 'City Centre Buzz': 65.

[22] See Sean Moffatt, 'Review Section', *Theatre Ireland*, 17 (Dec. 1988-Mar. 1989): 47; and Sean Moffatt, 'The Passion Machine', *Theatre Ireland*, 18 (April-June 1989): 8-12.

[23] Desmond Forristal, *Black Man's Country* (Newark, DE: Proscenium Press, 1975). John Brannigan discusses this play in his *Race in Modern Irish Literature and Culture* (Edinburgh: Edinburgh UP, 2009), but is mistaken in believing it is unpublished.

[24] J.M. Synge, *The Playboy of the Western World and Other Plays*, ed. Ann Saddlemyer (Oxford: Oxford UP, 1995); 146.

[25] In contrast, Declan Kiberd notes that in the 1990s, in spite of the significant presence on Irish streets of 'migrants, asylum seekers and

refugees, the literature produced in Tiger Ireland ... seemed largely incurious about the Other'. 'After Ireland?', *The Irish Times*, 29 August 2009, 'Weekend Review': 12.

[26] Theophilus Ejorh, 'Immigration and Citizenship: African Immigrants in Ireland', *Studies*, 96: 49.

9 | Audience expectation and the expected audience – writing for the international stage

Ursula Rani Sarma

I began writing plays in the late 1990s while a student at University College Cork, where I was studying English and History. The drama society of UCC, Dramat, was where I first enjoyed the experience of the theatre. Growing up in West Clare, my opportunities to see plays were few, and mostly consisted of whatever Theatre-in-Education company was touring whichever Shakespearean play was on the school syllabus at the time. So my first memories of theatre are of the three witches wearing tie-dyed leggings writhing about in some freezing cold school hall. It is interesting that, as I look back on those years now, I would not have considered that any of the theatrical productions taking place around the country were happening with me in mind. They merely existed; the idea that they would have taken me into account at the time of their conception was entirely beyond me. I did not see myself as the audience, and this is important, as it was that realization that informed the early plays I wrote while at UCC and in the years that followed.

After directing *Innocence* by Frank McGuinness in my first year at university, I spent several hours in the Boole Library looking for another project. I leafed through all the classics and some of the contemporary plays, and it occurred to me that so many of those plays simply did not speak to me. I had chosen *Innocence* over the better-known plays in the canon as I found a relevance and timeliness in McGuinness's questioning of the role of the church. At that time, the sexual abuse scandals within the church were beginning to break, and the manner in which they shook people's faith had a huge effect on me. Having being reared Roman Catholic but with a huge awareness of alternative religions such as my father's Hinduism, I had been used to questioning the church's teachings from a young age. The majority of my peers, however, were not. I remember a great sense of betrayal amongst many of the Irish people that I knew. I hadn't realized before discovering *Innocence* that theatre could challenge how we think about the world, and this continues to be the type of theatre that excites me and which I endeavour to create.

At that time, I had never seen a play which attempted to capture the experience of a young person growing up in rural Ireland – not the Ireland of Synge or O'Casey or Friel, but my Ireland and my generation who were caught somewhere between studying *Peig* and watching MTV. This was my history, my story, and I had yet to see it on stage. My first play, written while in my third year in university, was called *Like Sugar on Skin,* and it was my attempt to create the type of play which I would have liked to see, with young people from the countryside as central characters, dealing with their past and present and worrying about what kind of Ireland the future would bring. It was the success of that play at that year's Irish Student Drama Awards in Galway which made the prospect of becoming a playwright a possibility for me.

This desire to create the kind of work which I would have loved to have seen as a young person living in rural Ireland continued to sculpt the plays which followed once I left university. It seems ironic looking back that my first professional production *...touched...* premiered abroad at the 1999 Edinburgh Fringe Festival two months after I sat my final exams at UCC. Realistically, I had no concept of what an international theatre festival like the Edinburgh Fringe involved; all I knew at the time was student drama. I had no expectations about who would be sitting in the audience or about their nationality, and so once again I wrote and directed a play that I thought I would enjoy watching myself. The success of *...touched...* meant that I was suddenly given the label of a 'young up-and-coming Irish Female Playwright'. I had an international presence and within a year I had commissions from the Royal National Theatre (RNT) and the BBC. In a sense I began as I meant to continue, writing plays for an unknown audience abroad. I spent the following two years in Ireland, writing and directing *Blue* for the Cork Opera House in 2000 and *Gift* for the Belltable Theatre Limerick in 2001. Then I was offered a residency with the RNT in London and I left Ireland for the foreseeable future. Looking back, I consider that first wave of plays to be reflective of my own innocence at the time. I had little exposure to other contemporary plays, and was writing into a vacuum of sorts.

What followed was a number of commissions from UK-based theatre companies. I was commissioned by the BBC and the RNT some years before I was approached by RTÉ and the Abbey Theatre. While Writer-in-Residence for the RNT, I also received commissions from companies such as the Traverse Theatre in Edinburgh and Paines Plough in London. I was twenty-three with five plays to write including a new one for the Abbey. In 2002 and 2003, I experienced a phenomenon which I thought was writer's block but which, I realize in retrospect, was panic – and that directly related to my growing awareness of an expectant audience. I was suddenly very aware of the pressure of a particular theatre company having a pre-existing audience of people who were used to seeing a certain type of play. There was an expectation of what the work would be like before I had even chosen the title of the play. I was somewhat intimidated by the audiences who attended the plays I was seeing at the Royal Court and the Bush in London amongst others, and I was preoccupied with a question: what did I possibly have to say to them? It also struck me as disconcerting at some level that, at the time, many of my experiences at these theatres involved a middle- to upper-class, predominantly white audience watching gritty plays about inner-city Black or Asian kids with drug and social problems. I simply could not imagine where my work would fit in.

While still coming to terms with this block of sorts, I remember returning home to west Clare and standing on Lahinch golf course, with my mother explaining why I kept swinging the club without managing to actually hit the ball. Apparently if you lift your head too soon to see where the ball is going to go, you will end up missing it entirely. I flew back to London with this analogy in my head: if I kept worrying about who was going to receive the work, I would never get the work done at all. In order for me to create work for an audience I had to begin by ignoring them, or more accurately by treating myself as the first audience member. And so I reverted to my initial tactic: write for yourself and send it out there. The 'block' eventually disappeared. It was possibly the most important lesson I learned in my career in terms of dealing with my audience.

I remained in London to take up the Position of Writer-in-Residence with Paines Plough. The longer I stayed away from Ireland, the more I became aware of my own identity, not only as an Irish playwright but as a mixed-race female Irish playwright. I recall having to fill out an equal opportunities form for the company and realizing that I didn't tick the white or Irish box but instead the mixed-race one. I couldn't recall ever having being faced with this option in Ireland. The idea of boxes and the need for people to assign one to me fascinated me. I began to write a play for Paines Plough entitled *Without You* which was not set in Ireland, a trend which continued with my short play *When the War Came*, which was written for and produced by The New Theatre Company in London in 2005, and with *The Spidermen* written for the RNT's *Connections* series in 2006. I wondered at the time if they would describe these pieces as Irish plays despite the fact that neither the setting nor my own name would mark them out as such. I began to think about what made me an Irish playwright to an international audience. Was it my passport, my accent, the tone of the language itself, or none of those things?

In the years that followed, I was fortunate to have a string of commissions from companies outside of Ireland. In some ways I suppose this has kept me from forging the kind of relationships with theatre companies in Ireland that would have ensured that more of my work would be seen at home. As it stands, I have had more productions of my new plays abroad than at home, with some recent productions in New York, San Francisco, Edinburgh and Greece. I believe there are a few reasons for this. Firstly, there are simply more companies in the UK that are in a position to commission new work and with whom I now have a good working relationship. Secondly I myself have spent much of the period since 2000 outside of the country. And thirdly, there has been a lack of interest in producing the work of female Irish playwrights within the more heavily-funded companies in Ireland. There is a noticeable change in this trend over the past couple of years and I am optimistic that the future will hold many more opportunities for female playwrights to be produced at home. However, the reality remains: if I had not been so strongly supported outside Ireland in my formative years, as a playwright it is unlikely that I would have produced the body of work which I have written to date.

There are so many aspects of audience expectation that I could discuss but I thought it might be of interest to mention briefly my experiences of translation and how this has opened up an unintended audience to my work (in the sense that they were not anticipated at the time of writing). My work was first translated in 2002 when *Blue* and *...touched...* appeared in German. It shocked me at the time that these plays – which for me were so specific to Ireland and the world of my childhood – would find a home in Germany. *How would they get the cultural references?* I worried. What, in effect, would become lost in the translation? The translator, Anna Opel, was appointed by my German agents Felix Bloch, and I was somewhat relieved when I began to receive her emails, which asked me about specific details that she did not understand and which, when translated literally, did not achieve the desired effect in German. This series of emails between us was educational for me as I began to realize that, often with my work, it was not so much the words themselves which were important: instead, it was a certain beat or tone shift within a scene that really mattered. For example, I had to let Anna find a suitable joke to replace one in a scene that gave much-needed relief after a moment of intensity. This meant relinquishing a certain amount of control over the work itself, which took some getting used to. This experience is not the typical one, however – as I was to discover. There have been many translations of my plays where the translator has never been in touch. This concerned me at first, despite my being assured that my agency would only approve the highest-quality translators. Still, I continue to wonder about those tricky tonal switches, which are so important in the work, and how the moments of particularly Irish humour or pathos translate to Romanian, Polish, or Dutch.

The most positive experience of translation which I have experienced came in 2003 when the RNT commissioned me to translate Italian Playwright Luca de Bei's play *The Dogs in Front of the Hare*. At the time, the National Theatre Studio had a specific model in place for translating contemporary new work. They would try to match a foreign playwright with an English-speaking one who they felt shared a similar aesthetic sense. A literal translation was commissioned first: that is, an individual translates the text word for word. After this, Luca and I spent a week together at the studio with the person who had carried out the literal translation and we worked through the play line by line. I thoroughly enjoyed the experience and wished that I could have had an opportunity to have one of my own plays translated in a similar process. Again, it became apparent to us both that the literal translation at times did not serve the original. I empathized with Luca's initial concerns that the play he had written in Italian would not be the same play in English. After a period of six months, the translation was complete and we both found the process entirely fulfilling.

It seems to me now that the longer and more widely a play lives and travels, the less control you have over it as an author. Translation is an area which continues to fascinate me as more and more of my work is staged internationally in languages I will never understand. There have been more productions of *Blue* and *..touched...* in Germany than in any other country. I certainly did not think when writing the play in 2000 that the expected audience would be in Hamburg. In 2005, I was commissioned by a theatre company in Heidelberg to write a short play, which would be then translated into German. This in itself posed another interesting concept: the first time the play would be heard, it would be in German. I was present in Heidelberg for the premiere of the play, which is called *Patriotism* and which is set in an undefined location. I wondered as I sat there with a predominantly German audience if anything at all marked the play out as an Irish one, besides the programme note.

As these experiences watching my work abroad continued, I began to accept that the more specific the human experience documented in a play, the more universal its appeal. The three teenagers dealing with their lost innocence in rural Ireland in *Blue* were relevant to audiences in Athens, New Jersey, or New Zealand. *Orpheus Road*, written for Paines Plough in 2002 about the young love between a Catholic boy and an atheist girl in Belfast during the Troubles, was quickly translated, produced, and published in Romania. I have never even been to Romania and it often strikes me as strange that my work has visited places I have yet to see.

I continue to write predominantly for an international audience and am currently under commission from several theatre companies that are based outside Ireland. I still believe that to a huge extent it is necessary for my own best practice that I deliberately *not* think of the audience or of what they expect from my work. The moment I begin to think about what the audience might want or not want is a dangerous one, as with it comes the natural second-guessing of the artistic impulse. This impulse is the seed from which the play grows and it needs a certain amount of time and space free from expectation and judgement.

I have a natural affinity with the kind of art which considers less what the audience wish to see and perhaps more what the artist believes they need to see. I don't say this from any position of self-importance, or from a belief that the artist is a prophet; I am merely speaking of personal preference. I respond to work which attempts to hold a mirror up to society and reflect it back onto itself, exposing both the favourable and unfavourable elements. In an entertainment industry that measures success in terms of box office sales, I believe it is important to continue to create this type of theatre. As more and more of the general public seem drawn to escapism and entertainment at the level of reality TV shows, it is important to me to produce plays which I find personally stimulating, and which encourage audiences to think about the world they are in and the society they make up.

The themes which concern me at present are in some way expressed by these words from the comedian Bill Hicks:

> Go back to bed, America, your government has figured out how it all transpired.
> Go back to bed America, your government is in control. Here, here's American Gladiators.
> Watch this, shut up, go back to bed America, here is *American Gladiators*; here is 56 channels of it! Watch these pituitary retards bang their fucking skulls together and congratulate you

on living in the land of freedom. Here you go America – you are free to do what we tell you! You are free to do what we tell you![1]

I am interested in the concept that people eventually end up trading their voice and sense of empowerment for economic prosperity and a peaceful socio-political environment. And I am also interested in looking at those individuals who are not willing to make this exchange, either consciously or unconsciously, and in asking what happens to those who do not or who cannot conform. I try not to think if these themes are of interest to whatever audience will eventually watch these plays. All I know is that they are fuelling my artistic impulse at present.

In conclusion, I would say that the notion of audience expectation and the expected audience is one which I return to often, because it challenges me to redefine which box I fit into. The more expectation there is placed upon me to write a particular type of play, the more determined I feel to write the work that I want to see myself. I do not feel limited by the labels of Irish, mixed-race, or female; nor do I believe that my being able to be described as these things should indicate the tone or subject matter of the work I have created. I began writing for theatre because I wanted to create engaging stories, which attempt in some way to show a glimpse of the human experience, an experience, which I believe, transcends gender or ethnicity or language. All I expect from my audience is that they might take the time to come and see my work, and all I hope that they expect from me is a play written out of genuine need and desire to document some small element of the human experience.

---

[1] Bill Hicks, *Love all the People: Letters, Lyrics and Routines* (London: Constable and Robinson, 2004): 129.

10 | 'The Words Look After Themselves': The Practice of Enda Walsh

Jesse Weaver

Enda Walsh erupted onto the Irish theatrical scene in mid-1990s with *Disco Pigs*, a dynamic two-hander that brought Cillian Murphy to the attention of a worldwide audience. The play's success also brought Walsh a great deal of recognition, but not nearly as much as his contemporaries Conor McPherson, Marina Carr, and Martin McDonagh. Walsh's profile has grown considerably in Ireland and abroad over the subsequent years, however, thanks in part to the commitment to his work of Galway's Druid Theatre, which produced *The Walworth Farce* (2006), *New Electric Ballroom* (2008), and *Penelope* (2010). Most striking is the extent to which Walsh's work has been embraced by other European cultures; his drama is a constant presence on the German stage and has been performed in numerous linguistic and cultural contexts. Bizarre characters and settings such as a deadly talent show at the bottom of an empty swimming pool in *Penelope*, or a fallen furniture magnate arguing with his polio-stricken daughter in a filthy bed in *bedbound* (2000), are a hallmark of Walsh's dramaturgy. Yet, despite the seemingly postmodern preoccupations of Walsh's plays, his practical focus remains on opening a dialogue between the play and the audience. His own background as an actor and director has informed his attitudes towards the role of the audience, as well as his all-inclusive approach to drafting playscripts in terms of scenography, while also developing an anti-literary approach to language.

Drawing heavily on a conversation with Walsh from 2009, this essay will touch on Walsh's influences as a young writer, his beginnings with Cork's Corcadorca Theatre Company, his treatment of space, his own understanding of himself as an Irish playwright, and the interrelationship of the local and the global in staging new work in the twenty-first century.

Influences

Walsh grew up in the northside Dublin suburb of Raheny in the 1970s and 1980s. During that time, there was a resurgence and expansion of theatrical energies in both Dublin and Ireland as a whole. The dominant role of the Abbey as the producer of new voices for the Irish theatre was challenged both inside and outside Dublin by companies such as Rough Magic, which sought to articulate the aspirations of a new generation of theatre-makers. Enda Walsh cites specifically the Rough Magic production of Donal O'Kelly's *Bat the Father Rabbit the Son* (1988) as

> a really significant piece of work in Irish theatre – one that had a huge impact on me stylistically. I thought it was very unusual; O'Kelly had a sort of a James Joyce thing going on which at times I couldn't access but really enjoyed – and that had a big influence on me.[1]

Also significant about O'Kelly's play was its cast size: one. Relying on syntax to express extremes of emotion and characterization, O'Kelly's play was particularly well suited to the needs of Rough Magic, at that time a young company with limited staffing and resources. This would become an important model for Walsh and other emerging theatre-makers during the 1990s.

That said, limits on cast-size and narrative scope were not always a consideration for Walsh as a young writer. He claims to have once written a 180 page play with over fifty characters based on *Gone With the Wind*, for instance.[2] Looking back on his genesis as a writer, Walsh states that:

> in the late 1980s, I was reading lots of poetry, and I really liked Shakespeare. I had a conversation with someone recently about Shakespeare and the scale of those stories – the breadth of his narrative. There are times where you think, wouldn't it be great to do a play with fifteen, twenty people in it? But I've been doing this for thirteen years now and we're all being confined by casts of two to four – five maybe, if you're lucky. It makes things domestic, it makes things small, insular – and I think that has a big impact on the work, which becomes characters in rooms talking to one another. What if they got out of the room? What if they went multigeographical? And yes, you can do that with five characters, but would that dilute the work then? I presume

Mark O'Rowe and Conor McPherson must have a similar semantics. Our plays are small; they're contained, and they're all psychological, particularly Conor's. The characters are lonesome and deep, but the plays are small, tiny little plays.

A limited cast and a single set are hallmarks of Walsh's work. This is evidenced in examples like *misterman* (1999, rev. 2011), *bedbound*, and *The Small Things* (2005), all of which feature one or two characters who find themselves compelled to tell and retell the story of a past event that has defined the cruel circumstances of their present. In *bedbound*, a father and his crippled daughter both inhabit separate ends of the same bed, compulsively reciting the story of how the daughter contracted the polio that has imprisoned her there. This compulsion to tell stories is more a curse than an attempt at some kind of lyrical expression of emotion. Language gushes forth almost against the will of the speaker, much as it does for Mouth in Samuel Beckett's *Not I* (1972), possessing the speaker and acting on him or her as if it were a force completely beyond control. For example, the daughter from *bedbound* fights to ward off a deathly silence after her father finishes speaking:

> **DAUGHTER.** He stops/it stops/his panic putting an end to him and a start to me/I see that silence/oh Christ/fill it fast!/feel it race towards me all full of the loneliness/think fast of of of of of /my body![3]

As a result, much of the conflict in Walsh's plays comes from the attempts by characters to connect with each other beyond the compulsion to tell each other's stories, rather than from a direct, dialogic conflict between characters.

As Walsh mentions, a number of his contemporaries have also structured their plays around the reporting of dramatic events rather than their direct depiction. Conor McPherson's early plays feature characters narrating dramatic events in monologue rather than enacting them. For instance, Mark O'Rowe's *Howie the Rookie* (1999) has two characters telling the story of a single day from two different points of view. These dramaturgical strategies ultimately make the act of narration as central to the drama as the events they report. Even when the cast size and setting have been determined by theatrical rather than economic motives, the mobility of plays with a single setting (or no setting whatsoever) and a small cast makes it easier for independent producers to stage and tour new work. Walsh's *Disco Pigs*, which features a male and female performer and no set, played successfully in Cork before touring to Dublin, Edinburgh, and later around the world. The play's mobility as much as its energetic performances and exquisite treatment of Cork's cityscape helped make it a success for both Walsh and Corcadorca.

Cork

Cork city has served as a setting for a number of Walsh's plays, and Walsh spent most of his formative time there in the 1990s as a member of Corcadorca.

> I was going nowhere in Dublin and I got an acting job with [Cork-based] Graffiti Theatre Company, in a theatre and education show. I loved Cork as a city, and I couldn't believe people talked the way they talked. The people just didn't sound like me and I really loved that. I loved the fact that it was a second city and not Dublin. There were many things going for it: the language of the place, the shape of it, its close proximity to a beautiful landscape. Cork was a very interesting place at the time. There was an incredible amount of energy from the place. And while I was there I was very lucky to meet Pat Kiernan of Corcadorca Theatre Company.

> I think it was Corcadorca's second show that I saw. It was called *We Have Your Little Man*. It was an improvised show, and I was really impressed by it. I also liked Pat as a person. Triskel Arts Centre gave us a little space to work with and we used to do shows there every week, devised pieces and things like that. I was sort of the 'designated writer' – and happily so. I had a play called *The Ginger Ale Boy* in my back pocket which I originally wrote in Dublin, but I knew I was going to re-write it for Cork.

Together with Pat Kiernan and sound designer Cormac O'Connor, Walsh helped to form the nucleus of Corcadorca. The company set out not only to disrupt traditional dramatic form, but also to redefine the audience's relationship to that work. This was done primarily by staging work in site-specific spaces that reflected or reinforced the play's intended setting or thematic concerns. Walsh's writing also developed further with a commission from Graffiti: a play for young children called *Fishy Tales*. That drama features a number of the thematic and dramaturgical tropes that inform Walsh's work to this day. It is a single-character play in which the protagonist – here a prince who's been swallowed by a giant fish – relates the story of how he ended up in a space as physically and spiritually confining as a fish's stomach.

Walsh's time with Corcadorca proved a creatively fertile one, where a constant dialogue with Kiernan helped to inform Walsh's own approach to theatre making:

> It was an incredibly productive time, and we made a lot of work. It was all bad – really bad – but we knew it was bad. We just got up and did it, and then asked the audience why it was bad: 'Let's try and learn together what the work is,' we said. What

happened then was that the audience got to know us, they
became like our mates. We built an audience over a year by just
asking after each [performance], 'Ok. That was a little bit better
than the last time. Why do you think it was better? Can you see
what we're getting at?' During that period we did *The Ginger Ale
Boy*. That was a bit of a hit for us; it was a flawed play, but as a
writer I'd sort of arrived. And I suppose Cork sort of arrived in
it.

Walsh's preoccupation with Cork as a setting for his plays marks a
kind of performative strategy for the playwright, where the language
and locale of Cork acts as a mask Walsh puts on to erase himself from
the aesthetic equation.

You're always looking for a perspective to try and disappear
into, so that your writing isn't about you. So going down to Cork
was great because I forgot about me. I actually just loved
listening to people and fell in love with the city. There was less
of me in it, weirdly.

Translations

The success of *Disco Pigs* marked a turning point for both Walsh and
Corcadorca. Walsh had also created a private subculture shared by
the two teenage protagonists, Pig and Runt. The unique cadence of
Cork's regional dialect was refashioned into a kind of personalized
patois, a baby talk that both Runt and Pig utilize in retelling and re-
enacting the circumstances of their seventeenth birthday. During the
play's development and subsequent performance, it became clear to
Walsh and the company that they had created an affecting piece of
theatre.

As we were making *Disco Pigs*, I knew that we were making
something really good. Pat's direction and my writing came
together, and Cormac O'Connor's sound work was immense. I
wrote it for Eileen Walsh, who played the character Runt, and
we were fortunate to get Cillian Murphy, who played Pig. He was
unknown then and he and Eileen just gelled. It was a fun piece
to do. Once we went to Edinburgh the show was successful. We
were invited all over the world, and suddenly we were out there
looking at other people's work and going, 'Well, actually, we're
not that bad ...'

It took me a while to understand why I was good and that was
important: why *Disco Pigs* worked and what was in it that
worked. *Disco Pigs* was unusual in that it was an urban play that
was lyrical. That really took everyone by surprise, that we could

allow these characters to talk about the city that way and develop their own universe like that.

Given the specificity of Runt and Pig's dialogue, one wonders if a Cork audience was able to access and appreciate the play in a way that was different from other audiences' responses. Walsh doesn't think so.

> The way that Cork people had to understand *Disco Pigs* is the same way people in America or wherever we played had to understand it. It was the same sort of journey. Cork people could only initially understand thirty percent of the language. That was exactly the same for anyone in Toronto or wherever we were playing. The audience still had to learn about the play as they watched it. The theme of the play is very simple; it's just that our take on the subject was unusual. The language was unusual, the characters were unusual, but the actual story is incredibly naïve. The theme is very sweet, very romantic. The words look after themselves and the language looks after itself. It's how the theme is played and how the story is told and the perspective of the makers of that sort of story that's interesting. That's where the real work is being done.

For Walsh, the essential element of the play is the action of telling the story as opposed to displaying any kind of literary or linguistic aptitude. In claiming that 'the words look after themselves,' Walsh emphasizes that the process of storytelling is carried out through the performance of the play's action rather than on a faithful and literal interpretation of the language. In the case of *Disco Pigs*, the lack of a set and the fact that the two performers must embody the world of the play places the emphasis on the actors' presence and their physicality. It is perhaps for this reason that Walsh's work has translated so well to other languages and cultures. In considering this, Walsh states that:

> Plays of mine work in different countries. I'm sure loads of things are lost culturally, but then there must be loads of things added. *The Small Things* is huge in Greece – and I think, why is *The Small Things* huge in Greece? I know nothing about Greece, but there must be something within that play that resonates with them. I know that specifics are lost, jokes and references are lost. Weirdly, the Germans find it incredibly exotic because it's unknown to them. They can't access it, but for them that's a good thing. So there are things that are lost, but there are other things that are gained that are unknowable to me. But that's fine.

It is this exoticism in terms of Walsh's language, his at times bizarre scenarios, and the demands he places on his performers that make his work such an exciting challenge for European theatre practitioners. However, for the same reasons, it should be mentioned that Walsh's plays are exotic even within an Irish cultural context. Walsh's uncanny ability to make specific Irish idioms and locales wholly unfamiliar even to other Irish people helps to explain the immediacy and the wider communicability of his theatre. Rather than diminishing the global impact of his work through the evocation of Irish places and dialects, Walsh has instead opened spaces within his plays for other cultures to generate vastly different readings of their potential meaning in performance.

Being an Irish Playwright

Despite Walsh's assertion that 'the words look after themselves,' it must be noted that characters in his plays talk to excess, in a kind of grotesque parody of the traditional idea that the Irish are blessed with the 'gift of the gab.' Language gushes out of Walsh's characters, with dialogue appearing to 'speak' the characters, rather than the other way around. Here the 'gift of gab' is a vindictive curse rather than a charming cultural trait. Walsh does admit that while the Irish may possess a propensity for wordplay and loquaciousness, this trait should be seen as an act of proclaiming a sense of cultural individuality.

> I think Irish people proclaim quite a bit. They're not just talking for talking's sake. It's a proclamation, it's getting yourself out there, it's an analysis of where you are in relation to everyone else. I think it has to do with being at the edge of Europe: we're about to slip off the edge of Europe so we'd better proclaim ourselves culturally: 'This is who we are!' When you go to some pub in Ireland, it doesn't take long for you to get into a conversation where you're hearing stories and people are talking politics and so on. Chance meetings can become important. Nowhere else, in any sort of English speaking country, do I find that – in America or Australia or Britain. Not to the same extent.

Living as an Irish writer in London since the early 2000s has also given Walsh a more acute sense of himself as Irish.

> I do feel more Irish in the UK than I do back home. That happens to many writers who live abroad: you've got a perspective on Ireland, on what it is to be an Irish person. I'm Enda Walsh over here in England, but the second thing is that I'm an Irish person also. I do feel more Irish [in Ireland] now and I'm glad of that. I suppose it also has to do with working with Druid and being able to draw on their tradition of producing plays in the 1970s and 1980s. I feel part of a theatre

company, part of a history. I've been thinking more about that and feeling a lot more comfortable with the notion of being part of a long line of Irish playwrights.

Actually, sitting down and beginning to write you do feel the companionship of the many writers who came before. Shaw and Wilde, Synge and O'Casey, Behan and Beckett: you feel the strains of their work and their plays and their themes and their approach to character. I look back at *New Electric Ballroom* and I see images and strains that are part of our theatre history. I know my contemporaries – Martin McDonagh, Conor McPherson and Marina Carr: I think we live in our own bubbles, and people can say whatever they want to say about our work. But really we're probably our best critics and we'll annihilate stuff of our own that isn't good enough. We have the luxury of actually investigating our work in the theatre, and we introduce new, difficult work to try and move things on a little bit within the Irish tradition. We're part of a great lineage of Irish writers and it is important that we just keep developing. I'm very proud of the fact that going round the world people seem to welcome us, based on the history of Joyce and Beckett, or Wilde and Shaw. I'm very proud also, between me and my contemporaries, of what we've done and what we've achieved.

Walsh has also found the English response to his work to be indicative of an English perspective on Irish theatre as a whole.

I think English people have a very strange relationship with Irish theatre. They're a very literal audience. Irish people and the rest of the world take my work as it's intended: they see that it's a piece of theatre. Over here in England, they have issues with the reality of the people in *The New Electric Ballroom* living in a fishing village, with fish being stored under the ground: 'What does that mean? Is there a refrigerator there? Where are they?' They think the playwright is a journalist of some sort who takes life and puts it in theatrical form. We don't have that; as Irish people that's not our sensibility. Irish people deal in metaphor. We just allow plays to exist and be suspended in whatever world they are in. And we enjoy learning about the world of a Conor McPherson play or a Marina Carr play. We can reference it easily without it actually being like a piece of television – and over here in England a lot of the theatre is televisual.

Walsh's generalization does not take into account the work of English companies like Complicite, which stage work that utilizes highly theatrical and metaphorical expressions of the performer's body. This is true also of Theatre O, a company that Walsh worked with in 2006 to adapt Dostoevsky's *The Brothers Karamazov* for the stage. Theatre O combines text, movement, dance, music, and digital imagery in constructing its *mise en scène*, and is far from a journalistic theatre of reportage. Nonetheless, like Complicite and Theatre O, Walsh's own approach to making theatre seeks to disrupt received notions of a play's performance being merely a literal representation of the playscript.

Practice Makes Perfect

Walsh's construction of language is indicative of a writing process that is exceptionally quick and fluid. Walsh writes his plays in a matter of a few weeks, start to finish. The speed with which he conducts the process of writing has, Walsh states, allowed him a level of objectivity that he would not have if he had laboured over the text in a kind of literary, 'writerly' way.

> I write straight onto the computer. As I'm writing I might begin to make little notes or ask questions about the piece. With *Penelope* there were many times where I stopped and thought, 'There's a couple of big questions here. Will I actually begin to answer them, or will I completely ignore them? Where will I take this?' It doesn't all come out at once; it never does. But day by day I'm excited because I'm thinking, 'God – I have no idea where these characters are going to end up, but they're going to be ten minutes down the road in their lives.' And the day that they're living is an extraordinary day, and that's the day they are going to die. As soon as you figure out what the risk is for the characters, what they are facing, then you know something really, really big. Then it's just a joy to write.

> I tend to write very quickly. I have great perspective and objectivity on whatever I've written because I can't remember writing the thing. I think about the plays a lot, then write them, and then they're gone – I completely forget about them. I mean, I read *The Small Things* and I think, 'Ok, where did this play come from, and where is it going?' The structure is interesting: the way the story accumulates along the way ... But I can look at it and have no idea where it came from. It's like what Sarah Kane said when she worked on a play: 'Oh, I haven't written a word, but I can hum it.' And that's actually what playwriting is. The words look after themselves. What you're looking for is the music of it, the atmosphere of it, and the shape of it. *Penelope* formed in my head quickly – the atmosphere and the shape and the rhythm of it.

The apparent speed with which Walsh writes is contextualized by the amount of time and energy spent simply allowing the idea of the play to ferment. Walsh usually develops his ideas in conversation with dramaturge Tilman Raabke, who has championed his work in Germany. After the idea of the play is clear in his mind, the act of writing the play down occurs. This does not necessarily mean the detailed action of the play has been outlined for Walsh beforehand, and it is merely a matter of following a predetermined template for the play. Writing the play down has an open, improvisatory and performative element to it.

> There's only one time that I actually formed a play before writing it, where I've actually thought, 'Right, *this* is going to happen.' And it was an absolute piece of shit. There was no drama in it, there was no life in it, there was no theatre in it. I just have to trust in the process, as I've always done. The play is going to find its way. I know enough about the craft of writing and storytelling that the play and the characters will find their way, and will find some sort of resolution. And that's where you want the audience to be. At every second you want them to feel, 'I've no idea about the direction of this piece or the sense of it', because the characters are feeling exactly the same thing. And I'm feeling exactly the same thing as I write; I have no idea what's going to happen on the next page.

The play may then undergo cuts or alterations in preproduction, as in the case with *The Walworth Farce*, directed by Mikel Murfi. Walsh cites Murfi's input into the workshopping of the play as influential in developing the rehearsal draft.

> With *The Walworth Farce*, myself and Mikel did a lot of cutting. He came over to London and we read it and cut it, and then we found the ending – the repetitious moment of one of the characters playing at being in blackface. That scene wasn't in the original. I couldn't commit that character to that ending initially, because it broke my heart. I just couldn't do it; but then of course it has to end like that.

Once the play enters rehearsal, it is, for the most part, set; however changes can still occur, even deep into the run of a play.

> Once it gets into the rehearsal space, it will bend and some things will change a little to fit into the actors' mouths. Rhythmically there are things I would like to change. Things come out well-formed usually, though. With *The New Electric Ballroom* I added a line that wasn't in the original text during the run at the Traverse Theatre in Edinburgh. I felt the audience needed the line or else they would have been completely lost. It was a terrible anxiety on my part, that I didn't trust the play and didn't trust the audience's understanding the play. The line existed for quite a long time – for about a year. Finally, during the Dublin Theatre Festival in 2009, the play came back into

rehearsals and I said 'we have to lose that line'. And as soon as we lost it, there was the play. Suddenly I was asking, 'Why didn't I do that?' That's why I'm not a director: I really made the wrong decision there. I think if I stayed out of the business of changing the text during rehearsals, I would have probably had the strength and sensibility to know what the right thing to do was.

Despite protestations that he's not a director, Walsh writes with a kind of directorial intention, one that seeks to define the play not just in terms of an expression of narrative, but as an event as well. The construction of space, so important for his plays' meaning in performance, his appreciation of the potential for multiple meaning as expressed in the moment of speaking, and his understanding of the provisional nature of play development all suggest that Walsh is as much a theatre practitioner as he is a writer.

---

[1] Enda Walsh, personal interview, London, 9 November 2009. All subsequent quotations of Walsh are taken from this interview.

[2] Louise East, 'Creator of restless souls,' *The Irish Times*, 11 June 2005: C6.

[3] Enda Walsh, *bedbound & misterman* (Nick Hern Books: London, 2001): 12.

11 | 'Strangeness made sense': reflections on being a non-Irish Irish playwright.[1]

Elizabeth Kuti

A few months after I had arrived in my new home of Dublin, a friend wrote me a letter from England (this was in 1993 when people still wrote letters), enclosing Philip Larkin's poem, 'The Importance of Elsewhere' and asking me if it struck a chord:

> Lonely in Ireland, since it was not home,
> Strangeness made sense. The salt rebuff of speech,
> Insisting so on difference, made me welcome:
> Once that was recognised, we were in touch.[2]

Larkin's feeling of being 'separate, not unworkable' in Ireland was indeed very resonant for me then; now it strikes me as an apt description of my adventures in Ireland, and in Irish theatre in particular. The poem expresses a feeling that is a familiar one to me, and perhaps to many people who find the dislocation of the 'expat' experience paradoxically more comfortable than attempting to fit in to what ought to be 'home'. The final stanza of Larkin's poem ironically compares 'not home' with 'home', revealing the deeper – or 'more serious' – loneliness of feeling like an outsider in one's own country where there is no 'excuse' for it:

> Living in England has no such excuse:
> These are my customs and establishments
> It would be much more serious to refuse.
> Here no elsewhere underwrites my existence.

Many of the plays that I wrote in, and then, latterly, about Ireland, seem to me in retrospect to have allowed me to explore these very issues of home and exile, of belonging and not belonging: three of them, *Treehouses* (2000), *The Sugar Wife* (2005) and *The Six-Days*

World (2007) I shall discuss here. Ireland gave me so much, so many blessings, in the eleven years I lived there: not the least of which was the chance to become an actor and a playwright in the Irish theatre. As it seems to have been for Larkin, my time in Ireland was an education for me in the 'importance of elsewhere.'

The first full-length, original play I ever wrote came about as a result of a conversation with Karin McCully, who was then the Literary Manager at the Abbey Theatre. Karin had called me up for a chat in response to the three unsolicited scripts I had posted in to the Abbey's Literary Department. She told me that the Abbey had some 'Seedlings' money – not a full commission but £1000 to offer to a handful of promising playwrights in whom they were interested, for a first draft of a play, with no commitment from either side to take it any further. She asked if I had a play that I wanted to write, and I (of course) said yes. When she asked what it was about, I told her that it was about a man building a treehouse for his daughter. I had an image in my mind of the opening scene where the girl was looking up and saying 'I can see the moon', and I thought that perhaps this idea might have some connection with my father's family history in Europe and the story of how he survived the war and settled in England. But I wasn't sure yet how all that came together; I just knew that they were connected. Karin seemed to be satisfied with this rather whimsical description, though, and to my utter joy and astonishment, sent me a contract and £1000: my first bit of genuine playwriting money. So I wrote *Treehouses* and it turned out in fact to be fairly close to the idea that I had told Karin about, even containing the line, 'I can see the moon' somewhere in the opening scene. It was an attempt, partly, to answer the question, where are you from?

When I first arrived in Ireland in 1993 that question was everywhere. Irish people seemed to ask it constantly, not just of me but of each other. And Irish people always had a really clear and satisfying answer – Kilkenny, Cork, Wexford, Derry. Irish people seemed always to know without a shadow of a doubt where they were from. I always stuttered and mumbled, 'England ... London ... well, I grew up in Kent. My dad's Hungarian. So ... well, Kent really, I suppose'. None of it felt very secure.

It would be untrue to say that I 'felt' myself to be Hungarian in any way – my father had made no attempt to teach me the language – and I wasn't raised with any sense of Jewishness, either. I was a Home Counties girl. But somehow there was something worrying away at that identity which made it feel like something of an act – something not quite to be relied upon. When I asked why I had been named Elizabeth, and not Ilona (which had been my parents' second choice and the name of my father's mother) I was told that my father felt that as Ilona, 'no one would believe you were English'. Obviously identity was something that you had to persuade other people to believe in; and if they didn't 'believe' you – what then? Some sense of threat or danger lurked in my father's impulse to reject the name Ilona in favour of Elizabeth; giving me the name of the Queen of England was clearly something of a precaution. Looking back, I wonder if I grew up affected unconsciously by this sense of instability: the idea that identity, and nationality, was an act, a performance, that needed to be convincing to onlookers, where a flaw, or mark of difference of any kind, might give you away. I certainly had that anyway in the form of my 'very unusual' not to say unpronounceable surname.

Not speaking Hungarian, lunch at my grandparents' house in Croydon (they had all fled Hungary in 1956) meant people breaking into a percussive, staccato language I couldn't understand; strange, angry arguments about Communism and the Soviet Union that I didn't understand; and black-and-white photographs of unknown family members. When I asked who these people were, I was given uneasy, evasive answers that (as I know now, and perhaps, unconsciously knew then too) weren't the whole truth. I don't blame anyone in the least; there's never going to be an easy moment to explain to a seven-year-old what Auschwitz was. But there was mystery and subterfuge everywhere, and always a feeling of secrets, and of being protected from some truth that was too awful to be mentioned. I think this pervasive sense of a subtext that I barely understood and from which I had somehow to be 'protected', was perhaps the provocation that made me start writing, and writing drama in particular. Drama ignites where the subtext exerts an intolerable pressure on the surface of things; where the spoken clashes with the unspoken; where words and deeds diverge. And what's more, as Einstein said, 'Imagination is more important than knowledge.' What you knew, it seemed to me, or rather, what you thought you knew, was slippery and subject to endless revision and change. I thought my name was 'really' Kuti; it turned out in fact to be 'Kunzlinger', 'Kuti' being a post-war invention of my grandfather's. That type of revision of the past was constantly taking place for me. What I thought I knew and understood turned out to be not what it seemed; the simplest piece of knowledge that ought to have been reliable, set in stone, was liable to crumble into dust when poked or prodded.

Imagination, however, seemed paradoxically to offer more stability than knowledge. In making plays one could choose, determine and possess every facet of the world being created. There was no lie because it was all invented. That seemed oddly secure. Your feet were on solid ground not shifting sands. And yet drama is – must be – inevitably about uncovering the truth. 'For the subject of drama is The Lie', David Mamet writes. 'At the end of the drama, THE TRUTH – which has been overlooked, disregarded, scorned, and denied – prevails. And that is how we know the drama is done.'[3] Through writing plays – making it all up – it seemed one might perhaps, paradoxically, edge closer to truth, to wholeness of some kind.

I think *Treehouses* was an attempt to make something whole out of the scraps of what I knew of my origins. It was a rendering of what you might term a 'personal mythology', and as such perhaps the classic 'first play' or 'first novel' that the beginning writer sets out to write – sometimes, possibly, to his or her own detriment as a writer. I remember a conversation at the Tyrone Guthrie Centre at Annaghmakerrig with the wonderfully insightful Graham Whybrow, for many years the Literary Manager at the Royal Court Theatre in London, where he spoke with a tinge of weariness of how the first-time playwright in his view so often ended up 'blowing their personal mythology' on their first play. That key story, the one novel that they say everyone has in them, the writer's own, unique narrative of origins, then gets thrown away on a less than competent piece of work. Whereas, Graham implied, if only they had waited for play number three, four, or five, how many more good plays, and playwrights, might we have?

So I committed the classic wrong move of the beginning playwright and blew my personal mythology on my very first play. However, at first, it seemed that perhaps I'd got away with it. The Abbey Literary Manager, who was now Judy Friel, told me that 'the Building' liked the first draft sufficiently to transform my 'Seedlings' commission into a full commission, and to develop the script towards a full production. It was unbelievably exciting and unexpected.

What gradually happened, however, with the production was that I progressively lost my nerve and backed away from what I'd written. This is a syndrome that I now regularly detect in myself. Writing a draft can be private, fearless, you can dare yourself to say the unsayable, you can write to please yourself. You are making a map to a solitary place, an uninhabited island, with yourself the only castaway. The thrill of writing is the departure from the everyday and the plunge into the ocean of the unconscious and the imagination – to experience whatever sharks, coral-reefs, islands of paradise or cannibals that the journey may reveal.

It's quite another thing to put this stuff on public display with your name plastered all over it, and the reputations of other people – actors, designers, directors – pinned to it. Then the fear sets in; repression sets in. In truth, what I had written was indeed what the classifiers-of-plays would probably call a 'Holocaust play.' The play moved between three zones of time and place: one strand of the play followed the story of a young woman called Eva in 2000, on the day of her father's funeral. A second story strand, also set in 2000 and on the same day, follows the story of Magda, an elderly woman, a refugee from somewhere in Europe, talking to a care-worker in a care home. Old Magda reminisces about the summer during the war when she hid a runaway boy in the hayloft of the barn on her father's farm. A third story strand shows Magda's young self during the 1940s in an unnamed European country, during which she risks her life by hiding a persecuted Boy, and then has to choose whether to flee with him, or to stay and marry her childhood sweetheart, Stephen. Magda chooses Stephen; but the end of the play reveals that 'the Boy' was in fact Eva's father. From this we realise that the Boy escaped, survived and lived a full and interesting life in exile. Thus Eva's and Magda's stories are brought together.

The play itself as a text was in fact already rather shy about its origins, and I deliberately left the settings open and ambiguous. In my head, Eva and Old Magda were both living in England. But, as I knew I was writing for the Peacock in Dublin, I felt the need to cover the tracks a little. So it is never specified exactly where either of them are: Old Magda, who has clearly left her country of origin and taken up a new life in a new country, talks of coming to 'this island'. She speaks of the sea, and how her room overlooks the sea. In my head, this aspect of Magda was suggested by my Hungarian Great-Aunt Irmus who had a room in a care home in Dover, close to the sea. For audiences at the Peacock though, it could perhaps be Killiney or Howth; my guess is that audiences of other productions, such as at the Northcott Theatre in Exeter in 2001, would assume that the care home and Eva's home were both in England. I avoided specifically naming any towns, cities, or even countries. Old Magda chats with one of the care assistants in the home, whose name is Ger and who is clearly Irish; but such a person might easily be found in a British setting as well as in Ireland. Young Magda's European home is also unspecified, though a snatch of a song in Hungarian is a clue for those who know their Magyar from their Polish. The Boy describes trains leaving the city's stations at night-time, taking people away for 're-settlement' in the east. The words Jew or Jewish, ghetto, Nazi, Holocaust and so on never appear in the play.

In some ways this lack of specificity was part of the aesthetic of the play. The visual images I had in mind, and had stuck above my desk to remind me of the mood I wished to create, were some wood-cuts, which showed very simple, almost Biblical scenes of sowing and harvesting in clear, simple black outlines. Another influence was the dream-like, magical quality of Marc Chagall's paintings: a violinist, a man and woman flying through the sky over little houses and woods. The intention with the play, therefore, was not to be historically realistic nor photographically naturalistic, but to give the play a simple, fable-like quality: to create a mood of lyricism, the sense of the seasons passing, and the presence of death and danger and other unspoken dangers in the midst of sensuous childhood elation, so that the play might have the simple, universal feeling of a nursery rhyme or of the Bible.

By avoiding specific labels, the aim was perhaps to tell the story in such a way that the Boy's persecution, and the choices faced by Magda, retained some openness, and could resonate with other conflicts and with contemporary events. Perhaps in this way I hoped to sidestep the problem that an Irish audience's relationship with the Second World War is necessarily different from the British one. As an Irish friend said to me, 'We didn't have a war, we had an Emergency.' The 'war', in which Ireland had been neutral, had not even been named as such in Ireland. For British people born in the twentieth or even twenty-first century, the Second World War is both personal and family history, and also a key piece of national mythology. For Jewish people, it is of course another mythology, and a terrible legacy that casts a long shadow over past, present, and future. For most Europeans, surely, that war – what happened at Dachau, Birkenau, Auschwitz, what happened in cities right across our continent, the slaughter committed by all of us, inflicted on all of us – is a scar that fifty or sixty years on, has faded, but still retains its power to provoke – if not such profound guilt or despair as perhaps was the case in the immediate post-war period – then at least serious reflection.

But for an Irish audience the weight and meaning, the very naming of the Second World War, is specific and different. The emotion at the heart of *Treehouses* is a struggle with guilt, essentially in relation to the horror of the Holocaust. Magda laments a failure that is not hers alone but a collective human failure: 'Not even one. I couldn't even save one little boy ... I lacked courage. I promised – and I broke my promise'.[4] The last speech of the play is a plea for the chance to make some kind of reparation or to replay history: 'I will bring a bowl of salt and water to bathe your feet. I will save you from the fire. I will make an ark and set it among the rushes for some Pharaoh's daughter to find' (81). The play shows Magda's personal story, but the guilt she expresses goes beyond the personal.

However, it seemed in the late 1990s that this theme was obscure or irrelevant to Irish audiences. When the playwright Thomas Kilroy commented on the play in an open public workshop at the Peacock Theatre, the word 'Holocaust' was, I think, never mentioned. Tom described it throughout the two days as a 'memory play', and that seemed a category that Irish theatre, and Irish audiences, were much more comfortable and familiar with. This was a play about the past, about memory and about secrets: and this was how the play ended up being described and interpreted to audiences. The Holocaust issue was not merely downplayed; it was entirely unmentioned. The image on the flyer for the Peacock production was ghostly and atmospheric, but ambiguous, with nothing to indicate the play's setting or content; and the copy on the back was equally non-specific, describing the play as 'a magical tale of refuge, treachery, and of love lost and found'.

Not that I didn't comply with, in fact even encourage, this vagueness; it was probably largely my own fault. I remember talking to the Press Office at the Abbey and discussing the copy for the flyer, and anxiously suggesting that the Holocaust or World War Two should not be mentioned. The director, Jason Byrne, and the Press Office, seemed to be very much in agreement that we shouldn't stress the Holocaust angle – so that I am not sure now how much it was their decision, how much my own, or whether I had picked up on the rather ambivalent and lukewarm signals in response to the play's depiction of the war and the Holocaust (theatre productions come about in such a collaborative way that these matters are often confused). By avoiding specifics I think I hoped that contemporary resonances with other conflicts in Europe might more easily emerge. Parallels with refugees fleeing from 'ethnic cleansing' in Bosnia, Kosovo, Rwanda and so forth, might, I hoped, engage Irish audiences more perhaps than a play specifically depicting the Holocaust. After all, persecution and genocide, flight, migration and emigration were pretty big issues throughout the 1990s, and even Ireland was changing as Bosnians, Rwandans and others made their way here in increasing numbers.

Furthermore, the themes of 'home' and of 'exile' in the play had wider relevance – not just in the sense of homeland or nation, but in a wider sense of the 'home' of our first family, which changes and is dismantled by the passage of time, as children grow up, and parents die. The constant re-grouping of 'home' was a thread going through the play, and it is the thematic thread which connects Eva's narrative with that of Magda and the Boy. Eva's is an Oedipal drama in which she describes feeling 'exiled' from her home through her father's second marriage to her stepmother:

> today this garden his garden this day of all days it is so full of that summer the summer I was twelve that last summer when everything I saw from my nest in the tree belonged to us to me and him, before it all ended, before I had to share it, before I stopped being the one and only and became one of three and everything stopped being mine and his and became something he shared with someone else and I was no longer queen but minion in some occupied territory. (17)

Figure 6: the Peacock Theatre Flyer for *Treehouses*

Through telling their stories in parallel, the play connects the childhood psychological drama of Eva, dispossessed by her father's re-marriage, with the displacement and dispossession that her father himself went through as a Jewish child in the Second World War. Connecting these two stories was a problem for some critics, who saw Eva's story as far too minor a trauma to be compared in any way to that of the Boy. However, this pairing and comparison was central to my conception of the play and its imagery. The temporary nature and impermanence of 'home' was expressed in my very first visual image of the 'treehouse' which I had told Karin about right at the very beginning; the treehouse is a makeshift, easily-dismantled, temporary structure, belonging to childhood only: just as one's childhood 'home' is dismantled by the passage of time, as children grow up and leave or are ejected from it to form new family structures. The instability of all homes and refuges is a key theme as all the characters are ejected in some way or another from a 'home' to which they can never return. So the play was concerned with nationality and exile; but it was about 'home' and homeland on other metaphorical, psychological levels too.

Downplaying the Holocaust aspect, especially in terms of the way in which the play was described and marketed, did, however, I think probably result in the play becoming more perplexing for Irish audiences rather than less. Some over-cutting of the text which made the pay-off at the end of the play less than clear, and the general 'wrongness' of the Irish setting for Old Magda and Eva, meant that the play was robbed of its true identity, and was shoehorned into an identity that didn't really fit. Perhaps it was this that audiences perceived, even if unconsciously, and that made the evening unsatisfying. It was noticeable to me that American and English audience members were the most positive in their responses to the play, and seemed to enjoy it more. The play had been sent out as it were in an Irish costume and with an Irish accent and its true nature was therefore disguised and obscured.

The contrast between the marketing of the Peacock production with that of the first production of the play in the UK, at the Northcott Theatre in Exeter, was very marked. The flyer and poster for the Northcott's production was resolutely literal and unambiguous, showing a 1940s steam-train emblazoned with a Nazi swastika against the background of an Autumnal forest (see fig. 5).

Figure 7: Northcote Theatre Production of *Treehouses*

Audiences in Devon knew exactly where they were and it all made sense. The move towards clear historical specificity was also reflected in the set – a much more solid affair than Johanna Connor's beautiful, delicate, abstract design for the Peacock. I liked the subtlety of the choices for the Peacock production in terms of visually realising the play; however, the robustness of the Northcott's refusal to shy away from making it very firmly a 'Holocaust play' certainly lent clarity to the evening. Interestingly, it was a reviewer of the Northcott production who pointed out the contemporary parallels that had received no mention or comment in Dublin at all. A reviewer for the *Plymouth Extra* (22 March 2001) wrote a positive review and commented that this current production of the play had particular resonance now, 'at a time when history seems to be repeating itself, when the victims of war are again seeking asylum in our country, having been displaced from their own'. Perhaps the lesson of this is that if you attend carefully to the particulars, then the universals will emerge.

Strangely this play, despite its rather lukewarm reception at its premiere in Dublin, has probably been my most successful play to date, in terms of the number of productions it has received, and the distance it has travelled. A production at the Oregon State University in the United States chose for its poster a sombre but beautiful painting in dark tones of a bird in flight heading into a cloudily lit sky (a reference to the song in the play, 'Repülj madár, repülj', which means 'Fly bird, fly away'). A tag-line on the poster itself promised, with crystal clarity, 'a story of World War II Hungary, memory, love, lost and found'. Another production in London chose an eerily empty snow-filled landscape with the tag-line, 'Courage or kindness – which is the greatest virtue?' which sums up the emotional and moral dilemma facing Magda at the climactic moment of choice that the play is balanced upon. The tightrope walk between how much to reveal and how much to conceal, the line between delicate ambiguity and obfuscating evasion is one that the playwright negotiates at every word, line, scene, and act of the play; and it is negotiated again by designers, directors and even by the way that the play is marketed and explained to its prospective audience. Both clarity and ambiguity are essential qualities for an evening of good theatre. The poster image and the wording chosen to publicize a production may seem like a relatively minor matter, but it is the face your play wears to the world. It sends strong signals to your audience and shapes their expectations. It sets your audience up for satisfaction or disappointment. Furthermore, like the image formed for the eye by a Rorschach inkspot, it is a hugely revealing insight into the director's 'take' on the play: a kind of shorthand symbol for the entire interpretive angle that a particular production will pursue.

Despite the kind assurances I had received prior to its production from the Abbey's Literary Department that the script of *Treehouses* was indeed 'Irish' enough in its themes and concerns, as I have tried to convey above, my hunch remained that the play had not in fact been 'Irish' enough, and I felt strongly that my next play would need an unambiguously Irish setting and Irish concerns. At this point I had a commission for a new play for Rough Magic Theatre Company, and I was facing the same problem all over again: all the material that a playwright needs to draw on – experience of family life, of growing up, relatives, the kind of cultural concerns and reference points that you take in with your mother's milk and are hardly aware of – none of these were available to me in an Irish context. So the solution seemed to be the past – an Irish past, but so distant that it had slipped from the reach of living memory. 'The past is another country', as L.P. Hartley puts it, and this past would be my country, my own creation, and its authenticity would come from my own imagination. The Quaker community in Dublin just after the Famine offered me a setting that was very resonant for me: an immigrant household, so the characters would have an outsider's perspective (like my own), but as citizens living and working in Dublin they were insiders too. After all these years in Dublin I wanted to write something about the city I loved: Dublin itself was important to this play, and Bewley's Oriental Tea-houses in particular. The sign out on the pavement, 'Bewley's, established 1845' (now sadly to be seen no more) was my starting-point. Like many Quaker businesses – Cadbury's, Rowntree's, Jacob's biscuits – Bewley's was a highly successful and long-lasting one, and like many Quaker businesses, sugar was central to its trade. The paradox of its simultaneous involvement in philanthropic work as well as the campaign for the abolition of slavery whilst also having trading interests in sugar, a crop so central to slavery, seemed very ripe for dramatic exploration. These kinds of paradoxes are increasingly being explored by Quaker historians: Coalbrookdale (the real-life model for Slatebeck) had indeed been involved in the manufacture of guns and other goods used in the slave trade, and had also pursued philanthropic activities, including the charitable shipping of soup urns to Ireland during the Famine. In an Irish context these ironies were particularly striking. Bewley's was established during the same decade as the Famine; the Quaker contribution to Famine relief has been widely acknowledged. The transatlantic coffin-ships carrying thousands of dispossessed Irish people were a grim echo of the slave-ships that had sailed for America from Africa, bringing enslaved Africans to work on sugar plantations.

The parallels and paradoxes were enticing but the play refused to take shape for many drafts, as the ideas and research refused to knit together into the right story. To my rescue again came Graham Whybrow who at Annaghmakerrig gave me perhaps the most helpful advice I've ever been given. I had made Bewley's into the fictional 'Tewkley's', but I still felt the need to get everything as right and historically accurate as I could, and this was scuppering my ability to write the play; I couldn't get hold of the story whilst trying to honour historical accuracy. 'Why don't you just make it up?' said Graham. Along with Loughlin Deegan's advice on rewriting ('Just don't make it worse'), this ranks as my number one favourite piece of playwriting advice. This is a play, not history; I can make this up – and with that liberating thought the play started to come alive. Yes, it's a *roman* (or *pièce de théâtre*, if you like) *à clef*: Sarah Worth is a version of Sarah Parker Redmond, a former slave who gave a lecture tour in Dublin; the D.L.A.S.S. (Dublin Ladies Anti-Slavery Society) existed. But everything in the play is invented; it is a parallel, if you like, but utterly imagined, fictional universe.

So with complete authority over this imagined universe I felt at ease to write without fetters. Every character in *The Sugar Wife* is a stranger and an outsider, who has either chosen or had exile of some sort forced upon them. Hannah and Samuel Tewkley are Irish but members of the Society of Friends (Quakers), and as such are descended from members of a dissenting seventeenth-century sect who fled from persecution in England and settled in America, especially Pennsylvania, but also in Germany and Ireland. Alfred Darby is an English Quaker who has turned his back on his family, religion, and country of birth; Sarah Worth is a freed slave, now American citizen, of African descent. Martha Ryan is the only Catholic Irish character, and, as a working-class woman, is a marginalized and exploited figure with an outsider's perspective. The views in the mid-nineteenth century on Ireland that I came across as I read more – Harriet Jacobs' *Diary of a Slave-girl* and Asenath Nicholson's *Annals of the Famine in Ireland* – provided more and more startling perspectives on Ireland, viewed from the 'outside'. Where before Ireland and its history had either seemed a fiercely-guarded Irish possession, or else a closed dialogue locked solely into its colonial/post-colonial relationship with Britain, these outsider perspectives from the nineteenth century slowly helped me see Ireland and its history on a world stage, connected to worldwide patterns of refuge, exile, justice and injustice.

Bernard Klein, a German academic writing about history plays in the Irish theatre, has commented that, 'Public acts of memory define *us*, not *them*' – that is, such acts are about the rememberers, not the remembered. Klein cites the widespread theory of memory that, '...."cultural memory" (as opposed to "personal memory", most influentially discussed by Freud) is shaped not diachronically in relation to events of the past, but synchronically in relation to the social contexts of the present'.[5] Thus *The Sugar Wife* was a play in many ways 'about' Dublin of the late twentieth, early twenty-first century that I was living in: it was inspired by the climactic roar of the Celtic Tiger that had produced pockets of astonishing affluence in the city of Dublin, right next to pockets of extreme poverty and deprivation. Irish emigration had long had a voice in the culture and the national narrative; immigration into Ireland from the outside was a relatively new phenomenon, one that had barely existed when I arrived in 1993. By 2005, Dublin had become an ethnically diverse society, and the idea of strangers coming to these shores as immigrants was becoming a part of Irish experience, even if it was not (yet) expressed in Irish culture.

Interestingly, the image chosen for Rough Magic's production of the play, and for the cover of the published play-text, was another delicate and oblique image: a detail from an Oriental design, showing two cranes flying upwards against a red background (see fig. 6).

It did not give much away about the play's content, though it recalled the Chinese silk robe embroidered with kingfishers that features in the play, and that Hannah wears to have her photograph taken by Alfred Darby, in her pose as 'Maid of the Orient'. It is an attractive, lyrical image, with the flight of the two birds also suggesting love, and perhaps the (failed) elopement of the lovers. But it is ambiguous and does not signal the harsher aspects of the play.

Perhaps this choice of a rather oblique image revealed something of the same tentativeness with which *Treehouses* had been promoted. A first production of a new play is a risky and nerve-wracking time for all involved. No one, not even (perhaps especially) the playwright, knows yet what kind of animal the play is, having never seen it in front of its audience; and so it is hard to get it right in terms of introducing it to the public. When Rough Magic's production at the Cube at the Project Arts Centre had received a warm response from critics and audiences, and had been invited by the Soho Theatre in London to transfer there for a run in January 2006, everyone's confidence was much higher. When the Soho requested a different image to publicize the play, we discussed various options and it is interesting that the one chosen (in agreement as far as I recall with Soho, myself and with Lynne Parker and Rough Magic's team) was a much more literal image (see fig. 4), which shows a black woman in a white muslin dress and head-scarf photographed from behind (on the flip side of the flyer the image was reversed and shown in a ghostly negative, so that it appears to be a white woman in black clothing, thus foregrounding the idea of photography and enclosing Hannah Tewkley as well as Sarah Worth in the 'sugar wife' of the title).

Figure 8: Rough Magic's production of *The Sugar Wife*

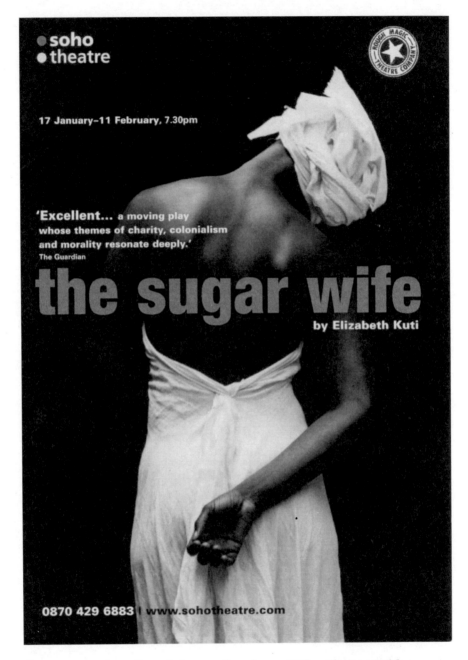

Figure 9: Soho Theatre's production of *The Sugar Wife*

The image on the flyer for the Soho signals very clearly that the play is concerned with race and slavery, and the centrality of a female figure might also suggest that the play is imbued with a feminist perspective. Again, the production of this play aimed at a British audience was promoted via a very upfront, literal image which made the themes crystal clear; while the production aimed at the Irish audience seemed to be given a more lyrical, understated, open image, which side-stepped the obvious 'issues' and sent ambiguous signals.

I couldn't on the evidence say whether this delicate ambiguity versus upfront literalism is a widespread and observable national difference in the marketing of plays in Ireland versus the UK; I can only make the obvious point that in my experience the same script – even the same production – is treated very differently depending on where the production is taking place, and that the process, anecdotally at least, *appears* to reveal national differences and concerns in an interesting way. For example when *The Sugar Wife* was translated as *Die Zuckerfrau* and produced in Stuttgart, the production demonstrated the greater control exercised by the director in Germany over the script than is the case either in Ireland or the UK. The actress playing Sarah Worth was made into a kind of narrator or ringmaster for the whole play, and in the first minutes of the play she delivered an opening prologue in her native language of Portuguese (with German subtitles) explaining that she – the actress – came from Mozambique, and therefore spoke the language of the European colonial power that had appropriated her country; for the rest of the play she would speak, as her character Sarah Worth, in English with German surtitles, while the other characters replied to her in English. The rest of this Brechtian framing prologue drew attention to the strange mixture of influences at work in this 'Irish' play by an English author translated by a German for the audience in Stuttgart. For the first ten minutes of the performance, I wondered if I was in the right theatre ... but it is this process of transformation and metamorphosis, through the sharing of ideas that is the joy of writing plays. I feel very honoured to have had some very interesting responses from people in Germany, where this play has seemed to strike a chord and find favour. I received this email from a student in Bremen, whose lecturer had included *The Sugar Wife* as a text on one of her courses:

> My friends and I feel that the topic of your play is not out of date at all. It is set in the 1850s; however, we can easily draw comparisons to the world we live in today, in 2009. We mean all the richness in Western societies, and that of course includes the privileged life we are enjoying in Germany, are based on the suffering and poorness of others (we just have to think of China, massive cheap labour, India, child labour, the clothes made by children, being successfully sold in Europe ... etc this could be an endless list). Necessarily there comes the guilt question. We

grew up with all that plenteousness so naturally, that it does seduce us at times to forget that this is everything else but a worldwide standard life, and even worse that we solely have this privilege, because it is denied to others – just because it happened that they were born by coincidences as well, into this world that has already followed the mechanisms of exploitation long before we could even have actively contributed to those mechanisms; are we then automatically born with guilt – a guilt that already adheres to us before we could even make the first step or form a conscious thought?[6]

This German student interestingly saw the play's central question as 'Are we then automatically born with guilt?' Given, as she argues, that we are born purely by coincidence into a nation which 'has already followed the mechanisms of exploitation long before we could have actively contributed to those mechanisms', to what extent do the crimes – if that is the right word – committed by our forefathers and mothers rest on our shoulders? And though this student is talking here about economic guilt, perhaps there are other subtexts to her words. As a British person in Ireland, as a German child born long after the end of the Second World War, as an American born centuries after the end of slavery, the question of the extent of our responsibility for oppressive systems set in place 'long before we could have actively contributed to those mechanisms' remains an urgent one. I am grateful for, and touched by, this eloquent response to the play from Isabella Steiner. Finding that *The Sugar Wife* could travel from Ireland to England to Germany to the U.S. and still resonate there for readers or audience members was a wonderful and very heartening experience.

By the time *The Sugar Wife* was being produced in 2005-6, I had already accepted a job in England and had made the poignant but seemingly necessary leap back across the water – to England and to Essex. A play that had been brewing for several years suddenly demanded to be written and tumbled out in a matter of weeks in 2007. It was set at Christmas and was in part a play about England, fuelled by my experience of 'elsewhere' after my eleven-year sojourn in Ireland. In particular it was about the absence of all religious belief in England, and what results when a society has nothing to believe in beyond the literal concrete everyday world. There was a feeling I wanted to get at, which was something to do with asking the question: Are we simply working and shopping to survive in an utterly empty universe? – in a world the gaudiness of which increases in inverse proportion to the shrinking of any kind of collective belief in a spiritual dimension to life? And can that possibly be enough? The play's title, *The Six-Days World*, came from a line from George

Herbert's sonnet, *Prayer*, where he finds a series of images for prayer, seeing it as a powerful force, ascending from man to God:

> Engine against the almighty, sinners towre,
> Reversed thunder, Christ-side-piercing spear,
> The six-daies world transposing in an houre.

The 'six-days world' meant to me the 'Monday to Saturday' grind, the working bit of the week: the bit unleavened by any sense of otherness or transcendence. In the play Ireland functions as a sort of mirror for England, in which England's spiritual emptiness is contrasted with Irish traditions of faith and belief. Eddie, the play's central character, is an Englishman, a musician in his thirties living a sort of extended adolescence in Ireland with his girlfriend Cat, to whom he is unable to commit fully. The play is set in his parental home over Christmas when he and Cat arrive to stay for a short visit. Eddie's rage about some of the repressed sadness in his parental home takes the form of diatribes against England as a spiritual wasteland in contrast to an Irish spirituality:

> This fucked-up culture, this English thing, this miserable, tight-arsed, joyless fucking culture – I'm even too afraid to say the word love. That's what this is about – it's about an absence – a lacuna – a deep-seated fundamental lack of love! It's a yearning fucking gaping chasm in all our hearts! And it's everywhere! It's hollowing us out! Perfect example – why is it called Boxing Day? I don't know! I bet no one in this room knows! It's just another fucking example! In Ireland they call it St Stephen's Day after the first Christian martyr so that simply by saying the name of the day you engage with the insane but beautiful notion that people throughout history have died in the name of Christ, have actually died by piercing and stoning and wounding and crucifixion for what they think is the glory of God and mad as the entire enterprise is at least it's not gift solutions and two-for-fucking one at Boots and value Christmas at Tesco's and the whole performance we get dragged through year after bloody year; at least in Ireland they know why the day has the name it has! And there's blood and loss and sacrifice in it![7]

Eddie's rants against England and the 'epidural of our non-culture' are partly explained by his personal circumstances and are an expression of his own pain and alienation; they are meant to raise a smile or at least to be taken with a pinch of salt. But there was also a kernel of something real that I wanted to express; a disillusion with the values of an entirely secular and de-culturized country, where no one sings at weddings, and no one has the words to express grief at funerals; where pop music and widescreen TVs and shopping have replaced real connection and communication. It's an impossibly naïve view, of course, the idea of 'holy Ireland': I lived in Ireland long enough to know how that kind of misty-eyed romanticization of Irishness is derided, regarded accurately as a fiction promoted by Bord Fáilte to fleece German and American tourists. But nonetheless something still persists in Ireland which you could argue has disappeared from the repressed England of *The Six-Days World*. Even if it only exists in a particular kind of joy in story-telling or in the 'noble call' of singing during the small hours of a lock-in: there is something which both Eddie and his father Ralph crave, and which is to do with non-material nourishment; with connection; with community, with the soul, if that word is allowed. In a wholly secular world there can be no respite from the six-days world of shopping and material production. If you take away symbolism and ritual and heightened language and replace it only with consumerism, there will be little help for pain for any of us, when death and disaster strikes. Eddie's anguish was meant to convey something of this idea; while Ralph's memory of pilgrims climbing Croagh Patrick represents a ritual act for which he has no equivalent. With his son's apparent suicide weighing on his conscience, and no recourse to acts of faith, he can see no end to his own spiritual suffering:

> I shouted after him, Go, you bloody fool – go, you fool, you want to waste your life, then go, I wash my hands. I wash my hands.
> He had this orange coat and I saw just one bright flash of it – I saw him running. Out towards the marsh. The railway. The crossing.
> And that moment has been visited on me –
> I have paid for that moment ten thousand times. Ten thousand times. All the suffering of hell.
> How much blood would I have to shed for that? How many times would I have to climb Croagh Patrick for that? (58)

The Six-Days World was a meditation on England and on Ireland, and strangely it had its roots in an odd piece of factual misinterpretation. The 1993 census revealed a sharp drop in the number of young men under the age of 35 living in England. The statistics revealed apparently that hordes of disenchanted young men, like my brother who left at around that time too, had taken flight from Thatcher's Britain and fled the country. This became a standard interpretation of the figures, that England was driving its young men away. It was an idea that interested me and became part of my thinking as the play took shape in my mind. However it was later revealed that this was an inaccurate narrative imposed upon the census results that had somehow taken hold of the imagination, and had been widely reported in the quality press. It was however a misinterpretation of the figures, and a story that was later discredited and corrected when the figures were looked at again less emotively. So-called facts, even those as seemingly black and white as the results of a census, are slippery creatures and not to be trusted. Much safer to avoid them and stick to the avowed fictions of the imagination.

In conclusion, then, I am honoured to be a non-Irish Irish playwright and I am probably more proud of my tiny entry in Volume 4 of the *Field Day Anthology* than perhaps anything else in the world, bar my children. I have overcome my terror that I have violated the rule that you must only write about your own backyard -- or as Sebastian Barry put it sternly in the Trinity College Writers' Workshop, that writers must only write about their own field, and mustn't go around taking someone else's. This seemed a rather frightening rebuke at the time – that by attempting to write plays set in or about a country that is not your birthplace, you might somehow be stealing someone else's field: committing the literary equivalent of an act of colonial misappropriation. But perhaps I took his words over-literally, or as a British interloper in Irish theatre, I was overly sensitive to the connotations of the 'field' metaphor! Now I am not so sure. I think the fences between our fields are more permeable and flexible than we thought. We set up our homes in each other's dreams. And anyway, as Virginia Woolf said, 'As a woman I have no country ... as a woman, my country is the world'.[8] Where are you from? The true answer to the question will not be found in the census statistics. The theatre gives us time-travel, it gives us dream-space, it allows us to see the past walking into the present moment. It is always an education in the importance of elsewhere.

Productions

Treehouses. Peacock Theatre, at the Abbey Theatre, Dublin. April 2000 Directed by Jason Byrne; designed by Johanna Connor.
Treehouses. Northcott Theatre, Exeter. March 2001. Directed by Ben Crocker; designed by Kit Surrey.
*Treehouses.*Oregon State University, April 2005. Directed by Charlotte J. Headrick; designed by George Caldwell.
The Sugar Wife. Rough Magic Production at the Cube, Project Arts Centre, April 2005. Directed by Lynne Parker; designed by Paul Keogan.
The Sugar Wife. Rough Magic Production, transferred to the Soho Theatre, London; January-February, 2006.
The Six-Days World. First reading at National Theatre Studio, July 2007. Produced at Finborough Theatre, London, November-December 2007. Directed by Jamie Harper.

Publications

Treehouses. (London: Methuen, 2000).

The Sugar Wife (London: Nick Hern Books, 2005)
The Six-Days World (London: Nick Hern Books, 2007).

---

[1] I would like to dedicate this essay to the memory of my much missed friend and colleague, Ros Dixon.

[2] Philip Larkin, 'The Importance of Elsewhere', in *The Whitsun Weddings* (London: Faber and Faber, 1987): 34.

[3] David Mamet, *Three Uses of the Knife: On the Nature and Purpose of Drama*, (London: Methuen, 1998): 69.

[4] Elizabeth Kuti, *Treehouses* (London: Methuen Drama, 2000): 78. Subsequent quotations appear in the text.

[5] Bernhard Klein, *On the Uses of History in Recent Irish Writing* (Manchester and New York: Manchester University Press, 2007): 6.

[6] Isabella Steiner, University of Bremen, personal email, 23.01.09.

[7] Elizabeth Kuti, *The Six-Days World* (London: Nick Hern Books, 2007): 37-8.

[8] Virginia Woolf, *Three Guineas*, ed. Naomi Black (Oxford: Blackwell for the Shakespeare Head Press, 2001): 99.

Texts Cited

Adigun, Bisi. 'In Living Colour', *Irish Theatre Magazine*, 19 (summer 2004).

Alberge, Dalya, 'After Sikh Riot, Theatre Stages Muslim Brothel', *The Times*, 22 March 2005.

Allen, Brooke, 'Summer Offerings (New York Theater)', *New Criterion*, 25.1 (1 September 2006): 89.

Anderson, Benedict, *Imagined Communities: Reflections on the Origin and Spread of Nationalism*, revised ed. (London: Verso, 1991).

Beller, Manfred and Joep Leerssen (eds.), *Imagology: The Cultural Construction and Literary Representation of National Characters: A Critical Survey* (Amsterdam: Rodopi , 2007).

Bill, Stephen, Anne Devlin, David Edgar, *Heartlanders* (London: Hern, 1989).

Birmingham Mail, 'Trouble at the Birmingham Repertory Theatre', *Birmingham Mail*, 16 May 1917: 3.

Birmingham Repertory Theatre, 'Library of Birmingham', <http://www.birmingham-rep.co.uk/about/library-of-birmingham/>

Brannigan, John, *Race in Modern Irish Literature and Culture* (Edinburgh: Edinburgh UP, 2009).

Broadway World, 'Pre-Lincoln Center DruidSynge Hits St Paul's Guthrie 6/27', *BroadwayWorld*, 22 June 2006.

Carolan, Mary, 'Copyright breach claim over modern production of "Playboy" at Abbey', *The Irish Times*. 18 May 2010

Cave, Richard, 'On the siting of doors and windows: aesthetics, ideology and Irish stage design' in Shaun Richards (ed.) *The Cambridge Companion to Twentieth-Century Irish Drama* (Cambridge: Cambridge University Press, 2004): 93-108.

Cave, Richard and Ben Levitas (eds.), *Irish Theatre in England*, Irish Theatrical Diaspora Series: 2 (Dublin: Carysfort Press, 2007).

Chamberlain, Franc, *Physical Theatres: A Critical Reader*, (London: Routledge, 2007).

Cherry, Gordon E. Birmingham: *A Study in Geography, History and Planning* (Chichester: Wiley, 1994).

Clark, W.S., *The Irish Stage in the County Towns: 1720-1800* (Oxford: Clarendon Press, 1965).

Cleary, Joe, *Outrageous Fortune: Capital and Culture in Modern Ireland* (Dublin: Field Day, 2007).

Cochrane, Claire, *Shakespeare and the Birmingham Repertory Theatre 1913-1929* (London: Society for Theatre Research, 1993).

Cote, David, Review of DruidSynge (Lincoln Center), *TimeOut* (New York), 564 (20-26 July 2006).

Crang, Mike and Nigel Thrift (eds.), *Thinking Space* (London: Routledge, 2000).

Crawley, Peter, '*The Trials of Brother Jero*: Samuel Beckett Theatre, Dublin', *The Irish Times*, 27 February 2009: 18.

--- Review of Solemn Mass for a Full Moon in Summer, *The Irish Times*, 11 March 2009: 16

Croghan, Declan, *Paddy Irishman, Paddy Englishman, and Paddy...?* (London: Faber, 1999).

Deane, Seamus (ed.), *Ireland's Field Day* (South Bend: Notre Dame University Press, 1986).

Decroux, Étienne, *Words on Mime*, Trans. Mark Piper, *Mime Journal* 1985.

Dennis, Anne, 'Étienne Decroux – An Actor, A Teacher of Actors, An Actor's Director', *Mime Journal* (Pomona CA), 1993/1994.

Derrida, Jacques, *Of Grammatology*, trans. Gayatri Chakravorty Spivak (Baltimore: Johns Hopkins Press, 1974).

Devitt, John, in conversation with Nicholas Grene and Chris Morash, *Shifting Scenes: Irish Theatre-Going 1955-1985* (Dublin: Carysfort Press, 2008).

Doyle, Roddy, *Brownbread and War* (London: Minerva, 1993).

---- *The Barrytown Trilogy* (London: Minerva, 1993).

---- *The Deportees* (London: Vintage, 2008).

Dziemianowicz, Joe, 'Something to Synge About', *The New York Daily News*, 12 July 2006: 35.

East, Louise, 'Creator of restless souls,' *The Irish Times*, 11 June 2005: C6.

Ejorh, Theophilus, 'Immigration and Citizenship: African Immigrants in Ireland', *Studies*, 96.

Falvey, Deirdre, 'Druid Returns to its Spiritual Home', *The Irish Times*, 28 March 2009, Weekend: 8.

---- 'On the break, or on the make?', *The Irish Times* 28 February 2009: 45.

Fay, W.G. and Catherine Carswell, *The Fays of the Abbey Theatre: An Autobiographical Record* (London: Rich and Cowan, 1935).

Feingold, Michael, 'Synge, Synge, Synge', *The Village Voice*, 19-25 July 2006: 45.

Finkle, David, Review of *DruidSynge* (Lincoln Center), *Theatermania*, 11 July 2006.

Fitz-Simon, Christopher and Sanford Sternlicht (eds.), *New Plays From the Abbey Theatre 1993-1995* (Syracuse: Syracuse UP, 1996).

Forristal, Desmond, *Black Man's Country* (Newark, DE: Proscenium Press, 1975).

Fricker, Karen, 'Druid Company Sings Synge Song', *Variety* 399.9 (25-31 July 2005): 54.

--- 'Expanding the Cottage Walls', *Irish Theatre Magazine* 5.24 (Autumn 2005) (22-24).

Friel, Brian, 'Talking to Ourselves', *Magill*, December 1980.

Gener, Randy, 'Synge Our Contemporary', *American Theatre* 23.6 (July-August 2006): 23.

Gleeson, Brendan, *Breaking Up* (Dublin: Passion Machine, 1989).

Grene, Nicholas and Chris Morash (eds.), *Irish Theatre on Tour*. Irish Theatre Diaspora Series 1. (Dublin: Carysfort Press, 2005).

Grene, Nicholas, *The Politics of Irish Drama: Plays in Context from Boucicault to Friel* (Cambridge: Cambridge University Press, 1999).

Hapgood, Robert, 'Introduction', in William Shakespeare, *Hamlet*. Edited by Robert Hapgood (Cambridge: Cambridge University Press, 1999): 1-97.

Heaney, Seamus, *The Cure at Troy* (London: Faber, 1990).

Hicks, Bill, *Love all the People: Letters, Lyrics and Routines* (London: Constable and Robinson, 2004).

Hoffmann, Barbara, 'Playing an Extended Run', *The New York Post*, 12 July 2006: 60.

Hughes, Wendy, 'Backlash Hampering Police – Warning', *Birmingham Post*, 25 November 1974: 5.

Huyck, Ed, 'New Guthrie Sets New Course, Honors Tradition', *BackStage* 12 July 2006.

Isherwood, Charles, 'Nasty, Brutish and Gloriously Long', *The New York Times*, 28 August 2005, Section 2: 1.

--- 'Theater; Waking Up the Rock Musical and Other triumphs', *The New York Times*, 24 December 2006, Section 2: 4.

--- 'Why Not Take All of Synge?', *The New York Times*, 12 July 2006: E1.

Johnston, Denis, *The Moon in the Yellow River*, in *Three Irish Plays*, ed. by E. Martin Brown (Harmondsworth: Penguin, 1959) (9-98).

Jordan, Eamonn, *Dissident Dramaturgies: Contemporary Irish Theatre* (Dublin: Irish Academic Press, 2009).

--- (ed.), *Theatre Stuff: Critical Essays on Contemporary Irish Theatre* (Dublin: Carysfort Press, 2000).

Keefe, John and Simon Murray (eds.), *Physical Theatre: A Critical Reader* (London: Routledge, 2007).

Klein, Bernhard, *On the Uses of History in Recent Irish Writing* (Manchester and New York: Manchester University Press, 2007).

Kuchwara, Michael, ' "DruidSynge" a 9-Hour Celebration', *The Washington Post*, 11 July 2006.

Kuti, Elizabeth, *The Six-Days World* (London: Nick Hern Books, 2007).

---- *Treehouses* (London: Methuen Drama, 2000).

Larkin, Philip, *The Whitsun Weddings* (London: Faber and Faber, 1987).

Leabhart, Thomas, *Modern and Post Modern Mime*, (London: Macmillan, 1989).

Lefebvre, Henri, *The Production of Space*, trans. Donald Nicholson-Smith (1974; Oxford: Blackwell, 1991).

Lonergan, Patrick, *Theatre and Globalization: Irish Drama in the Celtic Tiger Era* (Basingstoke and New York: Palgrave Macmillan, 2009).

Mamet, David, *Three Uses of the Knife: On the Nature and Purpose of Drama*, (London: Methuen, 1998).

Mansergh, Martin (ed.), *The Spirit of the Nation: The Speeches and Statements of Charles J. Haughey (1957-1986)* (Cork: Mercier Press, 1986).

McAuley, Gay, *Space in Performance: Making Meaning in the Theatre* (Ann Arbor: University of Michigan Press, 1999)

McCarter, Jeremy, 'Blackboard Jungle '06', *The New York Magazine*, 24 July 2006.

McGee, Celia, 'An Irish Director Arrives With 8½ Hours of Her Countryman', *The New York Times*, 2 July 2006, Section 2: 4.

Mengel, Ewald, Ludwig Schnauder, Rudolf Weiss (eds.), *Weltbühne Wien/World Stage Vienna, Vol. 1: Approaches to Cultural Transfer* (Trier: WVT Wissenschaftlicher Verlag Trier, 2010).

--- *Weltbühne Wien/World Stage Vienna, Vol. 2: Die Rezeption anglophoner Dramen auf Wiener Bühnen des 20. Jahrhunderts* (Trier: WVT Wissenschaftlicher Verlag Trier, 2010)

Moffatt, Sean, 'Review Section', *Theatre Ireland*, 17 (Dec. 1988-Mar. 1989): 47.

--- 'The Passion Machine', *Theatre Ireland*, 18 (April-June 1989): 8-12.

Mullin, Chris, *Error of Judgement: The Truth About the Birmingham Bombings. Fourth edition* (Dublin: Poolbeg, 1997).

Murray, Christopher, 'Unlocking Synge Today', in *A Companion to Modern British and Irish Drama 1880-2005*, ed. Mary Luckhurst (Oxford: Blackwell, 2006): 110-24.

--- *Twentieth-Century Irish Drama: Mirror up to Nation* (Manchester: Manchester University Press, 1997).

O'Casey, Sean, *Autobiographies*, 2 vols (London: Macmillan, 1963).

---- *Three Dublin Plays*. Edited by Christopher Murray (London: Faber, 1998)

O'Conor, Joseph, *The Iron Harp*, in *Three Irish Plays*. Edited by E. Martin Browne (Harmondsworth: Penguin, 1959): 99-164.

O'Darkney, George, *Die Blinden von Kilcrobally*, *Spectaculum*, 67 (1998): 175-210.

O'Faolain, Nuala, 'The Voice that Field Day Didn't Record'. *The Irish Times*, 11 November 1991: 14.

O'Hanlon, Jim, *The Buddhist of Castleknock* (Dublin: New Island, 2007).

O'Reilly, Kaite, *Belonging* (London: Faber, 2000).

O'Toole, Fintan, 'Theatre Has Nothing to Declare but an Innate Uncertainty', *The Irish Times*, 22 May 2010.

--- *Critical Moments: Fintan O'Toole on Modern Irish Theatre*, eds. Julia Furay and Redmond O'Hanlon (Dublin: Carysfort Press, 2003).

--- 'In the Theatre, the Audience Makes the Play', *The Irish Times*, 31 October 2009, Weekend: 9.

--- *Tom Murphy: The Politics of Magic* (Dublin: New Island Books; London: Nick Hern Books, 1994).

Parker, Stewart, *Plays 2* (London: Methuen, 2000).

Parry, Gareth, 'Bombs Hit Two Pubs', *Guardian*, 22 November 1974: 1.

Pelletier, Martine, 'Acts of Definition: The Field Day Anthologies of Irish Writing' in *The Book in Ireland*. Edited by J. Genêt, S. Mikowski & F. Garcier (Newcastle: Cambridge Scholars Press, 2006): 206-227.

Raab, Michael, 'The End of a Wave: New British and Irish Plays in the German-Speaking Theatre', *(Dis)Continuities: Trends and Traditions in Contemporary Theatre and Drama in English*, eds. Margarete Rubik and Elke Mettinger-Schartmann, CDE 9 (Trier: WVT Wissenschaftlicher Verlag Trier, 2002).

Rea, Stephen '"Creating Ideas to Live By": An interview with Stephen Rea', *Sources* 9 (Autumn 2000).

Reddy, Maureen T., 'Reading and Writing Race in Ireland: Roddy Doyle and *Metro Eireann*', *Irish University Review*, 35 (autumn/winter 2005): 374-88.

Richtarik, Marilynn, *Acting Between the Lines. The Field Day Theatre Company and Irish Cultural Politics, 1980-84* (Oxford: Clarendon Press, 1994).

Roche, Anthony, *Contemporary Irish Drama*, Second Edition (Basingtoke: Palgrave Macmillan, 2009).

Scheck, Frank, 'Fluid Druid at Fest', *The New York Post*, 12 July 2006: 60.

Sierz, Aleks, 'Still In-Yer-Face? Towards a Critique and a Summation', *New Theatre Quarterly* (69) 18.1 (2002)

--- *In-Yer-Face Theatre: British Drama Today* (London: Faber, 2001).

Siggins, Lorna, 'Druid Performs Three Plays in Three Time Zones', *The Irish Times*, 13 November 2009: 2.

Simon, John, Review of *DruidSynge* (Lincoln Center), Bloomberg 14 July 2006

Staunton, Denis, 'US Finds Synge Worth the Strain', *The Irish Times*, 15 July 2006, Weekend: 7.

Stephens, James, 'Foreword', *The Insurrection in Dublin* [1916], intro. John A. Murphy (Gerrards Cross: Colin Smythe, 1978).

Sutton, John, 'City Centre Buzz,' *Theatre Ireland*, 12 (1987): 67.

Sweeney, Bernadette, *Performing the Body in Irish Theatre* (Basingstoke: Palgrave Macmillan, 2008).

Synge, J.M. *The Playboy of the Western World and Other Plays*, ed. Ann Saddlemyer (Oxford: Oxford University Press, 1995).

Taylor, Charles, *The Ethics of Authenticity*, (Cambridge: Harvard University Press, 1991).

Teachout, Terry, 'All Synge, All the Time', *The Wall Street Journal* 14 July 2006: W5.

Theatre Record, Reviews of *Portia Coughlan, Theatre Record*, 6-19 May 1996: 608-612

--- Reviews of *The Plough and the Stars, Theatre Record*, 1-28 January 2005: 64-67.

--- Reviews of *The Shaughraun. Theatre Record*, 4-17 June 2005: 796-800.

--- Reviews of *Observe the Sons of Ulster Marching Towards the Somme* Theatre Record, 26 February – 10 March 1996: 303-305.

Tóibín, Colm, (ed.) *Synge: A Celebration* (Dublin: Carysfort, 2005): 34.

Trewin, J.C., *The Birmingham Repertory Theatre: 1913-1963* (London: Barrie and Rockliff, 1963).

Ubersfeld, Anne, *Reading Theatre*, trans. Frank Collins, eds. Paul Perron and Patrick Debbèche (Toronto: University of Toronto Press, 1999).

Voigt, Claudia, 'Schreib ein Stück!', *Der Spiegel* 28 (1998): 162-164.

Walsh, Enda, *bedbound & misterman* (London: Nick Hern Books, 2001).

Washington Times, 'Synge-ing Joy, but Mostly the Blues', *The Washington Times*, 7 July 2006

Weitz, Eric, *The Power of Laughter: Comedy and Contemporary Irish Theatre*, ed. Eric Weitz (Dublin: Carysfort Press, 2004): 76-86

Wilde, Oscar, *The Complete Works of Oscar Wilde* (London and Glasgow: Collins, 1966).

Wiles, David, *A Short History of Western Performance Space* (Cambridge: Cambridge University Press, 2003).

Woolf, Virginia, *Three Guineas*, ed. Naomi Black (Oxford: Blackwell for the Shakespeare Head Press, 2001).

Yeats, W.B. 'The Play, the Player and the Scene' in W.B. Yeats (ed.) *Samhain*, December 1904: 24-33.

--- 'The Reform of the Theatre' in W.B. Yeats (ed.) *Samhain*, September 1903: 9-12.

Zinman, Toby, 'Tragedy, Comedy, Repetition in Synge Marathon', *The Philadelphia Inquirer* 12 July 2006: C3.

Contributors

Richard Cave is Professor of Drama Emeritus at Royal Holloway, University of London. He is an authority on Renaissance and modern drama, particularly the plays of Yeats and his contemporaries. He co-edited *Irish Theatre in England*, the second volume of the Irish Theatrical Diaspora series. His other books include *Ben Jonson* (1991) and editions of Yeats's and Wilde's plays.

Nicholas Grene is Professor of English Literature at Trinity College Dublin and a Member of the Royal Irish Academy. His books include *The Politics of Irish Drama* (Cambridge University Press, 1999), *Shakespeare's Serial History Plays* (Cambridge University Press, 2002) and *Yeats's Poetic Codes* (Oxford University Press, 2008). He has co-edited two volumes in the Irish Theatrical Diaspora series, *Irish Theatre on Tour* (Carysfort Press, 2005), with Chris Morash, and *Interactions: Dublin Theatre Festival, 1957-2007* (Carysfort Press, 2008), with Patrick Lonergan

Werner Huber is Professor of English Literature at the University of Vienna, Austria, and has recently co-edited (with Seán Crosson) *Contemporary Irish Film* (Vienna: Braumueller, 2011). He is a director of the European Association of Centres and Associations of Irish Studies (EFACIS) and co-editor of its *Irish Studies in Europe* series.

Elizabeth Kuti is a playwright for theatre and radio, and Senior Lecturer in Drama at the University of Essex, where she teaches playwriting, drama and literature. She is currently writing a new play commissioned by the National Theatre, is researching the strolling players of nineteenth-century East Anglia, and has recently written a play about Aphra Behn, *Enter A Gentleman,* performed at the National Portrait Gallery in London.

José Lanters is Professor of English at the University of Wisconsin-Milwaukee, where she also co-directs the Center for Celtic Studies. She has published widely on Irish fiction and drama, including recent articles on Thomas Kilroy, Tom Murphy, and Martin McDonagh. Her latest book is *The Tinkers in Irish Literature* (Irish Academic Press, 2008). Her current project deals with the theatrical oeuvre of Thomas Kilroy. A past president of the American Conference for Irish Studies (ACIS), she also serves as Vice Chair for North America on the executive committee of the International Association for the Study of Irish Literatures (IASIL).

Patrick Lonergan is a lecturer in English and Drama at National University of Ireland, Galway. His first book, *Theatre and Globalization: Irish Drama in the Celtic Tiger Era* won the 2009 Theatre Book Prize. He has also published *The Methuen Drama Anthology of Irish Plays, Interactions – The Dublin Theatre Festival 1957-2007* (with Nicholas Grene), and a collection of essays from the Synge Summer School called *Synge and His Influences*. His most recent book is *The Theatre and Films of Martin McDonagh*. He has been the Director of the Synge Summer School since 2008.

James Moran is Head of Drama at the University of Nottingham, and presenter of the books feature on BBC Radio Nottingham. He has written the monographs *Irish Birmingham: A History* (Liverpool University Press, 2010) and *Staging the Easter Rising* (Cork University Press, 2005), and is editor of the collection *Four Irish Rebel Plays* (Irish Academic Press, 2007). His current research projects include work on the plays of Sean O'Casey, the 'regional' dimension of literary modernism, and the history of theatrical riots in the long nineteenth century.

Chris Morash is Head of the School of English, Media and Theatre Studies in NUI Maynooth. He is author of *A History of Irish Theatre 1600-2000*, and *A History of the Media in Ireland*; he is currently Chair of the Compliance Committee of the Broadcasting Authority of Ireland.

Christopher Murray is Emeritus Professor of Drama and Theatre History in the School of English and Drama, University College Dublin. A former editor of *Irish University Review* (1986-1997) and chair (2000-2003) of the International Association for the Study of Irish Literatures (IASIL), he is author of *Twentieth-Century Irish Drama: Mirror Up to Nation* (1997) and *Sean O'Casey Writer at Work: A Biography* (2004), and has edited *Brian Friel: Essays, Diaries, Interviews 1964-1999* (1999) and the RTE Thomas Davis

Lectures for Samuel Beckett's centenary, *Beckett at 100, The Centenary Essays* (2006).

Martine Pelletier lectures in English and Irish studies at the University of Tours, France. She has published widely on Brian Friel, Field Day and on contemporary Irish and Northern Irish theatre. Among her recent contributions are articles in *The Book in Ireland*, edited by Fabienne Garcier, Jacqueline Genêt & Sylvie Mikowski, published by Cambridge Scholars Press in 2006, in *The Cambridge Companion to Brian Friel*, edited by Anthony Roche (2007), in *Irish Literature since 1990*, edited by Scott Brewster and Michael Parker for Manchester University Press in 2009 and in the special issue of the Brazilian journal, *Ilha do Desterro,* on contemporary Irish theatre in 2010. With Alexandra Poulain she co-edited a special issue of *Etudes Irlandaises*, 'French and Irish Theatres: Influences and Interactions' (Vol 33 n2, Autumn 2008) presenting the proceedings of the ITD conference held that same year in Lille. She is currently prefacing the French translations by Alain Delahaye of twelve Brian Friel plays for Avant-Scène Théâtre, Paris.

Ursula Rani Sarma is an award-winning playwright, poet and screenwriter of Irish-Indian descent.. She has written plays for The Abbey Theatre, The National Theatre London, The Traverse Theatre, Paines Plough, and the BBC amongst many others. Recent productions include a new version of *Yerma* (West Yorkshire Playhouse), RIOT (A.C.T. San Francisco/Theatre Royal Bath), *The Dark Things* (Traverse Theatre), which won Best New Play and Best New Production at the Critics Awards for Theatre in Scotland (2010). She also writes for TV and Film and is Course Leader of the MA in Scriptwriting at Bath Spa University.

Rhona Trench is Programme Chair of the BA in Performing Arts (Hons) at the Institute of Technology, Sligo. She is Vice President for the Irish Society for Theatre Research, and is the author of *Bloody Living: The Loss of Selfhood in the Plays of Marina Carr*, Peter Lang, 2010. Ed. *Staging Thought: Essays on Irish Theatre, Scholarship and Practice*, Peter Lang 2012.

Jesse Weaver is an American writer based in Dublin, Ireland. His plays have been seen in Dublin, Chicago, New York and the U.K. Jesse also received his PhD from University College Cork, where his thesis focused on the role of the playwright in the production of Irish theatre over the last three decades. He is currently developing his thesis into a monograph.

Index

Carysfort Press was formed in the summer of 1998. It receives annual funding from the Arts Council.

The directors believe that drama is playing an ever-increasing role in today's society and that enjoyment of the theatre, both professional and amateur, currently plays a central part in Irish culture.

The Press aims to produce high quality publications which, though written and/or edited by academics, will be made accessible to a general readership. The organisation would also like to provide a forum for critical thinking in the Arts in Ireland, again keeping the needs and interests of the general public in view.

The company publishes contemporary Irish writing for and about the theatre.

Editorial and publishing inquiries to:
Carysfort Press Ltd.,
58 Woodfield,
Scholarstown Road,
Rathfarnham,
Dublin 16,
Republic of Ireland.

T (353 1) 493 7383
F (353 1) 406 9815
E: info@carysfortpress.com
www.carysfortpress.com

HOW TO ORDER

TRADE ORDERS DIRECTLY TO:
Irish Book Distribution
Unit 12, North Park, North Road,
Finglas, Dublin 11.

T: (353 1) 8239580
F: (353 1) 8239599
E: mary@argosybooks.ie
www.argosybooks.ie

INDIVIDUAL ORDERS DIRECTLY TO:
eprint Ltd.
35 Coolmine Industrial Estate,
Blanchardstown, Dublin 15.
T: (353 1) 827 8860
F: (353 1) 827 8804 Order online @
E: books@eprint.ie
www.eprint.ie

FOR SALES IN NORTH AMERICA AND CANADA:
Dufour Editions Inc.,
124 Byers Road,
PO Box 7,
Chester Springs,
PA 19425,
USA

T: 1-610-458-5005
F: 1-610-458-7103

What Shakespeare Stole From Rome

Brian Arkins

What Shakespeare Stole From Rome analyses the multiple ways Shakespeare used material from Roman history and Latin poetry in his plays and poems. From the history of the Roman Republic to the tragedies of Seneca; from the Comedies of Platus to Ovid's poetry; this enlightening book examines the important influence of Rome and Greece on Shakespeare's work.

ISBN: 978-1-904505-58-7   €20

Polite Forms

Harry White

Polite Forms is a sequence of poems that meditates on family life. These poems remember and reimagine scenes from childhood and adolescence through the formal composure of the sonnet, so that the uniformity of this framing device promotes a tension as between a neatly arranged album of photographs and the chaos and flow of experience itself. Throughout the collection there is a constant preoccupation with the difference between actual remembrance and the illumination or meaning which poetry can afford. Some of the poems 'rewind the tapes of childhood' across two or three generations, and all of them are akin to pictures at an exhibition which survey individual impressions of childhood and parenthood in a thematically continuous series of portraits drawn from life.

Harry White was born in Dublin in 1958. He is Professor of Music at University College Dublin and widely known for his work in musicology and cultural history. His publications include "Music and the Irish Literary Imagination" (Oxford, 2008), which was awarded the Michael J. Durkan prize of the American Conference for Irish Studies in 2009. "Polite Forms" is his first collection of poems

ISBN: 978-1-904505-55-6   €10

Ibsen and Chekhov on the Irish Stage

Edited by Ros Dixon and Irina Ruppo Malone

Ibsen and Chekhov on the Irish Stage presents articles on the theories of translation and adaptation, new insights on the work of Brian Friel, Frank McGuinness, Thomas Kilroy, and Tom Murphy, historical analyses of theatrical productions during the Irish Revival, interviews with contemporary theatre directors, and a round-table discussion with the playwrights, Michael West and Thomas Kilroy.

Ibsen and Chekhov on the Irish Stage challenges the notion that a country's dramatic tradition develops in cultural isolation. It uncovers connections between past productions of plays by Ibsen and Chekhov and contemporary literary adaptations of their works by Irish playwrights, demonstrating the significance of international influence for the formation of national cannon.

Conceived in the spirit of a round-table discussion, *Ibsen and Chekhov on the Irish Stage* is a collective study of the intricacies of trans-cultural migration of dramatic works and a re-examination of Irish theatre history from 1890 to the present day.

ISBN: 978-1-904505-57-0   €20

Tom Swift Selected Plays

With an introduction by Peter Crawley.

The inaugural production of Performance Corporation in 2002 matched Voltaire's withering assault against the doctrine of optimism with a playful aesthetic and endlessly inventive stagecraft.

Each play in this collection was originally staged by the Performance Corporation and though Swift has explored different avenues ever since, such playfulness is a constant. The writing is precise, but leaves room for the discoveries of rehearsals, the flesh of the theatre. All plays are blueprints for performance, but several of these scripts – many of which are site-specific and all of them slyly topical – are documents for something unrepeatable.

ISBN: 978-1-904505-56-3   €20

Synge and His Influences: Centenary Essays from the Synge Summer School

Edited by Patrick Lonergan

The year 2009 was the centenary of the death of John Millington Synge, one of the world's great dramatists. To mark the occasion, this book gathers essays by leading scholars of Irish drama, aiming to explore the writers and movements that shaped Synge, and to consider his enduring legacies. Essays discuss Synge's work in its Irish, European and world contexts – showing his engagement not just with the Irish literary revival but with European politics and culture too. The book also explores Synge's influence on later writers: Irish dramatists such as Brian Friel, Tom Murphy and Marina Carr, as well as international writers like Mustapha Matura and Erisa Kironde. It also considers Synge's place in Ireland today, revealing how *The Playboy of the Western World* has helped to shape Ireland's responses to globalisation and multiculturalism, in celebrated productions by the Abbey Theatre, Druid Theatre, and Pan Pan Theatre Company.

Contributors include Ann Saddlemyer, Ben Levitas, Mary Burke, Paige Reynolds, Eilís Ní Dhuibhne, Mark Phelan, Shaun Richards, Ondřej Pilný, Richard Pine, Alexandra Poulain, Emilie Pine, Melissa Sihra, Sara Keating, Bisi Adigun, Adrian Frazier and Anthony Roche.

ISBN: 978-1-904505-50-1   €20.00

Constellations - The Life and Music of John Buckley

Benjamin Dwyer

Benjamin Dwyer provides a long overdue assessment of one of Ireland's most prolific composers of the last decades. He looks at John Buckley's music in the context of his biography and Irish cultural life. This is no hagiography but a critical assessment of Buckley's work, his roots and aesthetics. While looking closely at several of Buckley's compositions, the book is written in a comprehensible style that makes it easily accessible to anybody interested in Irish musical and cultural history.   *Wolfgang Marx*

As well as providing a very readable and comprehensive study of the life and music of John Buckley, Constellations also offers an up-to-date and informative catalogue of compositions, a complete discography, translations of set texts and the full libretto of his chamber opera, making this book an essential guide for both students and professional scholars alike.

ISBN: 978-1-904505-52-5   €20.00

'Because We Are Poor': Irish Theatre in the 1990s

Victor Merriman

"Victor Merriman's work on Irish theatre is in the vanguard of a whole new paradigm in Irish theatre scholarship, one that is not content to contemplate monuments of past or present achievement, but for which the theatre is a lens that makes visible the hidden malaises in Irish society. That he has been able to do so by focusing on a period when so much else in Irish culture conspired to hide those problems is only testimony to the considerable power of his critical scrutiny." Chris Morash, NUI Maynooth.

ISBN: 978-1-904505-51-8   €20.00

'Buffoonery and Easy Sentiment':
Popular Irish Plays in the Decade Prior to the Opening of The Abbey Theatre

Christopher Fitz-Simon

In this fascinating reappraisal of the non-literary drama of the late 19th - early 20th century, Christopher Fitz-Simon discloses a unique world of plays, players and producers in metropolitan theatres in Ireland and other countries where Ireland was viewed as a source of extraordinary topics at once contemporary and comfortably remote: revolution, eviction, famine, agrarian agitation, political assassination.

The form was the fashionable one of melodrama, yet Irish melodrama was of a particular kind replete with hidden messages, and the language was far more allusive, colourful and entertaining than that of its English equivalent.

ISBN: 978-1-9045505-49-5   €20.00

The Fourth Seamus Heaney Lectures, 'Mirror up to Nature':

Ed. Patrick Burke

What, in particular, is the contemporary usefulness for the building of societies of one of our oldest and culturally valued ideals, that of drama? The Fourth Seamus Heaney Lectures, 'Mirror up to Nature': Drama and Theatre in the Modern World, given at St Patrick's College, Drumcondra, between October 2006 and April 2007, addressed these and related questions. Patrick Mason spoke on the essence of theatre, Thomas Kilroy on Ireland's contribution to the art of theatre, Cecily O'Neill and Jonothan Neelands on the rich potential of drama in the classroom. Brenna Katz Clarke examined the relationship between drama and film, and John Buckley spoke on opera and its history and gave an illuminating account of his own *Words Upon The Window-Pane*.

ISBN 978-1-9045505-48-8   €12

The Theatre of Tom Mac Intyre: 'Strays from the ether'

Eds. Bernadette Sweeney and Marie Kelly

This long overdue anthology captures the soul of Mac Intyre's dramatic canon – its ethereal qualities, its extraordinary diversity, its emphasis on the poetic and on performance – in an extensive range of visual, journalistic and scholarly contributions from writers, theatre practitioners.

ISBN 978-1-904505-46-4 €25

Irish Appropriation Of Greek Tragedy

Brian Arkins

This book presents an analysis of more than 30 plays written by Irish dramatists and poets that are based on the tragedies of Sophocles, Euripides and Aeschylus. These plays proceed from the time of Yeats and Synge through MacNeice and the Longfords on to many of today's leading writers.

ISBN 978-1-904505-47-1 €20

Alive in Time: The Enduring Drama of Tom Murphy

Ed. Christopher Murray

Almost 50 years after he first hit the headlines as Ireland's most challenging playwright, the 'angry young man' of those times Tom Murphy still commands his place at the pinnacle of Irish theatre. Here 17 new essays by prominent critics and academics, with an introduction by Christopher Murray, survey Murphy's dramatic oeuvre in a concerted attempt to define his greatness and enduring appeal, making this book a significant study of a unique genius.

ISBN 978-1-904505-45-7 €25

Performing Violence in Contemporary Ireland

Ed. Lisa Fitzpatrick

This interdisciplinary collection of fifteen new essays by scholars of theatre, Irish studies, music, design and politics explores aspects of the performance of violence in contemporary Ireland. With chapters on the work of playwrights Martin McDonagh, Martin Lynch, Conor McPherson and Gary Mitchell, on Republican commemorations and the 90th anniversary ceremonies for the Battle of the Somme and the Easter Rising, this book aims to contribute to the ongoing international debate on the performance of violence in contemporary societies.

ISBN 978-1-904505-44-0 (2009) €20

Ireland's Economic Crisis - Time to Act. Essays from over 40 leading Irish thinkers at the MacGill Summer School 2009

Eds. Joe Mulholland and Finbarr Bradley

Ireland's economic crisis requires a radical transformation in policymaking. In this volume, political, industrial, academic, trade union and business leaders and commentators tell the story of the Irish economy and its rise and fall. Contributions at Glenties range from policy, vision and context to practical suggestions on how the country can emerge from its crisis.

ISBN 978-1-904505-43-3 (2009) €20

Deviant Acts: Essays on Queer Performance

Ed. David Cregan

This book contains an exciting collection of essays focusing on a variety of alternative performances happening in contemporary Ireland. While it highlights the particular representations of gay and lesbian identity it also brings to light how diversity has always been a part of Irish culture and is, in fact, shaping what it means to be Irish today.

ISBN 978-1-904505-42-6 (2009) €20

Seán Keating in Context: Responses to Culture and Politics in Post-Civil War Ireland

Compiled, edited and introduced by Éimear O'Connor

Irish artist Seán Keating has been judged by his critics as the personification of old-fashioned traditionalist values. This book presents a different view. The story reveals Keating's early determination to attain government support for the visual arts. It also illustrates his socialist leanings, his disappointment with capitalism, and his attitude to cultural snobbery, to art critics, and to the Academy. Given the national and global circumstances nowadays, Keating's critical and wry observations are prophetic – and highly amusing.

ISBN 978-1-904505-41-9 €25

Dialogue of the Ancients of Ireland: A new translation of Acallam na Senorach

Translated with introduction and notes by Maurice Harmon

One of Ireland's greatest collections of stories and poems, The Dialogue of the Ancients of Ireland is a new translation by Maurice Harmon of the 12th century *Acallam na Senorach*. Retold in a refreshing modern idiom, the *Dialogue* is an extraordinary account of journeys to the four provinces by St. Patrick and the pagan Cailte, one of the surviving Fian. Within the frame story are over 200 other stories reflecting many genres – wonder tales, sea journeys, romances, stories of revenge, tales of monsters and magic. The poems are equally varied – lyrics, nature poems, eulogies, prophecies, laments, genealogical poems. After the *Tain Bo Cuailnge*, the *Acallam* is the largest surviving prose work in Old and Middle Irish.

ISBN: 978-1-904505-39-6 (2009)   €20

Literary and Cultural Relations between Ireland and Hungary and Central and Eastern Europe

Ed. Maria Kurdi

This lively, informative and incisive collection of essays sheds fascinating new light on the literary interrelations between Ireland, Hungary, Poland, Romania and the Czech Republic. It charts a hitherto under-explored history of the reception of modern Irish culture in Central and Eastern Europe and also investigates how key authors have been translated, performed and adapted. The revealing explorations undertaken in this volume of a wide array of Irish dramatic and literary texts, ranging from *Gulliver's Travels* to *Translations* and *The Pillowman*, tease out the subtly altered nuances that they acquire in a Central European context.

ISBN: 978-1-904505-40-2 (2009)   €20

Plays and Controversies: Abbey Theatre Diaries 2000-2005

Ben Barnes

In diaries covering the period of his artistic directorship of the Abbey, Ben Barnes offers a frank, honest, and probing account of a much commented upon and controversial period in the history of the national theatre. These diaries also provide fascinating personal insights into the day-to- day pressures, joys, and frustrations of running one of Ireland's most iconic institutions.

ISBN: 978-1-904505-38-9 (2008)   €35

Interactions: Dublin Theatre Festival 1957-2007. Irish Theatrical Diaspora Series: 3

Eds. Nicholas Grene and Patrick Lonergan with Lilian Chambers

For over 50 years the Dublin Theatre Festival has been one of Ireland's most important cultural events, bringing countless new Irish plays to the world stage, while introducing Irish audiences to the most important international theatre companies and artists. Interactions explores and celebrates the achievements of the renowned Festival since 1957 and includes specially commissioned memoirs from past organizers, offering a unique perspective on the controversies and successes that have marked the event's history. An especially valuable feature of the volume, also, is a complete listing of the shows that have appeared at the Festival from 1957 to 2008.

ISBN: 978-1-904505-36-5 €25

The Informer: A play by Tom Murphy based on the novel by Liam O'Flaherty

The Informer, Tom Murphy's stage adaptation of Liam O'Flaherty's novel, was produced in the 1981 Dublin Theatre Festival, directed by the playwright himself, with Liam Neeson in the leading role. The central subject of the play is the quest of a character at the point of emotional and moral breakdown for some source of meaning or identity. In the case of Gypo Nolan, the informer of the title, this involves a nightmarish progress through a Dublin underworld in which he changes from a Judas figure to a scapegoat surrogate for Jesus, taking upon himself the sins of the world. A cinematic style, with flash-back and intercut scenes, is used rather than a conventional theatrical structure to catch the fevered and phantasmagoric progression of Gypo's mind. The language, characteristically for Murphy, mixes graphically colloquial Dublin slang with the haunted intricacies of the central character groping for the meaning of his own actions. The dynamic rhythm of the action builds towards an inevitable but theatrically satisfying tragic catastrophe. ' [The Informer] is, in many ways closer to being an original Murphy play than it is to O'Flaherty...' Fintan O'Toole.

ISBN: 978-1-904505-37-2 (2008) €10

Shifting Scenes: Irish theatre-going 1955-1985

Eds. Nicholas Grene and Chris Morash

Transcript of conversations with John Devitt, academic and reviewer, about his lifelong passion for the theatre. A fascinating and entertaining insight into Dublin theatre over the course of thirty years provided by Devitt's vivid reminiscences and astute observations.

ISBN: 978-1-904505-33-4 (2008) €10

Irish Literature: Feminist Perspectives

Eds. Patricia Coughlan and Tina O'Toole

The collection discusses texts from the early 18th century to the present. A central theme of the book is the need to renegotiate the relations of feminism with nationalism and to transact the potential contest of these two important narratives, each possessing powerful emancipatory force. Irish Literature: Feminist Perspectives contributes incisively to contemporary debates about Irish culture, gender and ideology.

ISBN: 978-1-904505-35-8 (2008)   €25

Silenced Voices: Hungarian Plays from Transylvania

Selected and translated by Csilla Bertha and Donald E. Morse

The five plays are wonderfully theatrical, moving fluidly from absurdism to tragedy, and from satire to the darkly comic. Donald Morse and Csilla Bertha's translations capture these qualities perfectly, giving voice to the 'forgotten playwrights of Central Europe'. They also deeply enrich our understanding of the relationship between art, ethics, and politics in Europe.

ISBN: 978-1-904505-34-1 (2008)   €25

A Hazardous Melody of Being:
Seóirse Bodley's Song Cycles on the poems of Micheal O'Siadhail

Ed. Lorraine Byrne Bodley

This apograph is the first publication of Bodley's O'Siadhail song cycles and is the first book to explore the composer's lyrical modernity from a number of perspectives. Lorraine Byrne Bodley's insightful introduction describes in detail the development and essence of Bodley's musical thinking, the European influences he absorbed which linger in these cycles, and the importance of his work as a composer of the Irish art song.

ISBN: 978-1-904505-31-0 (2008)   €25

Irish Theatre in England: Irish Theatrical Diaspora Series: 2

Eds. Richard Cave and Ben Levitas

Irish theatre in England has frequently illustrated the complex relations between two distinct cultures. How English reviewers and audiences interpret Irish plays is often decidedly different from how the plays were read in performance in Ireland. How certain Irish performers have chosen to be understood in Dublin is not necessarily how audiences in London have perceived their constructed stage personae. Though a collection by diverse authors, the twelve essays in this volume investigate these issues from a variety of perspectives that together chart the trajectory of Irish performance in England from the mid-nineteenth century till today.

ISBN: 978-1-904505-26-6 (2007)   €20

Goethe and Anna Amalia: A Forbidden Love?

Ettore Ghibellino, Trans. Dan Farrelly

In this study Ghibellino sets out to show that the platonic relationship between Goethe and Charlotte von Stein – lady-in-waiting to Anna Amalia, the Dowager Duchess of Weimar – was used as part of a cover-up for Goethe's intense and prolonged love relationship with the Duchess Anna Amalia herself. The book attempts to uncover a hitherto closely-kept state secret. Readers convinced by the evidence supporting Ghibellino's hypothesis will see in it one of the very great love stories in European history – to rank with that of Dante and Beatrice, and Petrarch and Laura.

ISBN: 978-1-904505-24-2 €20

Ireland on Stage: Beckett and After

Eds. Hiroko Mikami, Minako Okamuro, Naoko Yagi

The collection focuses primarily on Irish playwrights and their work, both in text and on the stage during the latter half of the twentieth century. The central figure is Samuel Beckett, but the contributors freely draw on Beckett and his work provides a springboard to discuss contemporary playwrights such as Brian Friel, Frank McGuinness, Marina Carr and Conor McPherson amongst others. Contributors include: Anthony Roche, Hiroko Mikami, Naoko Yagi, Cathy Leeney, Joseph Long, Noreem Doody, Minako Okamuro, Christopher Murray, Futoshi Sakauchi and Declan Kiberd

ISBN: 978-1-904505-23-5 (2007) €20

'Echoes Down the Corridor': Irish Theatre - Past, Present and Future

Eds. Patrick Lonergan and Riana O'Dwyer

This collection of fourteen new essays explores Irish theatre from exciting new perspectives. How has Irish theatre been received internationally - and, as the country becomes more multicultural, how will international theatre influence the development of drama in Ireland? These and many other important questions.

ISBN: 978-1-904505-25-9 (2007) €20

Musics of Belonging: The Poetry of Micheal O'Siadhail

Eds. Marc Caball & David F. Ford

An overall account is given of O'Siadhail's life, his work and the reception of his poetry so far. There are close readings of some poems, analyses of his artistry in matching diverse content with both classical and innovative forms, and studies of recurrent themes such as love, death, language, music, and the shifts of modern life.

ISBN: 978-1-904505-22-8 (2007) €25 (Paperback)
ISBN: 978-1-904505-21-1 (2007) €50 (Casebound)

Brian Friel's Dramatic Artistry: 'The Work has Value'

Eds. Donald E. Morse, Csilla Bertha and Maria Kurdi

Brian Friel's Dramatic Artistry presents a refreshingly broad range of voices: new work from some of the leading English-speaking authorities on Friel, and fascinating essays from scholars in Germany, Italy, Portugal, and Hungary. This book will deepen our knowledge and enjoyment of Friel's work.

ISBN: 978-1-904505-17-4 (2006)   €30

The Theatre of Martin McDonagh: 'A World of Savage Stories'

Eds. Lilian Chambers and Eamonn Jordan

The book is a vital response to the many challenges set by McDonagh for those involved in the production and reception of his work. Critics and commentators from around the world offer a diverse range of often provocative approaches. What is not surprising is the focus and commitment of the engagement, given the controversial and stimulating nature of the work.

ISBN: 978-1-904505-19-8 (2006)   €35

Edna O'Brien: New Critical Perspectives

Eds. Kathryn Laing, Sinead Mooney and Maureen O'Connor

The essays collected here illustrate some of the range, complexity, and interest of Edna O'Brien as a fiction writer and dramatist. They will contribute to a broader appreciation of her work and to an evolution of new critical approaches, as well as igniting more interest in the many unexplored areas of her considerable oeuvre.

ISBN: 978-1-904505-20-4 (2006)   €20

Irish Theatre on Tour

Eds. Nicholas Grene and Chris Morash

'Touring has been at the strategic heart of Druid's artistic policy since the early eighties. Everyone has the right to see professional theatre in their own communities. Irish theatre on tour is a crucial part of Irish theatre as a whole'. Garry Hynes

ISBN 978-1-904505-13-6 (2005)   €20

Poems 2000-2005 by Hugh Maxton

Poems 2000-2005 is a transitional collection written while the author – also known to be W.J. Mc Cormack, literary historian – was in the process of moving back from London to settle in rural Ireland.

ISBN 978-1-904505-12-9 (2005)   €10

Synge: A Celebration

Ed. Colm Tóibín

A collection of essays by some of Ireland's most creative writers on the work of John Millington Synge, featuring Sebastian Barry, Marina Carr, Anthony Cronin, Roddy Doyle, Anne Enright, Hugo Hamilton, Joseph O'Connor, Mary O'Malley, Fintan O'Toole, Colm Toibin, Vincent Woods.

ISBN 978-1-904505-14-3 (2005) €15

East of Eden: New Romanian Plays

Ed. Andrei Marinescu

Four of the most promising Romanian playwrights, young and very young, are in this collection, each one with a specific way of seeing the Romanian reality, each one with a style of communicating an articulated artistic vision of the society we are living in. Ion Caramitru, General Director Romanian National Theatre Bucharest.
ISBN 978-1-904505-15-0 (2005) €10

George Fitzmaurice: 'Wild in His Own Way', Biography of an Irish Playwright

Fiona Brennan

'Fiona Brennan's introduction to his considerable output allows us a much greater appreciation and understanding of Fitzmaurice, the one remaining under-celebrated genius of twentieth-century Irish drama'. Conall Morrison

ISBN 978-1-904505-16-7 (2005) €20

Out of History: Essays on the Writings of Sebastian Barry

Ed. Christina Hunt Mahony

The essays address Barry's engagement with the contemporary cultural debate in Ireland and also with issues that inform postcolonial critical theory. The range and selection of contributors has ensured a high level of critical expression and an insightful assessment of Barry and his works.

ISBN: 978-1-904505-18-1 (2005) €20

Three Congregational Masses

Seoirse Bodley

'From the simpler congregational settings in the Mass of Peace and the Mass of Joy to the richer textures of the Mass of Glory, they are immediately attractive and accessible, and with a distinctively Irish melodic quality.' Barra Boydell

ISBN: 978-1-904505-11-2 (2005) €15

Georg Büchner's Woyzeck,

A new translation by Dan Farrelly

The most up-to-date German scholarship of Thomas Michael Mayer and Burghard Dedner has finally made it possible to establish an authentic sequence of scenes. The wide-spread view that this play is a prime example of loose, open theatre is no longer sustainable. Directors and teachers are challenged to "read it again".

ISBN: 978-1-904505-02-0 (2004) €10

Playboys of the Western World: Production Histories

Ed. Adrian Frazier

'The book is remarkably well-focused: half is a series of production histories of Playboy performances through the twentieth century in the UK, Northern Ireland, the USA, and Ireland. The remainder focuses on one contemporary performance, that of Druid Theatre, as directed by Garry Hynes. The various contemporary social issues that are addressed in relation to Synge's play and this performance of it give the volume an additional interest: it shows how the arts matter.' Kevin Barry

ISBN: 978-1-904505-06-8 (2004) €20

The Power of Laughter: Comedy and Contemporary Irish Theatre

Ed. Eric Weitz

The collection draws on a wide range of perspectives and voices including critics, playwrights, directors and performers. The result is a series of fascinating and provocative debates about the myriad functions of comedy in contemporary Irish theatre. Anna McMullan

As Stan Laurel said, 'it takes only an onion to cry. Peel it and weep. Comedy is harder'. 'These essays listen to the power of laughter. They hear the tough heart of Irish theatre – hard and wicked and funny'. Frank McGuinness

ISBN: 978-1-904505-05-1 (2004) €20

Sacred Play: Soul-Journeys in contemporary Irish Theatre

Anne F. O'Reilly

'Theatre as a space or container for sacred play allows audiences to glimpse mystery and to experience transformation. This book charts how Irish playwrights negotiate the labyrinth of the Irish soul and shows how their plays contribute to a poetics of Irish culture that enables a new imagining. Playwrights discussed are: McGuinness, Murphy, Friel, Le Marquand Hartigan, Burke Brogan, Harding, Meehan, Carr, Parker, Devlin, and Barry.'

ISBN: 978-1-904505-07-5 (2004) €25

The Irish Harp Book

Sheila Larchet Cuthbert

This is a facsimile of the edition originally published by Mercier Press in 1993. There is a new preface by Sheila Larchet Cuthbert, and the biographical material has been updated. It is a collection of studies and exercises for the use of teachers and pupils of the Irish harp.

ISBN: 978-1-904505-08-2 (2004) €35

The Drunkard

Tom Murphy

'The Drunkard is a wonderfully eloquent play. Murphy's ear is finely attuned to the glories and absurdities of melodramatic exclamation, and even while he is wringing out its ludicrous overstatement, he is also making it sing.' The Irish Times

ISBN: 978-1-90 05-09-9 (2004) €10

Goethe: Musical Poet, Musical Catalyst

Ed. Lorraine Byrne

'Goethe was interested in, and acutely aware of, the place of music in human experience generally - and of its particular role in modern culture. Moreover, his own literary work - especially the poetry and Faust - inspired some of the major composers of the European tradition to produce some of their finest works.' Martin Swales

ISBN: 978-1-9045-10-5 (2004) €40

The Theatre of Marina Carr: "Before rules was made"

Eds. Anna McMullan & Cathy Leeney

As the first published collection of articles on the theatre of Marina Carr, this volume explores the world of Carr's theatrical imagination, the place of her plays in contemporary theatre in Ireland and abroad and the significance of her highly individual voice.

ISBN: 978-0-9534257-7-8 (2003) €20

Critical Moments: Fintan O'Toole on Modern Irish Theatre

Eds. Julia Furay & Redmond O'Hanlon

This new book on the work of Fintan O'Toole, the internationally acclaimed theatre critic and cultural commentator, offers percussive analyses and assessments of the major plays and playwrights in the canon of modern Irish theatre. Fearless and provocative in his judgements, O'Toole is essential reading for anyone interested in criticism or in the current state of Irish theatre.

ISBN: 978-1-904505-03-7 (2003) €20

Goethe and Schubert: Across the Divide

Eds. Lorraine Byrne & Dan Farrelly

Proceedings of the International Conference, 'Goethe and Schubert in Perspective and Performance', Trinity College Dublin, 2003. This volume includes essays by leading scholars – Barkhoff, Boyle, Byrne, Canisius, Dürr, Fischer, Hill, Kramer, Lamport, Lund, Meikle, Newbould, Norman McKay, White, Whitton, Wright, Youens – on Goethe's musicality and his relationship to Schubert; Schubert's contribution to sacred music and the Lied and his setting of Goethe's Singspiel, Claudine. A companion volume of this Singspiel (with piano reduction and English translation) is also available.

ISBN: 978-1-904505-04-4 (2003) €25

Goethe's Singspiel, 'Claudine von Villa Bella'

Set by Franz Schubert

Goethe's Singspiel in three acts was set to music by Schubert in 1815. Only Act One of Schuberts's Claudine score is extant. The present volume makes Act One available for performance in English and German. It comprises both a piano reduction by Lorraine Byrne of the original Schubert orchestral score and a bilingual text translated for the modern stage by Dan Farrelly. This is a tale, wittily told, of lovers and vagabonds, romance, reconciliation, and resolution of family conflict.

ISBN: 978-0-9544290-0-3 (2002) €20

Theatre of Sound, Radio and the Dramatic Imagination

Dermot Rattigan

An innovative study of the challenges that radio drama poses to the creative imagination of the writer, the production team, and the listener.
"A remarkably fine study of radio drama – everywhere informed by the writer's professional experience of such drama in the making...A new theoretical and analytical approach – informative, illuminating and at all times readable." Richard Allen Cave

ISBN: 978- 0-9534-257-5-4 (2002) €20

Talking about Tom Murphy

Ed. Nicholas Grene

Talking About Tom Murphy is shaped around the six plays in the landmark Abbey Theatre Murphy Season of 2001, assembling some of the best-known commentators on his work: Fintan O'Toole, Chris Morash, Lionel Pilkington, Alexandra Poulain, Shaun Richards, Nicholas Grene and Declan Kiberd.

ISBN: 978-0-9534-257-9-2 (2002) €15

Hamlet: The Shakespearean Director

Mike Wilcock

"This study of the Shakespearean director as viewed through various interpretations of HAMLET is a welcome addition to our understanding of how essential it is for a director to have a clear vision of a great play. It is an important study from which all of us who love Shakespeare and who understand the importance of continuing contemporary exploration may gain new insights." From the Foreword, by Joe Dowling, Artistic Director, The Guthrie Theater, Minneapolis, MN

ISBN: 978-1-904505-00-6 (2002) €20

The Theatre of Frank Mc Guinness: Stages of Mutability

Ed. Helen Lojek

The first edited collection of essays about internationally renowned Irish playwright Frank McGuinness focuses on both performance and text. Interpreters come to diverse conclusions, creating a vigorous dialogue that enriches understanding and reflects a strong consensus about the value of McGuinness's complex work.

ISBN: 978-1904505-01-3. (2002) €20

Theatre Talk: Voices of Irish Theatre Practitioners

Eds Lilian Chambers, Ger Fitzgibbon and Eamonn Jordan

"This book is the right approach - asking practitioners what they feel." Sebastian Barry, Playwright "... an invaluable and informative collection of interviews with those who make and shape the landscape of Irish Theatre." Ben Barnes, Artistic Director of the Abbey Theatre

ISBN: 978-0-9534-257-6-1 (2001) €20

In Search of the South African Iphigenie

Erika von Wietersheim and Dan Farrelly

Discussions of Goethe's "Iphigenie auf Tauris" (Under the Curse) as relevant to women's issues in modern South Africa: women in family and public life; the force of women's spirituality; experience of personal relationships; attitudes to parents and ancestors; involvement with religion.

ISBN: 978-0-9534257-8-5 (2001)   €10

'The Starving' and 'October Song':

Two contemporary Irish plays by Andrew Hinds

The Starving, set during and after the siege of Derry in 1689, is a moving and engrossing drama of the emotional journey of two men.

October Song, a superbly written family drama set in real time in pre-ceasefire Derry.

ISBN: 978-0-9534-257-4-7 (2001)   €10

Seen and Heard: Six new plays by Irish women

Ed. Cathy Leeney

A rich and funny, moving and theatrically exciting collection of plays by Mary Elizabeth Burke-Kennedy, Síofra Campbell, Emma Donoghue, Anne Le Marquand Hartigan, Michelle Read and Dolores Walshe.

ISBN: 978-0-9534-257-3-0 (2001)   €20

Theatre Stuff: Critical essays on contemporary Irish theatre

Ed. Eamonn Jordan

Best selling essays on the successes and debates of contemporary Irish theatre at home and abroad. Contributors include: Thomas Kilroy, Declan Hughes, Anna McMullan, Declan Kiberd, Deirdre Mulrooney, Fintan O'Toole, Christopher Murray, Caoimhe McAvinchey and Terry Eagleton.

ISBN: 978-0-9534-2571-1-6 (2000)   €20

Under the Curse. Goethe's "Iphigenie Auf Tauris", A New Version

Dan Farrelly

The Greek myth of Iphigenie grappling with the curse on the house of Atreus is brought vividly to life. This version is currently being used in Johannesburg to explore problems of ancestry, religion, and Black African women's spirituality.

ISBN: 978-09534-257-8-5 (2000) €10

Urfaust, A New Version of Goethe's early "Faust" in Brechtian Mode

Dan Farrelly

This version is based on Brecht's irreverent and daring re-interpretation of the German classic. "Urfaust is a kind of well-spring for German theatre… The love-story is the most daring and the most profound in German dramatic literature." Brecht

ISBN: 978-0-9534-257-0-9 (1998) €10